D0464336

Small Futures

Other Books
of the Carnegie Council on Children

All Our Children: The American Family Under Pressure
by Kenneth Keniston and the Carnegie Council on Children.
Harcourt Brace Jovanovich, 1977.
First Harvest/HBJ Edition, 1978.

BACKGROUND STUDIES:

**Child Care in the Family: A Review of Research
and Some Propositions for Policy**
by Alison Clarke-Stewart.
Academic Press, 1977.

**Minority Education and Caste:
The American System in Cross-Cultural Perspective**
by John U. Ogbu.
Academic Press, 1978.

The Unexpected Minority: Handicapped Children in America
by John Gliedman and William Roth.
(Forthcoming)

SMALL
FUTURES

Children, Inequality, and the
Limits of Liberal Reform

by

Richard H. de Lone

for the Carnegie Council on Children

APR 18 1983

Harcourt Brace Jovanovich, New York and London

Copyright © 1979 by Carnegie Corporation of New York

All rights reserved. No part of
this publication may be reproduced or
transmitted in any form or by any means,
electronic or mechanical, including photocopy,
recording, or any information storage and
retrieval system, without permission
in writing from the publisher.

Requests for permission to make copies of
any part of the work should be mailed to:
Permissions, Harcourt Brace Jovanovich, Inc.
757 Third Avenue, New York, N.Y. 10017

This book is solely the work of the Carnegie Council on
Children and does not necessarily reflect the views or
opinions of Carnegie Corporation of New York, or of its
trustees, officers, or employees.

Printed in the United States of America

Library of Congress Cataloging in Publication Data
De Lone, Richard H
Small futures.
Includes bibliographical references and index.
1.   Children—United States.
2.   Children's rights—United States.
3.   Child welfare—United States.
4.   Equality.
5.   Liberalism—United States.
I.   Carnegie Council on Children.   II.   Title.
HQ792.U5D44   301.43'1'0973   77-92536
ISBN 0-15-183128-9

C D E

Acknowledgments

Any book about public policy draws on the work of many people: government officials who maintain and provide essential data; researchers whose analyses shape subsequent understanding of data; and scholars and writers whose contributions to any author's thoughts are hard to identify with precision but are still undeniable. In a sense, all books of this sort are collective works.

In addition, there are scores of individuals who have made direct and palpable contributions to this report. All the members of the Carnegie Council on Children provided criticisms and suggestions for various drafts. In particular, the wise insights and criticisms of Marian Wright Edelman, Kenneth Keniston, William Kessen, and Harold Watts, while not always heeded, were ample and extremely helpful to the author. Likewise, all the members of the Council's staff influenced the content of this book and its arguments. In particular, the works of Joan Costello, Peter Garlock, Katherine P. Messenger, and John U. Ogbu are reflected in various chapters and passages, while the critical readings of John Gliedman and William Roth constantly influenced the author's thinking.

The research assistance provided by Chris Buckley, Laura Eby, Nina Kraut, Phyllis Holman Weisbard, and, above all, the resourceful Georgia Goeters was invaluable. Without the typing support (and extraordinary patience in deciphering the author's hand) of Missle Wodajo Hankerson, Margaret Jackewicz, Michele McLean, and Sheila Meyers, backed up by the administrative support of Ethel Himberg, these words would never have reached the printer.

Finally, my special thanks to Jill Kneerim, the Carnegie Council on Children's editor. The sharpness of her excisions was matched only by the keenness of her suggestions. Her editorial judgment and restraint halted many a passage from its drift into "the night above the dingle starry."

What errors and vagaries persist are, of course, the author's responsibility.

Contents

Contents

Foreword

At the center of this book is a simple but far-reaching idea: that children have been assigned a key role in dealing with the deepest tension of American life, the conflict between economic and political liberalism. As an ideological move, assigning this role to children has been highly successful, for our faith in the effectiveness of child reform has helped defuse antagonisms between rich and poor that have torn other societies apart. But our faith in education and other strategies to improve children as a way of solving real social problems has been misplaced, for children's policy has never really acknowledged, much less addressed, the problems it was intended to remedy. Herein lies the irony of liberal reform, which has always counted on children to solve in the next generation the problems their parents could not solve in their own.

The impetus for this book can be summarized by two comments made early in the work of the Carnegie Council on Children. The first was made by one of our members, Catherine Foster Alter, when we were struggling to define our agenda. "We would be doing a lot," she said, "if we could help stop the hurting of children." That remark animated much of our preliminary work, an effort to identify what harms American children. The simplest summary of our answer is this: that virtually every index of harm to children, from death at birth to poor school performance, from malnutrition to low self-esteem, is firmly associated with poverty and race. And further, we found that although for more than century we have tried repeatedly to reduce the inequalities that adversely affect millions of children, we have made virtually no progress in that effort.

The second remark was made by an early adviser to our project, Dr. James Comer. "The first question," he said, "is why we Americans have failed to do for children what almost every other civilized nation has done." He meant, of course, our failure to provide to American children as a right what every child in the democratic nations of Europe can take for granted: for example, adequate health care, income supports for parents, public provision of child care. Were we a nation indifferent to the suffering of children or untroubled about human equality, Dr. Comer's question would be irrelevant. But paradoxically, every major reform movement in our history has been attuned to the suffering of children and has aimed at an increase in equality. To understand the failures in social policy that affect children, then, a historical inquiry was in order, and this book is one expression of that inquiry.

To understand the place of children we must look at the broader web of shared assumptions that define to a society what is important, real, and right—in short, at the society's dominant ideas and myths about itself. In the case of America, those ideas are commonly called economic and political liberalism—not the "liberalism" of one wing of the Democratic party, but that deep and largely implicit set of liberal assumptions shared by both major parties and by the overwhelming majority of Americans, a world view whose origins lie in the thought of men such as Adam Smith and John Locke.

American liberalism as an economic doctrine advocates a free-market, laissez-faire economy in which free competition between rational producers and free choice among rational workers and consumers is thought to produce optimal distribution of goods and effort. In practice, of course, the effort to create such an economy has been accompanied by numerous compromises: government interventions to increase social benefits by such means as the construction of canals, railroads, and highways; monopolistic or oligopolistic practices by producers that reduce the choices of workers and consumers; collective action by workers through unions; and so on. But even in its pure form, the free-market model of economic liberalism would produce a society with large disparities of wealth among its citizens. Indeed, economic inequalities are considered essential to the functioning of a liberal economy, in that they provide necessary incentives for effort, rewards for enterprise, and spurs to geographic and social mobility.

On the political side, however, classical liberalism is committed to the greatest possible equality. The creation of a separate judicial system designed to apply the laws with impartiality, the slow but effective extension of the vote, and the recurrent waves of reform aimed at removing barriers to equal participation in governing the society—all express the depth, vitality, and sincerity of this egalitarian commitment.

The problem lies in the inherent conflict between the inegalitarian consequences of a liberal economy and the egalitarian ideal of a liberal political democracy. At the level of everyday reality, this conflict can take many forms. In its most flagrant form, those who achieve wealth in a liberal economy gain the capacity to buy political influence and power, either directly through the purchase of corrupt politicians or through more subtle means such as financing the campaigns of sympathetic candidates. Then, too, the more prosperous have more power as consumers, more freedom to choose more goods, more capacity to buy the services of others, like housemaids and pediatricians, who make their lives easier and more agreeable.

Most crucial to this book, the rich and even the moderately well-to-do have a capacity to endow their children's futures that the poor do not possess. "Endowing" a child's future goes well beyond trust funds and the inheritance of wealth; the most vital endowments are those of body, mind, and spirit. Poverty at birth by no means irrevocably dooms a child to social judgments of infirmity, stupidity, or demoralization—there are millions of witnesses to the contrary—but it makes all three of these outcomes more likely. Almost every index of physical, human, and spiritual harm to children is strongly associated with inequalities of income and race.

In this accumulation of harm, psychological bias on the part of adults clearly plays a role. But even if personal prejudices did not exist, inequality in endowing children would persist. We do not need to assume racial prejudice in pediatricians to explain why black children receive less, and less adequate, medical care than white children. Medical care costs money, and black parents as a group have a good deal less of it than do white parents. Nor does class bias in educators take us far toward understanding why, in the 1960s among high-ability students, those from the wealthiest families were five times more likely to attend college than those from the poorest families. A good part of the explanation surely lies in the greater capacity of prosperous parents to pay college expenses.

But as this book shows, even the accumulation of external barriers to a decent childhood is not an adequate explanation for the shrinking of the futures of the poor. For children develop inner maps of the social world and of their future place as adults in it, and these maps become powerful determinants of their aspirations, of their self-images—and of their real futures. Constructed out of real-life experience, such maps go on to shape further experience and its interpretation, dictating, for example, that most children from poor families come to anticipate an adulthood not too different from that of their parents, while middle-class children routinely expect middle-class roles and lives.

The inequality of children's futures is the starting point of this book, just as it has been a central issue in American life ever since we as a nation began to confront the contradictions between a capitalist economy and a democratic polity. To be sure, as Americans we have rarely espoused radical leveling— complete equality of condition. But it is to our credit that we have always been uneasy with visible extremes of wealth and poverty—with the contrast between the seemingly limitless wealth of tycoons, robber barons, and successful top managers and the poverty of the millions of Americans who have lacked, by prevailing standards, the requirements for subsistence. Partly because we think of ourselves as a "people of plenty," the persistence of poverty has troubled the American conscience even in the absence of an impulse toward leveling.

Our unhappiness over large disparities in wealth has been especially acute where children are concerned. The advantages of wealthy *adults*, like the misery of poverty-stricken *adults*, could always be ascribed to their differential virtue, diligence, or talent and justified as necessary to preserve a proper hierarchy of economic incentives. But there has never been an easy way of rationalizing inequalities in the futures inherited by children. Awareness that babes in arms have very different life chances depending on the wealth, class, or race of their parents is clearly not consistent with the core American creed that all men are created equal. That inconsistency is one factor that has led to repeated efforts to equalize the life chances of children.

As Richard de Lone explains in this book, children have played a key role in our society's efforts to narrow the gap between our political ideals and our economic realities. Rather than try to modify directly the distribution of economic rewards and social standings, we have concentrated on uplifting the next generation. Education has been seen, in the words of Horace Mann, as "the balance wheel of society," and ultimately as the means of "preventing poverty." Confronted with unacceptable economic and social inequalities, we have reflexively channeled our moral indignation into efforts to improve the morality, character, skills, and intelligence of children—especially those who are poor, immigrant, or nonwhite—trusting that by so doing we would reduce social, economic, and racial inequality in the *next* generation. In other countries the same revulsion at economic inequality has led to widely debated proposals—in some nations at least partly implemented—to change the economic system itself. But in America such proposals have been few and unpopular, and one reason for their unpopularity is surely our alternative faith in the capacity of liberal reforms to improve our society by improving our children.

As de Lone acknowledges, things might have been much worse in the total absence of liberal reforms. But in the end, such reforms have failed in their lofty goals because they were not accompanied by more direct and structural change. Without structural change, education and efforts to equalize opportunity can at best only change the cast of characters who occupy pre-existing numbers of positions on the top and on the bottom. The

distance between top and bottom and the size of each group—
in short, the inequalities that spurred reform in the first place
—simply cannot be altered by education. Thus, every wave of
reform has inevitably failed to accomplish its equalizing mission
and has been followed by a wave of reaction, usually ending with
a declaration that the poor are constitutionally, racially, or genetically defective. The reason this has happened, the inevitability of its occurrence, and the pervasiveness of the assumptions
on which is founded the ironic failure of liberal reform—these
are the topics of this extended essay.

In calling it an extended essay, I want to underline its special
status as a work evolved in a dialogue of several years between
its author and the members and other staff of the Carnegie
Council on Children. It differs from the Council's core report,
All Our Children, in that the latter was in part drafted by and
in all respects thoroughly edited and approved by all Council
members. This book is instead a formulation of ideas that
emerged from and influenced the Council's thinking, but that
were given their present form by de Lone alone. The book has
been greatly modified to take account of suggestions by the
Council; and in its final form it has been approved by Council
members. Yet it remains in many ways a personal formulation of
the "structural" analysis that underlies the Council's thinking
and recommendations.

In the end, that analysis is what we hope will be influential
in our work. We have had many things to say about specific
programs, recommendations, and goals that we believe would
improve the lot of children and families. But our overall perspective seems to us more important than any of our specific
recommendations. That perspective, most fully amplified in this
book, can be summarized in two sentences. For well over a
century, we Americans have believed that a crucial way to make
our society more just was by improving our children. We propose instead that the best way to ensure more ample futures for
our children is to start with the difficult task of building a more
just society.

KENNETH KENISTON

January 1979

Small Futures

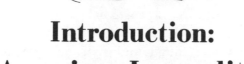

Introduction:
American Inequality

Nature hath made men so equall, in the faculties of
body, and mind; as that though there be found one man
sometimes manifestly stronger in body, or quicker mind
than another; yet when all is reckoned together, the
difference between man and man, is not so considerable,
as that one man can thereupon claim to himself any
benefit, to which another may not pretend, as well
as he.

—Thomas Hobbes, *Leviathan*

Jimmy is a second grader. He pays attention in school, and he
enjoys it. School records show that he is reading slightly above
grade level and has a slightly better than average IQ. Bobby is
a second grader in a school across town. He also pays attention
in class and enjoys school, and his test scores are quite similar
to Jimmy's. Bobby is a safe bet to enter college (more than four
times as likely as Jimmy) and a good bet to complete it—at least
twelve times as likely as Jimmy. Bobby will probably have at
least four years more schooling than Jimmy. He is twenty-seven
times as likely as Jimmy to land a job which by his late forties
will pay him an income in the top tenth of all incomes. Jimmy
has about one chance in eight of earning a median income.[1]

These odds are the arithmetic of inequality in America. They
can be calculated with the help of a few more facts about Bobby
and Jimmy. Bobby is the son of a successful lawyer whose annual salary of $35,000 puts him well within the top 10 percent

of the United States income distribution in 1976. Jimmy's father, who did not complete high school, works from time to time as a messenger or a custodial assistant. His earnings, some $4,800, put him in the bottom 10 percent. Bobby lives with his mother and father and sister. Jimmy lives with his father, mother, three brothers, and two sisters.[2]

The odds these two boys face remind us of facts easily forgotten or overlooked by the affluent and influential. There is great inequality in this country. With that inequality go tremendous advantages for people who have more, tremendous penalties for those who have less. These penalties fall hard on children—on something like one-quarter of the children in the United States.[3]

In the United States, as elsewhere, it is a penalty to be born poor. It is a compounding penalty to be born to parents with little education. It is a further penalty to be born to parents who are frequently unemployed and whose employment opportunities are limited to relatively uninteresting, dead-end jobs. All these penalties are increased still more for children in racial minorities. They are further increased for girls. Some of the penalties are immediate—the physical deprivations of poor nutrition, poor health, poor housing, inadequate medical care; some accumulate slowly, influencing the development of adult skills, aspirations, and opportunities. Together, they produce the odds that make Bobby's probable future a vista rich with possibilities and Jimmy's probable future a small door into a small room.

This book begins with the propositions that the odds against certain children consistently deny them the social and economic opportunity in which most Americans believe, and that these odds have not changed significantly throughout American history. It attempts to understand why American social policy, apparently aimed at providing equal opportunity for all, has not made much progress in that direction.

4

Poverty: Absolute or Relative?

A discussion of the extent of poverty in America, both today and in the past, requires an understanding of definitions. People disagree about how many Americans are born into poverty and about how much the proportion of those living in poverty has been reduced over the years, in part because two distinctly different conceptions of poverty exist. One considers poverty an absolute state, asserting that an individual living below a certain fixed level of income is poor, while an individual living above that level is not. The second conception assumes that poverty is basically a social condition, that a person is poor in relation to others in a given society.[4] A simple example can clarify how the ideas of absolute and relative poverty differ and can illustrate the importance of the distinction for social policy.

Imagine a highly simplified agrarian society in which earnings are directly proportional to landholdings and families have no source of income but their land. Assume that anyone holding less than 1 acre of land is considered poor, under the absolute definition of poverty. Suppose that a quarter of the families own 7 acres of land each, half of the families own 3 acres each, and the remaining quarter, the poor, own slightly less than 1 acre each. By the absolute definition, poverty would be entirely abolished if the society annexed more land and the poorest quarter of families received enough square footage each to bring it over the "poverty line" of 1 acre.

But also suppose that at the same time that the holdings of the poorest families increased by some fraction of an acre, the holdings of the middle range of families doubled, and the holdings of the richest families tripled. Now the poorest quarter of families would own an average of, say, 1.2 acres, the next 50 percent of families would hold an average of 6 acres, and the richest families would own an average of 21 acres. Instead of being a society in which the richest quarter of families held seven or eight times as much land as the poorest quarter, it would be one in which they held seventeen or eighteen times as much.

5

In absolute terms, the poorest families would no longer be poor. In relative terms, they would be worse off. Of course, if the annexed land had gone *only* to bring the poorest quarter above the poverty line, their relative as well as their absolute poverty would have been reduced. But this is not the way that economic rewards have usually been distributed in human societies.

The concept of absolute poverty may have meaning in a society in which survival is in doubt from day to day. But in our prosperous society it ignores the basic issue of inequality—the issue of how the goods and benefits in a given society are distributed. For poverty is not a state in itself. It is a *symptom* of broad social inequality. Yet most social programs designed to improve either the present or future opportunities for poor children have been aimed at helping individuals or families get over the poverty line, without paying adequate attention to how resources and benefits are distributed. They effectively ignore the issue of equality or, as it is sometimes identified, the issue of distribution.

The belief that poverty is just a state that people fall into when their income plunges below a certain level takes the subject out of its social context and treats it as a problem complete in itself, as if one side of a coin could exist without any reference to the other. This influential view is epitomized by the federal government's poverty line, widely used to judge who is and who is not poor (hence who is and who is not eligible for various government programs).[5] If people are lifted above the arbitrary poverty line, poverty is considered "cured." In recent years, in fact, some critics using this kind of index have concluded that poverty has been cut in half in this country[6] because the standard of living for all Americans, including the poor, has risen with economic growth. Several years ago the Mobil Oil Company, following this line of reasoning, ran this philosophic advertisement:

GROWTH IS THE ONLY WAY AMERICA WILL EVER REDUCE POVERTY
While the relative share of income that poor people get seems to be frozen, their incomes do keep pace with the economy. It's more lucrative to wash cars or wait on tables today than 20 years ago. Even allowing for inflation, the average income of the bottom tenth

6

of the population has increased about 55 percent since 1950. Twenty more years of growth could do for the poor what the Congress won't do.

There is no disputing the fact that the standard of living for everyone—including the poor—has risen substantially in the United States in the last generation. The average family in the bottom 20 percent of the income distribution has considerably more purchasing power than a similar family only twenty years ago, and it has more purchasing power than a great majority of the families that live in Bangladesh or India today. But it is scant consolation to a welfare mother in the South Bronx to know that in Calcutta she would be quite well off on her current income or that forty years ago her real income today would have seemed modestly comfortable. The point is simple: we judge our well-being by the here and now.

In fact, most Americans, whether they acknowledge it in these terms or not, consider poverty a relative thing. In survey after survey taken since World War II, a majority of the American public has regularly defined as "poor" any family of four living on an income that corresponds to about half that year's median income for a family of the same size.[7] This means that each year their definition of poverty has risen with the gross national product. When the distribution is consistently unequal, as the economist Dr. Bernard Anderson has put it, no matter how fast the engine proceeds, the caboose never catches up.

In 1976 (the most recent year for which complete data are available as this is written), 25 million Americans, including 10.1 million children under eighteen, lived in households below the official poverty line, which that year was $5,815 for a non-farm family of four. Children constituted over 40 percent of all persons in official poverty; 15.8 percent of all American children that year were poor by the government's definition.[8] But these figures understate the problem. If we use a relative definition of poverty and replace a bureaucratic definition of poverty with the American public's popular standard of half the median income, we find that *more than a quarter of all American children live in poverty.*[9] And by this definition, the percentage of poor children has scarcely changed in thirty years since the distribution of income (hence the percentage of families below half the median) has remained stable in that time.

Because our concern is with children, we will focus here on the distribution of family income. While all incomes have risen, family income *distribution* in this country has scarcely changed since the end of World War II.[10] (In this century the Depression and World War II both had modest equalizing effects on income distribution.)[11] For the last thirty years the top fifth of families (before income taxes but after income transfers such as welfare and Social Security payments are considered) has received somewhat over 40 percent of the country's net family income. The bottom fifth has received between 4 and 6 percent.*

Since incomes in the range of $35,000 to $40,000 are often seen as middle class by those who earn them, it may surprise

* In using these figures, we are fully aware that in the past several years a number of studies and articles have argued that Census Bureau definitions of income understate the income of the bottom fifth of families.[12] Their authors maintain that when the dollar benefits of food stamps, Medicare, Medicaid, and other noncash sources of income are thrown in, the income share of the poorest Americans rises considerably. But these studies and articles also exhibit a series of common flaws. First, with few exceptions, they are hypothetical; they compute the "in-kind" value of such benefits as if all families that are eligible receive them. In fact, many do not.[13] Second, many of them use the government's poverty line as an index, failing to note that relatively few families receiving all such benefits would rise above the low-income line of half the median.[14] Third, these studies are an example of how statistics can be used to perpetuate a double standard, for they count only noncash income of the poor, omitting such noncash benefits of the more affluent as health insurance and pension benefits paid by employers; Social Security paid by employers; capital gains not subject to taxation; other tax-exempt income, such as interest from government bonds; expense accounts and other perquisites that the affluent can write off as business expenses; imputed rental income from home ownership; and so on. One major study suggests that if such sources of income are counted, the share of income received by the richest 1 percent rises from the Census Bureau's 5 percent to 10 percent[15] or twice the amount of the bottom 20 percent of families. Others have suggested that once we include such noncash benefits of the affluent, a substantial portion of which result from tax loopholes, income distribution may not have become much more equal in the course of the entire century. This is contrary to Census Bureau definitions, which suggest that both the Depression and World War II, for quite different reasons, resulted in more equality.[16] Given these facts, we believe it is quite proper to use Census Bureau definitions that may, indeed, make distribution of income appear *more* equal than it is. Furthermore, without far more complete data than are available under any current collection system, the Census Bureau figures are the most widely used and thus the most commonly acceptable.

Distribution of Family Income (1976)[17]

Family Rank	Percentage of All Income	Income Range in $
Top 5 percent	15.6	37,047 and up
Top quintile	41.1	23,924 and up
2nd quintile	24.1	17,301–23,923
3rd quintile	17.6	12,401–17,300
4th quintile	11.8	7,442–12,400
5th quintile	5.4	Under 7,441

some readers to know that in 1976 an income of just over $37,000 was sufficient to put a family of four in the top 5 percent —the top twentieth—of American family income distribution. The net income of this top 5 percent of families almost equals that of the families in the bottom 40 percent. *In 1976, 20 percent of American families were living below half the median income, or what most Americans define as poverty.*[18]

These measures look at income alone. If we take a different measure, tangible and financial wealth (the net assets of families, including cash on hand, stocks, bonds, real estate, and so forth), inequality in the United States is even greater. In 1969 the top 4 percent of the population owned 37 percent of American net worth.[19] The net worth of the average family in the bottom 20 percent was zero.[20]

Of course, in any distribution there is a top and bottom tenth, or fifth, or fourth. The distributional issue is: how great is the distance between the top and bottom? Currently the average family in the top fifth has about eight times the income of the average family in the bottom fifth. Redistribution that brought all families' incomes above half the median would reduce the gap between the top fifth and bottom fifth to about four to one. We will argue in this book that such a change could substantially reduce the difference in odds—life chances—now facing the Jimmys and Bobbys, or the Marys and Janes, in the United States. Short of this kind of redistribution, we believe, the odds affecting Jimmy and Bobby are not likely to change. In other words, *the dynamics of our social structure are not likely to produce more equality of opportunity unless there is more equality to begin with.*

Social structure is a phrase that will be used throughout this book to describe the organizing principles (customs, ideologies, laws) of our society, with particular emphasis on its economic organization, and the social forms that spring from those principles. Main examples of these forms are institutional structures (e.g., the family, the educational system, and the corporation); the distribution of income, wealth, and power; and social class array.

Living in Poverty

In 1976 a family of four living at half the median for families of that size would have had an income of $7,480.[21] With about $1,000 going for income and Social Security taxes, such a family would have had about $635 a month left to live on—for food, rent, utilities, furnishings, transportation, clothing, and medical care, not to mention life insurance, vacations, entertainment, and personal expenses for four people.

It is no easy task to construct a comfortable budget out of this total.* Whatever allocation is made for food, say, may seem too low for a family of four to live on, but if one tries to increase it, the increase has to come out of other allocations already unbelievably low themselves, such as barely over $100 a month for rent, utilities, and furnishings. This difficult budget is still close to one and a half times the government poverty line; by the official estimate, families at this level are not poor.

Beyond Money

If money had nothing to do with such basics as power, health, a sense of well-being, a good education, or control over one's own time, inequalities in income and wealth might be as trivial as inequalities of height. But in a predominantly money economy,

---

* For an analysis of one possible way for a family of four to live on half the median income, see *All Our Children: The American Family Under Pressure* by Kenneth Keniston and the Carnegie Council on Children (New York, 1977), Chapter 2, p. 30.

where goods, services, and benefits are publicly provided only to those who live at the margin of poverty—and usually with stigmatizing strings attached—inequalities of income are associated with a host of other inequalities.

To take just one example, low-income families are most heavily concentrated in low-income communities such as the inner cities,[22] where the housing stock is oldest, the streets least safe, and city services poorest. In areas like this, redlining by banks and savings and loan institutions makes it difficult for families to get mortgage loans, diminishing the possibility of home ownership, the security it brings, and the economic incentives and tax breaks that make improving a house feasible.[23] Even if mortgage money is technically available, inner-city families have trouble getting owners' insurance,[24] which is often required to get a mortgage. Real estate speculation, urban renewal, and housing abandonment threaten residential stability. The costs to merchants of doing business in poor, crowded, and crime-ridden neighborhoods mean that consumers have to pay higher prices for basic goods such as food and for credit when they buy on time.[25]

Even more telling for low-income families than the inconveniences, hazards, and hardships of living in market backwaters is the high risk of unemployment for family earners. When a person in the lower range of incomes does find a job, it is generally a low-paying job that offers little security, none of the fringe benefits that a majority of American workers can take for granted, and none of the on-the-job amenities of leisurely lunch hours or air-conditioned offices that the white-collar worker enjoys, much less any on-the-job training that might be marketable later. Such jobs are generally dead ends with little or no chance for advancement. They are frequently monotonous, sometimes backbreaking, and often mentally enervating, yielding little pride, pleasure, or challenge to the worker.[26] This kind of low-paying work produces not only low incomes, insecurity, and limited prospects for advancement but also occupational hazards and higher rates of physical and mental illness.

Directly and indirectly, these aspects of inequality affect children. Unemployment, for instance, correlates strongly with mental illness, family breakup, and child abuse.[27] More subtly, when work—and life—become a grind, even parents who possess a superhuman resolve to hold their families together and rear their children with love, affection, and encouragement subtly and inadvertently communicate feelings of futility and worthlessness to their children.

Money, it should be noted, is not the solution to all family problems in the United States. The rich may have difficulties understanding and communicating with their children as often as the poor do. Well-to-do families and children experience setbacks and stresses, pain and disappointments like everyone else. Making incomes more equal would not eliminate personal problems of this kind. What it would do is help remove those harms that the sheer lack of money imposes. These harms are substantial, and they fall particularly hard on children.

Growing up "unequal"—if you are on the wrong end of the bell-shaped curve—has two kinds of effects.

First, there are hardships and hazards, the insults and injuries of poverty, which are self-evident and have been well documented for years. We need mention them only briefly. The problems start in the womb and continue through infancy: the chances of death in the first year (and every subsequent year) are much higher for poor children and highest of all for poor black children, whose infant mortality rates are double those of whites.[28] The prevalence of poor health, poor nutrition, and, with them, slower physical development is greater as income decreases. Inadequate childhood nutrition can cause health problems later in life.[29] Poverty is also strongly associated with mental retardation; some 90 percent of children labeled marginally retarded come from poor families but have no known organic brain damage.[30]

Second, while some recent evidence suggests some significant improvements as a result of federal health programs (poor children see doctors nearly as often as more affluent children, for example),[31] the fact remains that their health is much worse. A study of 1,178 children receiving Medicaid in Mississippi showed that collectively, they had 1,301 major health problems, ranging from cavities and anemia to poor eyesight, untreated cardiac anomalies, and parasites.[32] In a low-income Chicano community in Los Angeles, children had 4 times as much amebic dysentery as the national average, twice as much measles, mumps, and tuberculosis, and 1.4 times as much hepatitis.[33] In Nashville, Tennessee, a study of 1,266 poor families showed that 97 percent of children in those studies had serious health problems, yet only 13 percent of those with diagnosed medical problems were receiving proper treatment, as were only 10 percent of those with diagnosed dental problems.[34] A recent study in Rochester, New York, found that the impact of Medicaid there on the serious health problems of poor children was, at best, negligible.[35]

Poor children are more likely to live in substandard housing, where, despite publicity and programs to combat it, lead-paint poisoning remains a major health hazard.[36] Poor children are scattered through every community in America, but they are especially concentrated in central cities, where crime rates are high, social pathology such as drug abuse is endemic, and the services provided by government—from police protection to education—are of questionable quality.

No parent would wish hardships of this sort on a child. Yet it might be argued that all these hardships children face growing up in poverty would not be so important if most of these children could look forward to a better life as adults. In fact, most of them cannot. *The most destructive aspect of poverty for a child is not, in our view, the daily hardship, the compounding risks of death, disease, family breakup, miseducation, and the like; it is the fact that for most of them adult life will not be significantly better.* For most of them the future is a small future, a fact that, we will argue, exerts a profound influence on their development. And this is so despite the vaunted openness of opportunity in our society.

Social Mobility: How Big Is
the Escape Hatch?

Many people who acknowledge the hardship and difficulty that poverty can bring still find some hope in the belief that any child who combines a modest degree of ability and effort can "better himself," "rise in the world," or "make it," to cite typically American expressions of different vintage but similar meaning. Certainly the image of America as the New World, or the land of opportunity, an image that helped inspire the great waves of immigration to this country, has also meant that to an unusual degree American families have made children the bearers of their dreams. Mothers and fathers whose lives have not quite lived up to their expectations look to their children to study hard, work hard, and achieve what the parents themselves have been unable to do. Americans may never have believed firmly in equality for all, but they have certainly believed in equal chances for all.

But the power and the plausibility of this ideal are not supported by the facts. As the case of Bobby and Jimmy reminds us, it is not so easy for children to make futures independent of the social forces that shape their lives from birth. In the broad sweep of American history the promise of a more equal society implicit in equal opportunity ideology has not been fulfilled. Not only are inequality of income and wealth stable features of our society, but our social structure appears no more fluid than that of other industrialized nations.

The historian Stephan Thernstrom, reviewing evidence on occupational mobility from one generation to the next (intergenerational mobility) over the past century and a half, has concluded that the inequalities in life chances associated with social class have altered scarcely at all. There has been, he concluded, "an element of remarkable, almost eerie, continuity. There was a calculus of probabilities that governed the likelihood that a young man from a particular kind of family would himself enter a given occupational stratum, a calculus that was nearly identical for youths born at any time between 1840 and 1930."[37] Thernstrom's evidence, based on his own data and thorough review of other historical mobility studies, may surprise some readers, but it is entirely consistent with findings of the great bulk of studies that have looked at intergenerational mobility in the United States in the twentieth century. The conclusion reached by Otis Dudley Duncan and Peter Blau in their landmark 1967 study of the American occupational structure can stand for all: "The influence of social origins [on adult social status] has remained constant since World War I."[38]

Studies of the American class system by Joseph Kahl conclude that after one accounts for mobility produced by variations in birthrate or changes in the occupational structure itself (e.g., a higher proportion of white-collar jobs, which produces mobility by definition), only 20 percent of American males exceed the status of their fathers through individual effort and competition.[39] This is hardly the fluidity depicted in our social mythology, and most people do not climb many rungs up the social ladder. (Note that by definition, 20 percent also fall below parental status when mobility through competition is the criterion.)

Intragenerational mobility, or the ability of an individual to make significant gains in occupational status over a lifetime, is not much better. Even among white men in the labor force, only 57 percent improve their work status during a lifetime. That leaves 43 percent who do not. And for black males, the combined chances that they will either move down the ladder or remain at the same rung they began on exceed the possibility of their moving up.[40] This is only one example of the discrimination that forces some people—minorities and women—to bear a disproportionate share of inequality's burden.

Most mobility studies have focused on white males, but the few studies that have concentrated on blacks or women in the United States have found significantly lower rates of mobility, both intergenerational and within the same generation. Particularly striking is the finding that the typical black male ends up just about where he began in the labor force. His exclusion from the normal white pattern of career advancement and an increase in earnings with advancing age is one more tangible example of the profound nature of racial inequality in the United States.

Furthermore, even "upward" mobility can be deceptive since most people who improve their status move only a few short steps up the career ladder. Unskilled laborers become operatives; typists become secretaries. But few typists become executives, few laborers become foremen, and few foremen become managers.

Thus, while there is some social mobility in the United States, the odds that differentiate a Bobby and a Jimmy have been impervious to change. Mobility has not diminished, as some have feared it might in an economy increasingly dominated by large corporations, but neither has it increased.

In none of this is the United States unique. But neither is it true, as many believe, that the chances for mobility are greater here than elsewhere. From Pitirim Sorokin's pioneering mobility studies in the 1920s to the present, study after study has found that intergenerational mobility rates in the United States are roughly comparable to those of other industrialized nations.[41] The liberal ideology of the United States minimizes the importance of class distinctions and proclaims that opportunity is open. European societies, heir to a lingering feudal tradition, are imbued with a deeper sense and awareness of class distinctions and class membership. But the differences are merely in attitude; the facts of socioeconomic mobility are much the same in Europe and the United States.

The Discrimination Dividend

Since the great majority of families in this country are white families with two parents, the greatest number of poor children come from white two-parent households. But any child in a minority household or a household headed by a woman bears a much greater chance of being poor, for discrimination by race and sex in this country adds a "dividend" ensuring that such families bear an extra share of inequality's burden.

There should be no doubt as to the reason why minority-group men and women of all races who do work have low incomes; it

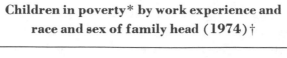

Children in poverty* by work experience and race and sex of family head (1974)†

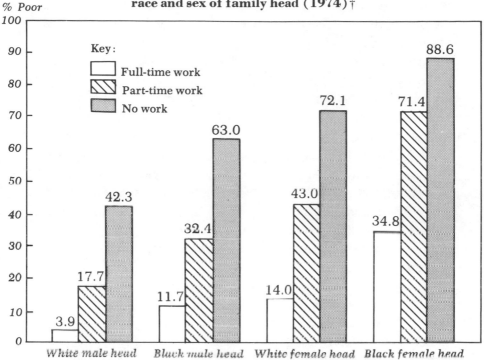

Source: *Characteristics*, Table 29
*Government poverty line
†Number of children under 18 as of March 1975

is because of discrimination. Sometimes a host of complex historical factors (including discrimination) combine to produce lower levels of educational attainment for women and minority-group members. Sometimes they are the victims of blatant discrimination in the workplace. The evidence comes clear from figures such as these:

When full-time black and white male workers *with the same amount of education and work experience* are compared in similar occupations, the salary of the average black man is 85 percent that of the average white man.[42]

If full-time male and female workers with similar back-grounds are compared, the difference is even larger. On the average, the salaries of women are 60 percent of those received by men. Among sales workers, a category in which women pre-dominate, the average annual woman's salary is only *40 percent* of the average man's.[43]

These figures do not necessarily mean that a woman or a black man in any given office is receiving lower pay than the white man at the next desk. Rather, it means that more women and blacks tend to get assigned to the lower-paying classifications within occupational categories and firms, to the lower-paying firms within industries, or to lower-paying industries. Often this kind of discrimination is masked by long-entrenched traditions, so women and minorities rarely even think to apply for certain jobs. This pattern of inequality is all the harder to unravel be-cause it is so deeply woven into the social fabric.[44]

Inequality between races or sexes is different from the basic distributional inequality we have discussed thus far. Some white males, who are not discriminated against as a group, end up in the bottom fifth because of social class stratification. Similar stratification also exists within the nonwhite and female groups: some blacks make much more money than others, and some women make much more than others. Indeed, the inequality in income between the top fifth of black wage earners and the bottom fifth is much greater than that between the average white and the average black.[45]

This does not mean that inequality between races and sexes is trivial; it just means that ending the discrimination that pro-duces these differences will still leave a long way to go to produce a more egalitarian society. Bringing the median income or the employment status of black families or female-headed families up to par with the majority would not necessarily diminish the unequal distribution of income and well-being that characterizes the society as a whole. It would simply eliminate the discrimina-tory mechanisms that now make the risk of low income much greater for children and families in these groups.

Children, of course, do not read statistics, surveys, or books like this. But in one way or another, directly or indirectly, they get the message. The child of a migrant worker reports: "Once a policeman asked me if I liked school and I said sometimes I did and then he said I was wasting my time there, because you don't need a lot of reading and writing to pick the crops, and if you get too much of schooling, he said, you start getting too big for your shoes, and cause a lot of trouble, and then you'll end up in jail pretty fast and never get out if you don't watch your step —never get out."[46]

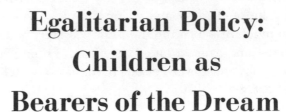

Chapter One

Egalitarian Policy:
Children as
Bearers of the Dream

Poverty, the poverty of civilized man, which is everywhere coexistent with unbounded wealth and luxury, is
always ugly, repellent and terrible either to see or to
experience; but when it assails the cradle, it assumes
its most hideous form.

—John Spargo, *The Bitter Cry of the Children* (1906)

Americans have not ignored the facts of social and economic
inequality in our society. Inequality often troubles the American
imagination, and for well over a century the nation has periodically tried to do something about it. Myriad programs, private and
public, have been devised to deal with aspects of poverty—to
help relieve the suffering of its victims and to improve their
prospects for good health, an adequate education, and economic
opportunity. To a considerable extent, these programs have
focused on children. It is also true that public policy in the
United States, when it addresses the needs of children, has
typically focused special attention on children who live in
poverty.

An explicit connection between children and equality in the
formation of public policy was first made 150 years ago at the
birth of free and universal public education in Massachusetts,
which its proponent, Horace Mann, proclaimed would end pov-

erty.[1] The same equation was made at the turn of the century, when every city saw the creation of settlement houses in part to improve family life, when the Progressives undertook to reform the public schools, and when the first White House Conference on Children was convened in 1909. More recently the same connection between a concern for equality and a concern for children can be seen in programs such as Project Head Start, compensatory education, and a host of programs for children's health and nutrition, all components of the War on Poverty in the 1960s.

Children and Equal Opportunity:
Tying the Knot

These public programs have typically been advanced on the grounds that social and economic inequality is at least partly the result of a vicious cycle that can best be broken by intervening in the victim's childhood—that poor children have poor parents who will rear them poorly to lead poor lives unless society steps in to "help." It has been generally assumed that programs of individual assistance to children caught in this cycle can enhance their social and intellectual development and therefore improve their life chances—that is, the likelihood that they will capitalize on opportunity to achieve secure, comfortable, or even rich status as adults. These are claims that programs to help individual children will help equalize *opportunity* for them, making the odds facing Bobby and Jimmy fairer. Whether or not programs of assistance to individuals can do this is a matter of debate (and is discussed at some length in Chapter 3). But the interesting point is how quickly the hopes for more equal opportunity for all have been confused with the presumption that making opportunity more equal will reduce the overall extent of poverty or economic inequality in the society. For 150 years this has been a recurrent claim of public policy concerning children and concerning inequality.

It is quite remarkable that the marriage of children's policy and egalitarian policy has lasted so long, for the facts suggest that it has served neither children nor equality well. Sometimes the laws and programs issuing from this marriage have had benefits for some particular children and their families, but at other times they have been so warped in practice that they actually damage their intended beneficiaries. And when we look at the results in broad perspective, the record shows a repeated failure to achieve more than minimal progress toward social and economic equality in the United States, a record particularly limited in the past third of a century.

Since World War II neither the heroic efforts of the civil rights movement nor the billions of dollars spent in domestic anti-poverty programs have dislodged our solid structure of inequality. In these thirty-odd years the distribution of income and wealth has been virtually frozen;[2] the historic differentials separating blacks and whites in earnings and unemployment have endured.[3] Despite affirmative action and the women's movement, women's salaries for comparable work remain substantially lower than men's.[4] Despite cycles of educational reform under the banners of "basic skills" in the post-sputnik 1950s, "the open classroom" in the 1960s, or "back-to-the-basics" in the 1970s, the correlation between the socioeconomic status of a child's family and the child's school performance and attainment (years of education) seems unshakable.[5] The extent of inequality—the gap between those at the top and those at the bottom—has not diminished.

Faced with these facts, some observers urge that we simply accept the biblical maxim "The poor ye shall have always with ye." Others argue that policies and programs aimed at eliminating poverty have been either badly designed or ineptly implemented. Yet the first proposition need not be true, and the partial truth of the second misses a deeper point. America's failure over 150 years to create a genuinely egalitarian society and to eliminate the hardships and lifelong denial of opportunity that inequality means for some children can be attributed to a tangle of misconceptions almost inevitable when egalitarian policy and children's policy are bound so closely together. That the misconceptions have held firm through so many failures is testimony to how deeply rooted they are in our culture. These misconceptions—perhaps better characterized as half-truths—are the beliefs that:

—*Poverty is an absolute state that one escapes by achieving a certain level of material well-being.*

This misconception, enshrined in the federal government's poverty line, misses the essentially relative nature of poverty: in a given society, one is poor primarily in relationship to others and the standard of living in that society. The idea that poverty is an absolute obscures the key issue—namely, distribution, or how great the income spread is between the richest and the poorest fifths of the population.

—*The cause of poverty lies in individuals and the way they develop.* Specifically:

First, it is widely believed that individual inadequacies are what determine who ends up poor. Anyone who wants to succeed can do so, says the myth. Therefore, those who don't succeed must somehow be choosing not to or must not have what it takes.

Second, it is generally assumed that if someone is inadequate, he either was born that way or suffered the wrong influences in childhood. American psychological and social thought widely subscribe to the idea that, as Wordsworth wrote, "the child is father of the man."

Third, it is widely believed that whenever inadequacy can be traced to environment rather than to genes, the probable environmental factors are no wider than the family or, at most, the neighborhood or school.

Together, these misconceptions naturally lead to assumptions that poverty can be treated by itself, without relationship to the rest of society, that the way to treat it is to "improve" the individuals who suffer from it, and that the most fruitful time to intervene in individuals' lives is during childhood.

These beliefs, and elaborations on them, have shaped American social policy in era after era, producing programs of assistance to individual children at earlier and earlier ages, either directly or through their families. The reasoning is that such assistance will give poor children a decent chance to become competitive, economically self-sufficient, successful adults. Unfortunately, when the state and the powerful members of society undertake to "help" poor children, they often cross the fine line between enhancing development and stamping out deviance, between assisting individuals and trying to control them. When this happens, egalitarian efforts stand on their heads and become means of reinforcing inequality.

Egalitarian children's policy has also been plagued by a deep cultural ambiguity about the concept of equality itself. Equality has long been a powerful ideal, but it is also an elusive concept that makes many people uncomfortable.

Americans have sometimes agreed that beyond one-man, one-vote and equal treatment before the law, things are not "as equal" as they should be. But it is always easier to argue that position than to answer the question "How equal should they be?" Some people maintain that we should pursue absolute equality for all, or equality of condition, but the only clear standard here is the empty concept of mathematical sameness. The more popular and enduring answer has been that society should provide equality of opportunity, specifically that no individual should be denied opportunity by virtue of race, creed, sex, national origin, or other such arbitrary characteristic. But without reference to the end results (which we know to be about as unequal as they ever were in this century), it is no easy task to decide whether equality of opportunity in the competition for social prizes and economic rewards is being achieved. Finally, it is important to remember that "equal opportunity" tells us nothing about equality of condition. To use a simple example, if society consisted of a rich king and 900,000 impoverished subjects, and the king were chosen by lottery, there would be perfect equal opportunity, but little equality to cheer about.

Changing Structure, Not Individuals

The ideal that makes sense to us is that no child should face systematic hardship in the present or systematic inequalities in life chances, as many children have faced for years in this society. At his desk in the second-grade classroom, Jimmy should have as good a chance as Bobby for living a rewarding and productive life. So should every child in the classroom, boy or girl, white or nonwhite, well-off or poor. It is the purpose of this book to argue that progress toward this goal will require that social policy eschew the half-truths and directly attack the issue of social and economic inequality.

A first step in our argument is to demonstrate that the beliefs we have called half-truths are indeed just that; next, to understand their source; beyond that, to appreciate how deeply the half-truths have conditioned our view of childhood and how deeply they are rooted in our culture and its dominant institutions.

The first necessity in this analysis is a reconsideration of the historic marriage between children's policy and egalitarian policy. Unless the conceptual framework binding children's policy and egalitarian policy is considerably altered, it is hard to be optimistic about the future prospects of either. If we Americans wish children to reap the equality of opportunity that is so honored a goal of our society, we must address an issue that has, ironically, been obscured by our focus on equality of opportunity; we must attempt to create greater equality of social condition directly, not indirectly through children.

To back up this sweeping statement, this book will veer away from children per se to a consideration of the tradition of American liberalism, which has provided the matrix for thinking about children, child and family policy, and equality. We will try to demonstrate the connections between liberal social policy and the way Americans think about children and their development, arguing that many aspects of children's policy in this country have been more an effort to *use* children to resolve deep-seated tensions and contradictions in adult society than a genuine effort to help children themselves. By and large, the effort has failed on both fronts.

The Origins of Our Liberal Ideology

Far beyond inspiring and sustaining the half-truths that plague children's policy and egalitarian policy alike, American liberalism has provided a continuum of political institutions and public values unmatched in any other industrial nation. "Liberalism" in this context does not mean the views of liberal Democrats, but a tradition of thought—a set of axioms about man and society —that emerged in late seventeenth- and eighteenth-century European thought and became embedded in Western culture, perhaps above all in American culture.[6] Since this book argues that contradictions in the liberal tradition are exactly what cause the repeated failure of many of our best-intentioned public programs, it is worth sketching in outline what the contradictions are and where they came from.

Three ideas dominate classic liberalism: one, that a rational natural law governs the universe; two, that this natural law can be deciphered and mapped by the operations of human reason, specifically the operations of the empirical mind (this idea attended the birth of modern science); and three, that individual well-being is the ultimate point of society, as opposed, for instance, to promotion of the church, the state, or any other institution as an end in itself. This third concept, the primacy of the individual, is directly derived from the first two; natural law, the philosophers of the Enlightenment argued, conferred on man certain "inalienable rights" which were the foundation of individual freedom, and through the development and exercise of reason the individual not only gained an understanding of those rights but became, in effect, their custodian. Liberal political theory, stressing the rights of individuals rather than inherited rights, gave birth to modern democracy. Similarly, the emerging economic order of the Industrial Revolution, also endorsed and sustained by liberal ideology, was built on the prerogatives of individuals to retain the rewards of their labor, not to work for the greater glory and profit of the local baron.

The peculiar irrationality of liberalism is not that it dismisses the existence of a dark, emotional, or irrational side of human nature, but that it believes that through a particular set of political arrangements called democracy and a particular set of economic arrangements called private enterprise or the free market, an ideal and eminently rational equilibrium will be achieved in the individual and in the society at large, and thus we will have "the best of all possible worlds."

An eloquent expression of this belief is Alexander Pope's poem "An Essay on Man," a pure piece of eighteenth-century liberal theory that builds to the famous conclusion that "everything that is, is right."

> Two Principles in human nature reign;
> Self-love, to urge, and Reason, to restrain;
> Nor this a good, nor that a bad we call,
> Each works its end, to move or govern all;
> . . . Self-love and reason to one end aspire,
> Pain their aversion, pleasure their desire;
> But greedy that, its object would devour,
> This taste the honey, and not wound the flow'r.

Liberal theory, as Pope's lines so deftly demonstrate, is at root a psychological theory ("Two Principles in human nature reign"). In liberalism, as it was developed in the Enlightenment, both political theory and economic theory reflect this individually focused psychological underpinning.

In the political theory of democracy, best exemplified by the second of John Locke's *Two Treatises of Government*, the origins of government were seen as a social contract formed among reasoning individuals who consent to a duly constituted form of government to preserve their own self-interest, including the protection of their natural rights. The opening paragraphs of the Declaration of Independence are often construed as an expression of Lockean social-contract theory.[7] "Natural law" gives individuals the right to withdraw from a government that no longer preserves their "inalienable" individual rights to "life, liberty and the pursuit of happiness." Governments derive their just powers from the consent of the governed, and "all men are created equal"; each has a vote, no greater in power or influence than any other's.

27

In liberal *economic* theory, epitomized by Adam Smith's *Wealth of Nations,* we can see the same combination of self-love and reason, and again the individual has primacy. The pursuit of self-interest, enlightened by rational choices in a marketplace governed by the laws of supply and demand (the economic equivalent of natural law), results, in theory, in a perfect equilibrium in which production is optimally efficient and the "unseen hand" of the market (the cumulative choices and decisions, based on self-interest, of rational individuals) determines which goods are produced. Quite literally the theory of free markets claims that when markets are free, "everything that is, is right." The implication is that in a free market all outcomes are fair, because every individual has been as free as any other to capitalize on his talents to the best of his ability. In such a situation, obviously, those who come out on top must be those who have the ability.

Political Equality vs. Economic Inequality: Who Wins?

There is, as many writers have observed, a deep tension in liberal thought between the political and the economic traditions. The political tradition emphasizes the equal *rights* of all individuals, rights conferred by the natural law from which human reason draws its strength. The economic tradition emphasizes not so much the rights as the *prerogatives* of individuals in the pursuit of self-interest, e.g., the accumulation of property and wealth. Rights and prerogatives often clash. The political tradition of rights embraces equality while the economic tradition of prerogatives leads to inequality. Perhaps this would not be troublesome if the political and economic domains were separate and distinct, but of course they are not. Economic monopolies have been widely acknowledged, from Adam Smith on, as being as potentially tyrannous as political totalitarianism, and economic power is regularly converted into political power.

The tension between the political and economic sides of the liberal tradition becomes a full-blown contradiction when history is considered. For although political rights are theoretically conferred anew as each individual reaches adulthood, economic privileges, capital, power, and opportunity can be, and are, passed on from one generation to the next. Being born rich (or poor) does not guarantee that one will stay that way, but it does make it much more likely. And liberalism, with its emphasis on the individual as maker of his or her own fate, has difficulty coming to grips with inequalities that are ordained at birth. In idealizing the individual, liberalism discounts the importance of historical forces beyond the control of the individual.

Liberal theory not only takes the individual out of time but also obscures the importance of social context. The political order is viewed as the product of individual "signatures" to the social contract, symbolized by the vote. The liberal economy is pictured as the result of individual choices, in both production and consumption. While it is obvious that, in fact, the society as a whole—its culture, classes, institutions—influences the way individuals think, act, develop, and choose and that the society as a whole shapes the opportunities and options available to individuals, liberal theory per se is at a loss to account for how. The "feedback" loop is generally missing: liberalism views the whole society as the product of its individual parts, and it frequently ignores the impact of the whole over time on the development of those parts. American psychology, for one highly influential example, has a propensity to focus almost exclusively on the individual and frequently fails to consider, except in a limited sense, the impact of social structure on individual development. This issue is discussed at length in Chapter 4; here, suffice it to say that while psychologists of various schools have focused on the interaction of the child and the child's environment, their definition of environment has been quite narrow, effectively limited in many studies to "Mom."

Psychology in the Liberal Tradition

The thought of John Locke was seminal in forming a binding connection between liberal social theory and modern psychology. His *Essay Concerning Human Understanding* bears much the same relationship to modern psychology as his writings on government do to modern political theory. In it he probed the nature of the individual who was elsewhere central to his social thought, arguing that there were no innate ideas—only senses that were the doorway to experience, which shaped the child's thought and in turn were shaped to coherence by the logical mind. In Locke's view, the child was both the object of experience and, to use a contemporary term, the processor of experience.[8]

Lockean psychology and, more generally, the psychology of the Enlightenment more or less originated the idea of development as we understand it today. The individual, acted on by experience and acting, through reason, on that experience, passes through a distinct stage of life called childhood. The child stands outside the social contract, and childhood, the time of development, is critical to the formation of the faculties that enable the individual to be party to the social contract. Proper shaping of the child, accordingly, was a way to shape a more perfect society. We can trace the influence of Locke, whose essay *Some Thoughts Concerning Education* wrestled with the best way to shape the experience of children, on much of pedogogic thought since the seventeenth century. It is reflected in the nineteenth-century pedagogies of Pestalozzi and Froebel and other Europeans, which in turn were the source for the pedagogic ideas of Americans from Mann through Dewey;[9] in the current stress on the importance of early childhood education; and in such apparently competing schools of educational thought as the open classroom and behaviorism, both of which share an underlying assumption about the importance of childhood experience in shaping adult patterns of thought or behavior.

The competing psychological theories from which educational theory is derived are likewise yoked together in the broad spectrum of liberal thought. Our psychologies, with only minor exceptions, are first and foremost psychologies of the individual. In Freudian theory, the pleasure and pain principles are as fundamental as they were to Pope, albeit differently treated, and both flow from experience acting on the individual. Piagetian psychology, with its emphasis on the formative influence of experience on cognition, mediated by the innate cognitive capacity of the child, can be seen as a subtle and sophisticated reworking of the Lockean dualism. The rewards and punishments of the behaviorists (whom many Freudians regard as their polar opposites) are themselves a reworking of the pleasure-pain dichotomy.

At this point it is possible to begin to draw together some of the threads that have constituted the fabric of liberal social policy over time and to begin to understand the centrality of the child to that fabric. What liberalism provided was a remarkably complete set of basic ideas.

No system of thought—in the West, at any rate—has since arisen to displace it. The ideas of science, progress, democracy, classical economics, and human nature—as it is formally studied by psychology—are all part of the same bundle, the same broad, encompassing view of human nature and society. This is not to suggest that liberalism is as simplistic as such a capsule treatment makes it sound or that all thought since has been a simple repetition of Locke. Quite simply, it is to suggest that the uses that liberal social policy has made of children are intrinsic, not incidental, to liberalism's basic precepts. In a nation that embraced those precepts with a "charming innocence,"[10] trying to achieve social reform by returning to the original precepts results in a powerful and peculiar conservatism. Reforms billed as "new eras" turn out to be replays of old efforts, with the same tragic flaws. This twist is particularly apparent when the logic of reform is applied to the salvation of children.

American Reform Movements

The continued power of the basic liberal misperceptions in shaping American views of children and social policy can be understood by reviewing the record of liberal reform in three crucial eras—the Jacksonian period (roughly 1828 to 1848), when the rudimentary precepts of equal opportunity ideology took shape; the Progressive era (circa 1895 to 1914), when these precepts became professionalized, bureaucratized, and deeply rooted in institutions and disciplines that are strikingly similar to those of the present; and the years from the inception of the Great Society era to the present. For while these periods differ in many important ways, and while each was characterized by internal disagreement about what to reform and how, there are striking continuities in the dominant theory and practice of reform in all three. The common concern with inequality and its handmaiden, poverty, helped produce in each era social reform movements that were expected to ameliorate social and economic inequalities. And in each era, the reformers' script was, in broad outline, a rewrite of the same play. The synopsis goes something like this:

Social protest is triggered or accompanied by shifting economic conditions, which always produce social dislocation that disturbs the patterns of all classes. The have-nots demand change, using protest, polemics, and sometimes violence to call attention to inequalities. The threat of disorder, together with genuine moral alarm, bestirs the more affluent and influential members of the society, who gradually reach a consensus on programs to restore social harmony.

In theory, two different strategies for ameliorating inequality are always possible. One is to make profound direct changes in the means of distributing wealth and privilege in the society, changing the ground rules, the focus of decision making, the means of decision making, and the nature of decisions in both the economic and the political spheres. Some such changes happened in each era. In the Jacksonian period the structure of banking was changed; in the Progressive era antitrust laws were established, and the income tax was instituted just thereafter; and the Great Society promoted affirmative action and briefly supported community action. But the primary emphasis of reform each time has been not on structural change, but on the second strategy—assistance to individuals.

This strategy has several familiar elements. First, instead of emphasizing redistribution of income as the means to achieve greater equality, reformers look to economic growth to make the pie larger and give everyone a bigger piece. The reformers put their faith in free-market economic theories, which argue that the market's distribution of goods, resulting from individual efforts and individual choices, is the best possible distribution. It then follows that the focus on stimulating economic growth will be

subtly transmuted into a focus on stimulating individual development. (It is more than semantic coincidence that *growth* and
development are key words in both psychology and economics,
for liberalism's emphasis on the primacy of the individual suggests that growth in these two realms is intertwined.) The three
periods of liberal reform each saw great emphasis placed on individual growth and development, primarily through education.
In each, individual development was perceived as both the strategy for enhancing equality *and* a means to enhance economic
growth.

It is at this point that the concept of equal opportunity comes
into play, and with it the emphasis on children. The economy has
developed inequalities, rooted in economic status but inevitably
accompanied by political and social inequalities as well. The reformers' chosen strategy for reducing inequality is, first, to
stimulate economic growth so that opportunity in general will be
increased; second, to make sure that anyone who has ability and
exercises effort can capitalize on that opportunity (for instance,
by the passage of antidiscrimination laws); and third, to provide
various kinds of compensating assistance to people whose backgrounds handicap them in the race to seize opportunity. Here,
liberal social theory and liberal psychology meet in policy and
programs to help children, for long before child developmentalists began arguing the importance of early years, liberal society
had begun to operate on the assumption that adulthood is too
late to do much to influence development. So the reform eras
whose histories we will review have seen the birth of common
schools, of settlement houses and social work aimed at improving family life, of juvenile courts given great power over family
life in the name of promoting the best interests of the child, of
early childhood health programs and education programs, of parent education, and, part and parcel of all these, the growth of
psychological and educational professions armed with theories
that are themselves profoundly shaped by liberal precepts.

What does the effort to manage individual development do
for equality? Very little of benefit to children, if we can believe
the data. But it does do something peculiar, even perverse, to
people's perception of the issue of equality. For as professional-

33

class reformers assume the management of individual development, *their* standards become the standards against which development is measured, and the child's task, as it were, becomes measuring up to these standards; the helper as manager has a substantial power over individuals. This may seem to conflict with liberalism's emphasis on "inalienable rights," but in our legal tradition, inalienable rights do not by and large apply to children.

In the liberal tradition the emphasis on individual assistance has an ironic footnote: when individuals fail to profit from the "help" they receive, the blame may be laid on the individual, not on the helper or the program. "Blaming the victim," as one writer has called it,[11] has been a pervasive habit in the history of liberal reform. At its most vicious, this practice takes the form of racism, proclaiming that the poor—especially members of a minority group who are predominantly poor—are genetically debased. Indeed, resurrection of the genetic hypothesis is often the final stage of reform. As the cycle completes itself, liberalism's emphasis on the individual proves to serve equally well as the rallying cry for social action and as the rallying cry for racism, individual blame, and reaction.

In a certain sense, the individualistic emphasis of liberal reform has been highly successful. Under the banner of equalizing opportunity, it has been possible to promote economic growth and preserve social harmony while holding out the promise of a millennium—the promise that, in the *next* generation, children will fulfill the dreams of their parents. As that peculiarly American admonition of parent to child, "Better yourself," suggests, the mission of childhood in this country has been defined to a considerable extent by the promise of equal opportunity.

Chapter Two

Political and Social Reform
in Three Eras

The ideas of economists and political philosophers, both
when they are right and when they are wrong, are more
powerful than is commonly understood. Indeed, the
world is ruled by little else. Practical men, who believe
themselves to be quite exempt from any intellectual
influences, are usually the slaves of some defunct
economist. Madmen in authority who hear voices in the
air, are distilling their frenzy from some academic
scribbler of a few years back. I am sure that the power
of vested interests is vastly exaggerated compared with
the gradual encroachment of ideas.

—John Maynard Keynes, *The General Theory of
Employment, Interest and Money* (1936)

Lord Keynes's well-known comments on the power of ideas in
history can serve as text for this chapter, if a corollary is added.
Ideas may be more powerful than vested interests, but when
vested interests support ideas, the resulting ideology is more
powerful still. The marriage of children's policy and egalitarian
policy is a case in point. The history of egalitarian social policy
in the United States is the history of a developing ideology so
powerful that it has reinforced the status quo even as it claimed
to change it.

The Jacksonian Legacy: Equality
with Limits

Some writers have dubbed the Jacksonian era "The Age of Equality," but historians differ on the real nature and extent of the egalitarian impulse in that period. Arthur M. Schlesinger, Jr., in his 1945 book *The Age of Jackson,* interpreted the emergence of the Jacksonian Democratic party in terms akin to class struggle.[1] Most historians, however, have supported Richard Hofstadter's argument that the real struggle was less interclass than intraclass, a battle between the established propertied families of the eastern seaboard states and the rising entrepreneurs of the frontier, of whom Jackson himself, a lawyer, merchant, and land speculator, was prototypical.[2]

Regardless of how one interprets the political conflicts of the era, it is clear that during the 1820s and 1830s there were widely conflicting interpretations of what *equality* meant in the United States and that in resolution of that conflict, both the Democratic party and the traditionally conservative Whigs adapted Thomas Jefferson's concept, equality of opportunity, which has since become a basic element in the American consensus.[3] In the process, the basic pattern of reform was established. Economic growth was emphasized. The actual achievement of equality was deferred to the next generation through a focus on children and equal opportunity. The reformers stressed the importance of managing individual development (for purposes of increasing economic productivity, restoring social harmony, and, presumably, fostering equality). Often the reformers' prescriptions were couched in moral rhetoric that could be read two ways: as an expression of altruism or as a self-righteous condemnation of the morality of the poor. The era even saw the emergence of one of the classic explanations of why reform didn't always work: the people who were the object of all the reform efforts were genetically inferior.

In the early years of the nineteenth century the Whigs, the direct descendants of Alexander Hamilton's Federalists, were the dominant political party, and the Hamiltonian view of equality prevailed. As Hamilton had put it years before, "All communities divide themselves into the few and the many. The first are rich and well-born, the other are the mass of the people. . . . The people are turbulent and changing; they seldom judge or determine right. . . . Give, therefore, to the first class a distinct, permanent share in the government. They will check the unsteadiness of the second and, as they cannot receive any advantage by a change, they therefore will ever maintain good government."[4]

It was axiomatic in this view, first, that wealth and good judgment would always be unequally distributed and, second, that wealth and good judgment always went hand in hand. The issue, accordingly, was simply how political power was to be distributed. As late as 1821 leading Whigs, such as Chancellor James Kent, would use terms very like Hamilton's to argue against extending the right to vote beyond those who owned property. "The disproportion between the men of property and the men of no property," he said, "will be in every society in a ratio to its commerce, wealth, and population." He went on:

The tendency of universal suffrage is to jeopardize the rights of property and the principles of liberty. There is a constant tendency in every human society, and the history of every age proves it; there is a tendency in the poor to covet and to share the plunder [*sic*] of the rich; in the debtor to relax or avoid the obligation of contracts; in the majority to tyrannize over the minority and trample down their rights; in the indolent and the profligate to cast the whole burthens of society upon the industrious and the virtuous; and there is a tendency in ambitious and wicked men to inflame these combustible materials.[5]

But by the 1820s the Whigs' resistance to more equal rights for all was crumbling. In state after state the franchise was being extended to all white men, whether they owned property or not. Inspired partly by European revolutionary thought, the doctrine of equality, while still cast primarily in terms of legal and voting rights,[6] was being broadened to include not only universal suffrage but also economic rights. Urban areas saw the rise of early trade unions and the first workingmen's parties, with platforms that called for free and universal education, and on the frontier a new class of entrepreneurs was developing. Under the rallying cry of "Down with monopoly and privilege," Jackson's Democratic party was becoming dominant in state after state.[7]

The old Hamiltonian view of "equality" as meaning only equality before the law and equal political rights among the propertied had lost its political viability. At the other extreme, an antithetical minority view embracing early socialist sentiments gave evidence of how broad a meaning the word *equality* was beginning to assume in the American lexicon. Such voices on the left, arguing that the concept of equal rights should be extended to include a right to property, alarmed the Whigs.[8] But the Democratic party espoused a far more restricted egalitarianism than some Whigs had feared. In vetoing congressional efforts to reestablish the U.S. Bank, President Jackson took pains to indicate the limits:

Distinctions in society will always exist under every just government. Equality of talents, of education, or of wealth can not be produced by human institutions. In the full enjoyment of the gifts of Heaven and the fruits of superior industry, economy, and virtue, every man is entitled to protection by law; but when the laws undertake to add to these natural and just advantages artificial distinctions, to grant titles, gratuities and exclusive privileges, to make the rich richer and the potent more powerful, the humble members of society—the farmers, mechanics, and laborers—who have neither the time nor the means of securing like favors to themselves, have a right to complain of the injustice of their Government.[9]

Although some of his supporters may have been thinking that more than opportunity should be equal, Jackson clearly was not. As Hofstadter points out, "This is not the philosophy of a radical levelling movement that proposes to uproot property or to reconstruct society along drastically different lines. . . . What is demanded is only the classic bourgeois ideal, equality before the law, the restriction of government to equal protection of its citizens. This is the philosophy of a rising middle class; its aim is not to throttle but to liberate business."[10]

Part of the ideology of equal opportunity is present in Jackson's veto message: the economy is to grow, and all are to have a chance at reaping its dividends. But he accepts the inevitability of social classes and treats them almost as a given not worth arguing about. Inequality is objectionable only when it is sustained by privilege and monopoly. So while Jackson's policies were designed to increase access to capital, he also warned that the "real people" of the country—the planters, farmers, mechanics, and laborers who were its "bone and sinew"—should not "expect to become suddenly rich by the fruits of their toil."[11]

As is often the case in the magic lantern of American political history, images blurred and faded into each other. Hamiltonian ends—the promotion of business and wealth—were to be achieved through Democratic means: extending the franchise to all white men and giving them access to capital through state banks. But there was no intent, at least on Jackson's part, to overhaul the social order. He was as certain as Hamilton or Kent that distinctions in society would continue. In arguing for more "democracy" in the marketplace, in fact, the Jacksonians were simply arguing a classic free-market position, endorsing the distribution of rewards through the means of individual competition in the market. If anything, as the historian Marvin Meyers has demonstrated, the Jacksonian Democrats were attempting in their attack on concentrated eastern wealth to achieve, amid social, economic, and territorial change, the tranquil world Thomas Jefferson had described in writings a half century earlier: a society of autonomous and hardworking individuals, rising or falling on their own merits.[12]

The Democratic version of a free, open, and growing economy was one of a cluster of ideas that merged in this period to provide the reform ideology of equal opportunity. But it remained for the Whigs—dropping their Hamiltonian ideology in a dramatic about-face—to put the finishing touches in place. It was primarily out of the Whig party (and the established middle and upper classes that formed the backbone of its constituency) that the prototypical liberal concern for individual development emerged. For the democrats, despite their reputation and sometimes their rhetoric, had a limited commitment to "equality" and even to "equal opportunity." Indeed, as one historian has put it, "with all their talk about providing opportunity for the largest number and eliminating restrictions blocking the economic and political progress of the American people . . . the Jacksonians were singularly unresponsive towards women's rights, prison reform, educational improvements, protection of minors and other forms of social betterment."[13] The Democrats supported slavery, and Jackson's policies toward Native Americans in opening the economic terrain of the West were almost genocidal. Early sentiment for abolition of slavery, protection for Native Americans, the temperance movement, the creation of asylums, and the promotion of free, universal education and curtailment of child labor were causes that although they did not attract all Whigs, received support and found their leaders among influential Whig politicians and businessmen, especially in the Northeast. Thus, in the Jacksonian era social reform assumed the patrician quality it has frequently exhibited since. In the process the remaining strands of equal opportunity ideology were woven into place.

So long as the Whigs stuck to the Hamiltonian line, with "their love of capitalism and their fear of democracy,"[14] they provided ready political ammunition for the Democrats, who had merely to accept Hamilton's description of the facts and advance a more popular explanation. Roger Taney, for instance, who was Jackson's secretary of the treasury, was simply inverting the logic of his predecessor Hamilton when he told the House of Representatives in 1834: "It is a fixed principle of our political institutions to guard against the unnecessary accumulation of power over persons and property in any hands. And no hands are less worthy to be trusted with it than those of a moneyed corporation."[15]

For reasons of sheer political expedience, the Whigs had to find a new "line," and they did. Inverting the old Whig emphasis on social distinctions, they now denied the importance—sometimes even the existence—of social class in America, asserting instead that capital and labor were interdependent and that opportunity was open to all. The conversion of Daniel Webster illustrates the Whigs' turnabout. In 1820 Webster was opposed to the extension of the franchise because "there is not a more dangerous experiment than to place property in the hands of one class and political power in those of another," but in 1838 he told the Senate that while Europe had a "clear and well-defined line between capital and labor," here we had "no such visible and broad distinction."[16]

Edward Everett, the governor of Massachusetts in the late 1830s, was another Whig who helped form the dogma of what Schlesinger has aptly called "the Whig counterreformation."[17] Everett praised the "comfort and elegance" of newly constructed mills; he told working-class audiences that he, too, was a workingman; he warned that "the blow aimed at the moneyed capitalists strikes over on the head of the laborer, and is sure to hurt the latter more than the former." And picking up Webster's theme, he declared that there were no classes in America since here "the wheel of fortune is in constant operation, and the poor in one generation furnish the rich of the next."[18]

Horace Mann's Perfect Balance Wheel

The Whigs' new doctrine was more than opportunistic rhetoric. The concept of interdependence expressed their real desire to restore social harmony. In the face of the dangers and the domestic strife that the industrialization of the economy was bringing, the Whigs promoted industrialization as diligently as did the Democrats, but they still worried about its likely side effects. Horace Mann, for instance, a Whig politician and a promoter of industry before his appointment as first secretary of the Massachusetts Board of Education, argued that steam represented not only a critical source of energy for the state's economy but also a source of dramatic and dangerous social change. He accurately foresaw that "if steam is employed, there is no assignable limit to the amount of manufacturing population that may be gathered into a single manufacturing district."[19] Like his friend Abbott Lawrence, the leading industrialist of the state, Mann feared the result would be cities like England's Manchester, where "great numbers of the laboring population live in the filthiest streets" and where parents "raise children dedicated to ignorance and vice."[20]

Mann went further than simply worrying about city slums. In

his *Twelfth Annual Report to the Board of Education* (1848), his analysis mixed moral alarm with an almost Marxist critique: Massachusetts, he wrote, "by its industrial condition and its business operations . . . is exposed far beyond any other state in the Union, to the fatal extremes of overgrown wealth and desperate poverty. . . . If this be so, are we not in danger of naturalizing and domesticating among ourselves those hideous evils which are always engendered between Capital and Labor, when all the capital is in the hands of one class, and all labor is thrown upon another."[21]

Mann was asking what, in effect, could be done to ensure that the "wheel of fortune" would keep lifting the poor out of poverty, as his friend and ally Everett had claimed it did. Mann was looking for a means that would somehow enable industrial progress —which he saw as inevitable *and* beneficial—to proceed hand in hand with social harmony. And the key to social harmony, he said, had to be the elimination of poverty. If the Jacksonians' extension of the franchise and creation of state banks would not do it, the prime question was how could it be done?

The solution Mann came up with was destined to be as enduring as it was popular, for it provided the final link in the ideology of equal opportunity that is still with us. In a famous passage from his *Twelfth Annual Report* Mann—after denouncing quasi-socialist schemes for sharing the wealth—declared, "Education, then, beyond all other devices of human origin, is the great equalizer of the conditions of men—the balance-wheel of the social machinery." And he added, in a less often quoted phrase, "It does better than to disarm the poor of their hostility towards the rich; it prevents being poor."[22]

Here, for the first time, public policy seized upon the child as the place to resolve the tensions of liberal capitalism. To Mann's view of education as a harmonizing and an equalizing influence —capable, he argued, of reconciling democracy and order in ways Whigs a few years earlier feared impossible—he added yet another benefit: education would simultaneously promote individual wealth and the growth of capitalism. "Beyond the power of diffusing old wealth," the *Twelfth Report* went on to say "[education] has the power of creating new." Education would make workers more productive, he said, in part by increasing their knowledge and in part by inculcating the proper values and behavior patterns (an argument that appealed to many business-men). And by increasing the general level of knowledge, education would stimulate technological improvements. "Education has a market value," he wrote to Abbott Lawrence. "It may be minted and will yield a larger amount of statutable coin than common bullion."[23] Lawrence preached the same message: "Let your common school system go hand in hand with the employ-ment of your people; you may be quite certain that the adoption of these systems at once, will aid each other."[24] It was obvious that Mann had struck a chord that seemed deeply right to some people who had already received many advantages from the wheel of fortune and apparently did not feel that Mann's new "balance-wheel" would dislodge them from the top. His salary as secretary of the state board of education was supplemented by some of the state's successful businessmen, who also put up the funds for his pet innovation: the first "normal school" or teacher-training college.*[25]

Mann—like other reformers then and since—urged that schooling be systematized and given over to a class of profes-sionals. His normal school was designed to train teachers, thereby making a profession of teaching. He argued for the appointment of professional administrators—superintendents—to replace citizen boards in running school districts. He advo-cated consolidation of local school districts into bigger units

* The common school was not the only form of education advanced as a means of simultaneously educating and civilizing the work force. The so-called Boston Associates, for instance, under the guidance of the fabulously successful in-dustrialist Francis Cabot Lowell, created the "Waltham system" of model fac-tory towns, which attempted to avoid the evils of a Manchester by organizing social, educational, and recreational activities for their employees (who at first were primarily young women)—an effort to blend the factory and the finishing school. As changes in the mode of production, the availability of cheap male immigrant labor, and the rising "cult of femininity" conspired to change the nature of the work force, this effort rapidly went by the boards. But if it be-came obvious that education could not be grafted onto the workplace in ways that turned every worker into a paragon of gentility, the hope remained that schools would have that effect.

and a strong role for the state board of education as central overseer. Thus, he felt, the "balance-wheel" could be founded on solid rock to ensure that every child in each generation would have an equal opportunity to compete for the benefits of an expanding economy. This did not, of course, mean that the benefits of the economy should be equally distributed themselves, only that everyone's chance to employ his talents in obtaining them should be as good as the next person's.

In Mann's day there were critics who argued that the tenets of equal opportunity were flawed. One of these was Orestes Brownson, who served briefly as a leading theorist for the Democrats in Massachusetts and was active in their unsuccessful effort to dismantle the state board of education in 1850. Brownson criticized Mann's claims that the common school would be an equalizer. "We regard the improvement of the adult as the means of advancing the child," he wrote, "rather than the education of the child as the means of advancing the adult." And he argued that the tools Mann advocated—a strong state board of education, normal schools, centralization of control—were designed less to promulgate knowledge than to achieve social control. Brownson declared that the creation of the business-backed state board was an effort to "imitate despotic Prussia," where "the King, seeing what the French Revolution has made quite evident, that the people will have education and that they cannot much longer be kept in submission to their masters by brute force, shakes hands with the schoolmaster." Brownson predicted, accurately, that once "they get their Normal schools into successful operation, they will so arrange it, if they can, that no public school shall be permitted to employ a teacher who has not graduated from a Normal school."[26]

Indeed, Mann was not denying these intentions; he explicitly stated that schools were an instrument of social control and said that they would "disarm the poor of their hostility towards the rich." He wrote that such an event as the French Revolution "would never have happened with free schools," that "the mobs, the riots, the burnings, the lynchings, perpetrated by men of the present day, are perpetrated because of their vicious or defective education when children."[27] Here the characteristic moralism of liberal reform creeps in, and the knot that binds moralism, upper-class dominance, and the instinct for social control together in an American ideology of managed development is apparent. It is even more pronounced in Mann's statement that the common or public school was "an instrument more extensively applicable to the whole mass of the children than any other instrument yet devised. [Through it] the good men in society can send redeeming influences to those children who suffer under the calamity of vicious parentage and evil domestic association."[28] In other words, both Mann and his antagonist, Brownson, agreed that schools were instruments of social control; they differed merely over whether that control was good or bad.

Mann argued that the common school would socialize children to the requirements of the new industrial order while simultaneously shaping individuals in ways that avoided the industrial world's excesses. It would, he hoped, restore the old moral order while promoting the new economic order. The experience of schooling would "hold out to the young mind the example of industry and perseverance and self-denial as indispensable requisites to greatness." (A cynic might observe that these also happen to be requisites to keeping a labor force poorly paid.) Throughout his reports Mann stressed that simply undergoing the school regimen would teach students the requirements of clock time, which the factory, unlike the farm, ran on, and would cultivate punctuality. (Mann was also a strong early advocate of health and physical education, which he believed would increase worker productivity by preventing illness.) And he and his followers were sympathetic to the pedagogy of European educational reforms because they believed this new "soft" pedagogy would prove far better than the old hickory stick at inculcating strong internal moral controls in children.[29]

The actual impact of the school on most children in the Jacksonian era is unclear, since school attendance remained sporadic and, for most children, brief throughout most of the nineteenth century.[30] But the role of Mann's thought in shaping the formulas of liberal reform and in helping create a powerful national mythology is beyond question. Mann's work, preaching the gospel of schooling, industrial progress, and social order, was enormously influential in the development of schools throughout the East and Midwest, in the West, and, after the Civil War, in the South.[31] Most important, the common or public school movement established the rationale that subsequent waves of reformers would seize on in their attempts to resolve contradictions and outright blemishes in the social fabric through children.

The Land of Opportunity and Its Underside

The Whig theory of a classless society that could be redeemed from its flaws through children, when coupled with the Jacksonian Democrats' insistence that opportunity was open to everyone, established the framework of equal opportunity ideology. As Louis Hartz has written:

We think of the Whigs in the age of Harrison as stealing the egalitarian thunder of the Democrats, but actually they did more than that. They transformed it. For if they gave up Hamilton's hatred of the people, they retained his grandiose capitalist dream, and this they combined with the Jeffersonian concept of equal opportunity. The result was to electrify the democratic individual with a passion for great achievement and to produce a personality type that was neither Hamiltonian nor Jeffersonian, but a strange mixture of them both: the hero of Horatio Alger.[32]

The importance of this transformation can hardly be overestimated. It created a political middle ground from which neither major political party has since been able to stray very far for very long. It codified an ideology that fulfilled the old Federalist yearning for a national identity (America, the land of opportunity), an identity that, after it survived the challenge of the South, proved a solid base for a country that was emerging as a political and economic power in the world. And this ideology of equal opportunity was what reformers of subsequent eras would return to again and again as they tried to resolve the continuing tensions in our system between political rights and economic prerogatives.

Horace Mann's optimistic predictions that education would be "the great equalizer of the conditions of men" did not prove accurate. Through most of the nineteenth century the economy grew apace with industrialization and the creation of a national transportation system and national markets, but at the same time American cities developed into the hellholes Mann and Lawrence had so dreaded, and the distribution of wealth and income appears to have been scarcely equalized at all.[33] Mann's invention was never up to preventing poverty, as he had dreamed it would be. Did it at least even the chances of all to obtain the unequal rewards at the end of the race? Not really. It may have contributed at least to keeping inequality from getting worse, but mobility patterns did not change from generation to generation any more than the distribution of income did.

However, the ideology of liberalism was established, and its mythology survived—in part because, whatever else they accomplished, schools were splendid instruments through which to propagate the gospel of liberal capitalism. A widely used mid-century textbook declared:

If he has good health and is industrious, even the poorest boy in our country has something to trade upon; and if he be besides well educated and have some skill in any kind of work, and add to this moral habits and religious principles, so that his employers may trust him and place confidence in him, he may then be said to set out in life with a handsome capital, and certainly has as good a chance of becoming independent and respectable, and perhaps rich, as any man in the country. Every man is the maker of his own fortune.[34]

The same story was virtually canonized later in the century by Horatio Alger in his best-selling novels about "ragged Dick" and other rags-to-riches heroes. And in the legend that grew up around Abraham Lincoln, the dream of the self-made man reached its apotheosis.[35]

A few extraordinary careers and a handful of novels did not change the facts that opportunity was not equal and equality did not increase. But the facts apparently could do nothing to subdue the myth of equal opportunity. For one thing, there was a certain measure of social mobility, then as now, and there was considerable economic growth. As David Potter has argued, the fact of abundance has long shaped the American social character, making it easy to gloss over injustice, inequality, and other blemishes in the social order.[36] Also, it was a broadly centrist belief capable of sounding either radical or conservative. So long as a few diehards maintained the original Federalist line or as newspapers such as the *Philadelphia National Gazette* opposed the common school as "an agrarian plot [for] compulsory application of the means of the richer for the use of the poorer classes," the liberal reformers sounded almost revolutionary. Indeed, contrasted with the remnants of European feudalism, their doctrine of equal opportunity *was* revolutionary.[37]

When common schooling for the mass of children failed to make good the liberal reformers' promises of an end to vice, crime, and poverty, people began to blame not the system or the ideas on which it was based, but the people the reforms were supposed to work for. As the first great wave of immigration peaked in the early 1850s, there arose a social and political movement holding that Americans descended from the early settlers were constitutionally superior to the German and especially the Irish newcomers.[38] Clearly, reform theory wouldn't work out perfectly in practice if it was applied to second-rate stock. For instance, Samuel Gridley Howe, an ally of Mann's who had been particularly active in creating the first of those ultimate schools, the reform school, finally despaired of his efforts and concluded: "The causes of evil are manifold, but among the immediate ones the chief cause is inherited organic imperfection, vitiated constitution, or poor stock."[39]

Thus, some of the disillusioned reformers of the Jacksonian era were able to find an explanation for the failure of their reforms in theories of genetic inferiority. Many people maintain that this genetic argument represents a rejection of liberalism and all it stands for; but since the argument has reappeared in the wake of nearly every social reform that has failed, it seems more accurate to describe the theory of genetic inferiority as the underside of liberalism's individualistic bias.

The Progressive Era: Equal Opportunity
in the Corporate State

As the nineteenth century came to a close, growing unrest over worsening economic and social conditions prepared the way for another period of reform. The 1880s and 1890s were decades of great economic instability: cycles of inflation and recession intensified; farm prices sank dramatically, and a fresh wave of immigration began, bringing people from the Mediterranean and Eastern Europe who swelled the ranks of the poor in large urban slums.[40]

At the same time, there developed a new class of highly visible millionaires; the sons of Horatio Alger had become the robber barons of the Gilded Age, the titans of industry and finance— Rockefeller, Morgan, Vanderbilt, Gould, Frick, Carnegie—whose opulent, ostentatious life-styles struck some as uncouth and others as immoral and no doubt excited envy in still more. Oil, steel, railroads, and finance, the sinew and muscle of the economy, were under their control, bound together by trusts and interlocking directorates. These were the visible manifestations of a new and rapidly growing form of economic organization— the heavily capitalized corporation.[41] Concentrations of capital on this scale had never been seen before. The funds raised for one monopoly, the steel trust, in 1904 would have been enough to run the federal government for two years.[42]

At the turn of the century the consensus supporting liberal ideas was shaky, the efforts to reconcile Jeffersonian pastoralism with industrial capitalism had obviously failed, and the liberal order was not functioning according to script. Poverty was widespread; living conditions were execrable for the poor, especially in the cities; the trusts and a variety of monopolistic business practices were making the idea of open, competitive markets obsolete; and political corruption was rampant. Many politicians' votes were for sale to the highest bidder, which meant a corporate bidder. The traditional liberal separation of political and economic systems was breaking down fast.

In rural America the Populist party began—and nearly elected William Jennings Bryan president in 1896. In urban America there was agitation on the left, exemplified by the Haymarket riots of 1886, and a new upsurge in labor union activity, often opposed with physical violence by employers. There was a flourishing Socialist party, which, at its peak, won close to one million votes (6 percent of the total) for Eugene V. Debs in the 1912 presidential election.[43]

This was a more complicated society than the United States of Jackson's time, and the specific political and social issues were different; but there is a striking similarity between both the broad issues and the instruments of reform in both eras. The precepts that had crystallized as the ideology of equal opportunity fifty years earlier reappeared as the guiding precepts of the Progressive reformers. The ambiguities and paradoxes in the reform program reappeared as well.

These conflicts are apparent in the Jacksonian era only with the hindsight of history. By the time of the Progressives, however, the effort to reconcile the basic political and economic tenets of liberalism with a society that was undergoing massive social and economic changes resulted in a strange tangle of means and ends, of modernism and nostalgia, of science and moralism, of efforts to control the corporate "octopus" and infatuation with the management technology of big business. The underlying tensions of the period are evident in reformers' efforts to come to grips with changing economic organization, most notably in the antitrust movement (the contrasting views of two very different "reformers," Theodore Roosevelt and Woodrow Wilson, illustrate some of the conflicting pulls that resulted from efforts to apply old formulas to new problems), and these tensions reappear as blatant contradictions in the area of social reform. Struggling to come to grips with a new set of social and economic forces through the application of an ideology that did not account for them well, reform theory unwittingly embraced sharp contradictions. In reforms aimed at helping poor children or their families, especially in the implicit effort to reconcile the new with the old and to resolve social problems through programs serving individuals, the Progressives established institutions, practices, and professions that are still with us. But in recasting and refining liberal ideology, they added strange new meanings to individualism and equality.

Economic Reform

"My problems," said Theodore Roosevelt, "are moral problems, and my teaching has been plain morality." These words could have been the motto of a generation of reformers.[44]

If Roosevelt's morality was "plain," it was only because he spoke with the absolute assurance of moral rectitude that social standing conferred on the upper-middle-class and upper-class reformers of the era. He was promoted as president by the business aristocrat Mark Hanna, and "the advisors Roosevelt listened to were almost exclusively representative of industrial and financial capital."[45]

Yet Roosevelt began his political career as a reform politician, active in municipal government and civil service reforms in New York. As president from 1905 to 1909 he gained the nickname "the Trustbuster" primarily because of his attacks on John D. Rockefeller and Standard Oil, although his administration initiated far fewer antitrust actions than the immediately previous and subsequent ones. In 1912, after four years out of office, he became the first presidential candidate of the new Progressive party, much to the chagrin of some members of that party.

An emblematic bundle of contradictions, the apostle of "rugged individualism" and often a jingoist, Roosevelt saw quite clearly that the economic map of the country had changed and that the precepts of liberal individualism, if they were to survive, would have to be reconciled with an increasingly concentrated and corporate economy. A number of people were arguing that economic individualism and the cutthroat competition that accompanied it had been the cause of economic instability. Roosevelt agreed. "Concentration and cooperation in industry in order to secure efficiency are a worldwide movement," he said in his acceptance speech at the Progressive party's 1912 convention.

Some governmental controls on the economy were needed "in order to protect the people," so "concentration, cooperation and control are the key words for a scientific solution of the mighty industrial problem which now confronts this nation."

Roosevelt never viewed antitrust action as a way to break up concentrated industries and restore the days of small firms and individual entrepreneurship; he saw it as a means to preserve the old moral order while promoting a new business order. He had told Congress in 1902: "Our aim is not to do away with corporations; on the contrary, these big aggregations are an inevitable development of modern industrialism, and the effort to destroy them would be futile unless accomplished in ways that would work the utmost mischief to the entire body politic. . . . We draw the line against misconduct, not against wealth."[46] In linking concentration, cooperation, science, efficiency—and morality—Roosevelt was in full accord with many Progressive thinkers.[47] But some reformers, nostalgic for a simpler era, disapproved of his tolerating large-scale corporate enterprise. Woodrow Wilson, for instance, also casting himself as a reformer (first as governor of New Jersey and subsequently in defeating Roosevelt and Taft in the 1912 presidential election), opposed Roosevelt's "New Nationalism" with his "New Freedom." He wrote nostalgically of that "ancient time in America" when "men were everywhere captains of industry, not employees," the days of "absolutely free opportunity, where no man is supposed to be under any limitations except the limitations of his character and of his mind."[48] Similarly, a U.S. circuit court judge, Peters Grosscup, wrote in the muckracking journal *McClure's* that there was an alternative to monopoly and the concentration of wealth in a few hands. It was "individual opportunity—the opportunity, actual as well as in theory, to each individual to participate in the proprietorship of the country."[49]

Roosevelt proved, perhaps, to be a better student of history than Wilson. He wrote in his autobiography that nostalgic formulas for re-creating economic individualism were "both futile and mischievous" since they sought to remedy "by more individualism the concentration that was the inevitable result of the already existing individualism. [People] saw the evil done by the big combinations, and sought to remedy it by destroying them and restoring the country to the economic conditions of the middle of the nineteenth century."[50]

Wilson had an equally incisive response to Roosevelt's call for concentration, cooperation, and government intervention. He said, "If the government is to tell big business men how to run their business, then don't you see that big business men have to get closer to the government even than they are now? Don't you see that they capture the government, in order not to be re-strained too much by it?"[51] In short, if Roosevelt foresaw the new economic order, Wilson foresaw the history of regulatory agencies. Their disagreement emerges as two horns of a di-lemma. Wilson wanted government action that would restore the economy to an innocent state in which government action would no longer be necessary. Roosevelt wanted the government to regulate industry without restructuring it, to curb its power without interfering with its efficiency. Both men were clearly operating within the liberal tradition, attempting to dissociate the economic and political systems, yet neither could find a version of the tradition that would work.

Political and Social Reform: Morality and Control

While Roosevelt, Wilson, and others struggled in various ways to reconcile the new economic order with an older version of morality, muckrakers, social scientists, civic leaders, and edu-cators struggled with the question of what to do about the cities and the urban poor. Many of them saw the source of trouble as industrial society and "greedy capitalists." Even Roosevelt took his share of potshots at "the dull, purblind folly of the very rich men; their greed and arrogance." Publications abounded with analyses that linked "urban problems" to economic sources, accusations that the trusts were buying and selling politicians, arguments that the great influx of immigrants was being de-liberately encouraged by big business to attract cheap labor (and undercut the wages of American laborers), and moralistic at-tacks on the business tycoons of the day. There were even sharper structural analyses arguing that the forms of production in industrial society inevitably led to social, economic, and political inequities and that poverty was intrinsic to the capitalist system.

Yet the reformers once again took it as their mission not to solve inequality—or poverty, the eyesore that bothered them the most—in the present, but to equalize opportunity for the future. The problems of poverty might be unsolvable for the present generation, but with the reformers to provide an antidote to family incompetence, the wheel of fortune would turn. By the next generation both moral excellence and material well-being would be achieved.

Like most liberal reformers, the Progressives looked backward for their prescriptions. In the mirror of the past they located a bucolic, predominantly rural America of harmony, equality, and moral probity, which they sought to re-create in urban form in order to produce the influences they felt would open the future for the children of poverty. The reformers would work with individuals in small settings—schools, settlement houses, neighborhoods, families—to re-create the benign environment of rural nineteenth-century America. John Dewey set out the essential argument in 1899: the school must attempt to mimic, in the midst of a growing industrial economy, conditions that pertained "one, two, or at most three generations" back, when "the household was practically the center in which were carried on . . . all the typical forms of industrial occupation." He went on to say:

The children, as they gained in strength and capacity, were gradually initiated into the mysteries of the several processes. . . . We cannot overlook the factors of discipline and of character-building involved in this kind of life: training in habits of order and of industry, and in the idea of responsibility, of obligation to do something, to produce something, in the world. There was always something which really needed to be done, and a real necessity that each member of the household should do his own part faithfully and in cooperation with others.[52]

Despite occasional passages like this one, Dewey generally avoided the moralizing and nostalgia that characterized the thinking of others who held this attitude.[53]

Juvenile Justice and the "Child-Saving" Movement:
A Case in Point

Nothing more clearly illustrates the ambiguities and inherent shortcomings of Progressive reform than the creation of the juvenile justice system or the "child-saving" movement. With antecedents in earlier decades, this movement—fundamentally an effort to take juveniles out of the adult corrections system and provide them with individualized, therapeutic justice— picked up a full head of steam in the 1890s, with state after state adopting laws for the special treatment of juvenile offenders and designating, at the same time, a special set of so-called status offenses (such as truancy, loitering, and incorrigibility) that applied only to juveniles. As one review of recent historical treatments of the movement summarizes it:

On the one hand, reformers were genuinely shocked at young people being housed in city and county jails with adult criminals. Out of humanitarian impulses, they sought separate facilities to hold them, and separate trials to process them. On the other hand, child-savers throughout the 19th century, and increasingly after 1870, sought to control or change the so-called "predelinquent" behavior of youth and thereby prevent future crime. In practice, this meant middle- and upper-class officials and reformers tried to control the social behavior of poor and immigrant children—the "perishing and dangerous classes." Successful inculcation of middle-class values in lower-class youths would help secure the position of the upper orders by removing the potential threats of individual crime and collective political protest.[54]

In an effort redolent of nostalgic pastoralism the child savers "sent out" tens of thousands of children to live in rural areas, assuming that rural life would instill virtue in them. They also attempted to replace incarceration in adult jails with detention in family-style "cottage homes"—sounding a theme not unlike that of current efforts to "deinstitutionalize" juvenile justice facilities in favor of group homes in community settings. In addition, the primitive tools of the emerging profession of psychology were used on juvenile offenders in an effort to diagnose individual needs.

No doubt it was an improvement, at least in the short run, for children to spend time in cottage homes rather than in sinkhole prisons in large cities, just as efforts to remove adolescents from contact with adult criminals in those prisons which have yet to do so make sense today. "Benign incarceration" is preferable to inhumane incarceration. But there was a price: once given "special status," juveniles lost the protection of due process. For better or for worse, they stood solely at the mercy of the court. And in the long run, it is apparent that the intentions of reformers were not realized in practice. Family-style cottages turned into mini-prisons; rural communities protested the exporting of these clearly stigmatized youths to the country; and, perhaps the crushing blow, the effort to inculcate middle-class values was often undercut by the simple fact that there were no jobs waiting to provide middle-class status. In fact, as some observers at the time discovered, sending urban youths to rural settings at a time when agricultural and rural employment was beginning a long contraction was a prescription for failure.[55] The traditional liberal effort to reform individuals—even at the price of social controls that ran afoul of traditional liberal concerns for civil liberty—was undercut by the traditional liberal failure to account for structural economic forces. Whether the half loaf of reform was better than none is not the central question here. Rather, it is (as discussion of the current juvenile justice system in Chapter 4 illustrates) that the main result of these reforms was to "save" children from adult jails only to make them the prisoners of benign intentions.

Trying to Make a Science

In many ways, Progressive reformers' underlying strategies for social reform, and the conceptual framework they relied on, resemble those of Jacksonian reformers. But a new note, a new faith in managerial solutions to basic social problems, is also present, and the mixture has strange consequences.

The complex, massive, and concentrated industrial economy was here to stay; children had to be taught how to adapt. Specifically, they had to learn cooperation; individual potential would have to be realized within the confines of the industrial order.

Reform efforts should thus adopt the tools, the techniques, and the organizational formats of that economic order. Scientific efficiency had to be introduced into reform methodology, just as the skills and moral values of efficiency had to be induced in children. Progress would lead to restoration; the chaos and disruption of the new corporate economy would be harmonized by application of its managerial tools to the individual and the family, as well as to the management of government. These trends that developed in the Progressive era produced a set of hybrid institutional practices that are still with us.[56]

Emphasis on reforming children and their family life distracted attention from the economic forces, differences in power, and the distribution of goods that were, then as now, both results and causes of inequality and its perpetuation. The effort to make a science of reform did nothing to counter this tendency, for it was, as one would expect in a liberal society, first and foremost a science of individualism, drawing on the individualistic psychology of William James, on the measuring and testing of individual intelligence, on early theories of child development, and on the growth of biological knowledge concerning hygiene and nutrition. To be more precise, the "science" of the Progressive era was concerned with explaining—and rationalizing—differences between individuals. This was indeed a perverse kind of concern for individuals, for individualization by the Progressive definition began to mean different, not equal, treatment.

The supposedly scientific discovery that people were different from one another—and the use of increasingly specialized instruments such as IQ tests to measure the differences—mirrored the increasingly specialized needs of the workplace at the turn of the century. Science was now being marshaled to explain those limitations that qualified Woodrow Wilson's vision of equality of opportunity: "No man is supposed to be under any limitations *except* [and we add the emphasis] *the limitations of his character and his mind.*" There was a nearly perfect fit between the requirements of the economy—increasing differentiation and specialization of roles in hierarchic organizations—and the postulates of this science. On the one hand, psychologists

57

had a battery of tests to prove that individuals had different talents and degrees of ability. On the other hand, the occupational structure required different talents and abilities. The challenge for the Progressive reformers, persuaded as they were of individual differences, became the creation of institutions that could detect and develop the different talents and abilities of individuals and funnel them into the right "slot" in the occupational hierarchy. Thus, liberal social theory and the ideology of opportunity were merged with the new doctrine of corporate interdependence (advanced by Roosevelt, Herbert Croly, and others)[57] and the science of individualism.

With this marriage *the tradition of individualism became a tradition of inequality*. Schools, a major concern of Progressive reformers, provide both the clearest and by far the most important example.

Inequality as Individualism: The Case of Schools

Progressive educational reformers were caught between several rocks and a few hard places. Everyone was telling them what to do. Theorists such as Dewey argued that schools had to take on a set of functions that had previously been lodged in the home. Muckrakers such as Joseph Mayer Rice were attacking the schools for corruption, archaic teaching methods, and incompetent teachers.[58] Other muckrakers, lashing out at the social conditions in the cities (especially in immigrant communities), demanded that schools become agents of social change. ("Dare the schools create a social revolution?" asked George Counts, a leading educator.) Others—including some immigrants—were insisting that the schools help Americanize immigrant children. Municipal reformers, alarmed by the cost of schooling and the prospect that it would multiply with the rapid growth of the high school, wanted whatever was done to be cheap. Social scientists, particularly in the burgeoning new field of psychology, were arguing that the schools needed to become more scientific, basing curriculum on sound learning theory and acknowledging the different capabilities and aptitudes of pupils. At the same time, school administrators influenced by Frederick Taylor, the efficiency expert and apostle of "scientific management," were urging an overhaul of school management to make the school system run more like a factory. Educators and businessmen alike were arguing that the schools had to assume new responsibility for vocational education, preparing students for the differentiated roles in the corporate structure which both scientific management, with its stress on hierarchic specialization of labor, and the evolving forms of production demanded.[59]

Out of this clash of demands emerged extraordinary educational innovation and activity which, as Lawrence Cremin has argued, transformed the American school and laid the groundwork for much subsequent educational theory and practice.[60] One kind of innovation was the "soft Progressivism" popularly, if erroneously, associated with Dewey's name today—the free, loose, child-centered approaches to schooling caricatured in *Auntie Mame*. But then, as now, only a small minority of cultural radicals, bohemians, and children of the affluent actually attended such schools.

The far more common result was "hard," or conservative, Progressivism, which emphasized bureaucratic efficiency, standardization of curriculum, assessment of students' achievement by comparison of each of them to the norm, and differentiation of school offerings, or "tracking," according to measures of individual ability.[61] What the reformers did not perceive, or perhaps acknowledge, was that all these measures tended to reflect strongly the social class of the child's parents.

Beginning with Harvard President Charles W. Eliot's call in 1888 for what we today describe as "ungraded" classes (without distinctions between, say, first and second graders, to permit each child to proceed at his or her own pace), the Progressives— true to their liberal roots—placed great emphasis on "individualizing instruction."[62] The aim was to break the "lockstep, all-children-are-alike" approach to teaching, as a *Ladies' Home Journal* article put it, but efforts to implement this goal included stronger and stronger administrative controls, which tended to reduce the teacher to a relatively powerless cog in the machine.[63] The teacher's individual judgments, proclivities, and talents were now subordinated to the dictates of the system.

The Progressives' approach to individualizing instruction was to standardize and divide the curriculum into small sequential units, prefiguring the programmed instruction of today. Theoretically this enabled teachers to decide what step a child belonged on (although there is little reason to believe that most children did not continue to progress step by step, side by side with other members of their class). And there was a major emphasis on measuring both pupils' achievement and their "potential." Toward the end of the Progressive era IQ tests were becoming more and more commonplace. The result of these reforms—all illustrative of efforts to apply science and modern management to education—was, ironically, that schooling became more and more routinized, while individualized instruction came to mean (as it still often does) little more than grouping children by ability or assigning them to tracks.[64]

At the same time the reformers' interest in individualization placed stress on developing the "whole child," a concept derived from Dewey's observation that the school had to assume many functions traditionally performed in the home. But the strange result of applying modern management to this task was the creation of more and more specialists—the school counselor, the school nurse and school social worker, the industrial arts teacher, and so on. Each specialist assumed responsibility for a fragment of the whole child, with planners and administrators at the top of the bureaucratic heap responsible for managing the system in a way that was supposed to put all the pieces back together.

As one result of these developments, many of the functions traditionally lodged in the home became the responsibility of the state. A complex bureaucratic apparatus, erected in the name of individual development and the preservation of family life, increasingly diminished not only the family's role in child rearing but the ability of parents to influence or control the presumed determinants of a child's growth. In the structure of business, government, and schools and other service organizations, the application of the emerging managerial technology of liberal capitalism was more and more at odds with the traditional liberal emphasis on individualism.

The Progressive era's administrative reforms helped transform education from a process of interaction between teacher and learner into a problem of instructional management. This extraordinary transformation, the prime contribution of Progressive reform to American education, is still affecting children.

In the process of bureaucratization, *individualization* took on a new meaning directly related to the world of work. The same thing was happening to two of Theodore Roosevelt's favorite words, *cooperation* and *interdependence*. Roosevelt and some other Progressive reformers rejected the cutthroat individualism that classic free enterprise then seemed to mean, because it produced economic chaos. They argued that the new industrial order of concentrated organizations required cooperation not only between industrial sectors (steel and the railroads, for instance) but between individuals within the organization—between owners and managers, managers and workers. Specifically, cooperation no longer meant a mutual relationship of equals, but the complementary interdependence of differentially ranked individuals in a hierarchy. Individuality, in turn, was to be achieved through cooperation, and an individual's "uniqueness" was increasingly defined by the role he or she had to play in the productive system.

For the Progressives, as for the common school reformers before them, the measure of an individual—his morality, his talent, his social worth—was, in the final analysis, an economic measure. The achievement standards urged on schools were those that presumably reflected the cognitive requirements of an emerging corporate economy. The moral and personal qualities in which students should be drilled and against which they were to be measured—diligence, cooperation, and, above all, efficiency —were seen as the prerequisites to the economy's growth. The effort to mold schools into specialized, consolidated, centrally managed bureaucracies was a conscious effort to copy industrial modes of production and to create an institutional environment in which children would be socialized to the relationships and procedures of the corporate world. To this end, the curriculum was busily revised so that its broad contents and individual tracks would teach the skills presumed necessary for the changing economy.

The Progressives' clear perception of the interplay between the economic system, on the one hand, and social life, family life, and secondary institutions such as the school, on the other, struck a new and distinctly modern note that was far more sophisticated and self-conscious than the perceptions of Mann and his contemporaries. Indeed, if one accepts the structure of the productive system as an immutable given, the Progressive reforms in education possess a compelling logic, for schools were definitely being redesigned to supply the different levels of a hierarchic labor force. But accepting this as inevitable is tantamount to an acceptance of social and economic inequality as a prerequisite to economic progress.

Individual instruction, in fact, explicitly meant differential instruction. But if children were to be differentially educated according to their abilities and taught to realize their individual potential by the single standard of becoming "cooperative" workers, special parts in the industrial complex, then both *individuality* and *equality*, words traditionally linked in liberal theory, had taken on perverse connotations. The meaning of *individualism* and *equality* in this revised liberal formula were summed up by the Boston superintendent of schools in 1908: "Until very recently, [the schools] have offered equal opportunity for all to receive *one kind* of education, but what will make them democratic is to provide opportunity for all to receive such education as will fit them *equally well* for their particular life work."[65]

The contradictory nature of reform educational thought is well represented in the work of Elwood P. Cubberley, one of the most influential educators of his day and, like Mann before him, a touchstone for reform thought. The tendencies and tensions we have identified as characteristic of liberal reform are all readily apparent in Cubberley's seminal work, *Changing Conceptions of Education*.[66]

Closely following Dewey's analysis in *Society and the School*, Cubberley argued that as the world had grown complex, parents were unable to fulfill the functions they once had. Inevitably "each year the child is coming to belong more and more to the state." He insisted that to restore the civic and moral virtues of an earlier era while further promoting economic growth, the schools had to play a larger and larger role. But true to the liberal tradition, Cubberley was full of contradictions. In the concluding chapter of *Changing Conceptions*, he wrote in an Algeresque vein: "Each man with us is the captain of his own fate and the carver of his own destiny." The implication was that differences in individual status simply reflect differences in individual talent and effort. But elsewhere Cubberley gave a sharper structural analysis of the causes of inequality that moved beyond individual traits. "With ever increasing subdivision and specialization of labor," he wrote, echoing Mann, "the danger from class subdivision is increasing."

Cubberley also looked to schools to resolve this contradiction, but his thoughts merely recapitulated it. On the one hand, the public school, which Cubberley portrayed in his influential history of American education as a "triumph" of democracy, would ensure that the social structure remained open. The school would be "a ladder for all who can afford it and have the mental capacity to use it." But Cubberley had doubts about how many actually had the capacity to climb very many rungs on that ladder, and the same writer who was concerned about "the danger from class subdivision" caused by specialization of labor wrote a few pages later that the urban schools, particularly, "will soon be forced to give up the exceedingly democratic idea that all are equal, and that our society is devoid of classes . . . to begin a specialization of educational effort along many new lines in an attempt to adapt the school to the needs of many classes."

Cubberley argued that "the great battles of the world in the future are to be commercial rather than military or naval. . . . The trained artisan is to be the private; the trained leader the captain; and an educated, sober, capable and industrious people the base . . . in a gigantic battle of brains and skill [for] the markets of the world." In this "battle" the school system, that erstwhile source of equality, could adapt industrial methods, particularly the methods of scientific management, to preparation of labor for an economic system premised on inequality. "The school," Cubberley declared, "is essentially a time and labor saving device." In a few short pages, "the captain of his own fate" had become the industrial private, the "carver of his own destiny" had become a cog in the economic army. The tension between the political tradition of individual equality and the economic tradition of individual prerogatives seems explosive, mediated only by Cubberley's implicit assumption of intrinsic differences in individual merit and his faith in the moral righteousness of school bureaucracies.

There was never any doubt who should control the centrally managed, professionalized, scientifically run bureaucracies Cubberley advocated or whose values and ideals should be promulgated in them: for Cubberley, as for Mann, it could be only the "best men" of the society. The most severe test for the schools, as he saw it, was posed by the Southern and Eastern European immigrant groups who had come to the country after 1880: "Illiterate, docile, lacking in self-reliance and initiative, and not possessing the Anglo-Teutonic conceptions of law, order and government, their coming has served to dilute tremendously our national stock, and to corrupt our civic life . . . and the problems of proper housing and living, moral and sanitary conditions, honest and decent government, and proper education have everywhere been made more difficult by their presence."[67]

The ready-made excuse for reform's failure—the intrinsic inferiority of the individuals whom reformers were claiming to help—was clear in these words, which echo the nativism of the mid-nineteenth century and prefigure the racism of the mid-twentieth. Social Darwinist thought, a strong undercurrent throughout the Progressive era,[68] simplistically translated the theory of evolution into the belief that the most powerful and successful in any given society were of a superior breed. Social Darwinism, coupled with the development and use of IQ tests, gave birth to the eugenics movement (which argued that the human race should be improved through selective breeding), which was rising in strength as the approach of World War I coincided with the decline of reform zeal. For the leaders of this movement, including many prominent figures in educational testing circles, the urban poor were not simply "illiterate, docile [and] lacking in self-reliance," they were inherently, genetically inferior. Henry Goddard, for instance, declared that 83 percent of all immigrant Jews were feebleminded.[69] In this mood, state after state (eighteen in all) passed laws permitting sterilization of criminals and persons judged mentally defective.

It is easy to cross that fuzzy line between reform and racism, between scientific analysis and moral condemnation, between environmental and genetic explanations of poverty, between social work and social control, between human development and the training of a docile work force, and the Progressive reformers often crossed it. They built the ironies and ambiguities of liberal reform into the intellectual tools, the analytic approaches, and the structural properties of the institutions and professions that became their legacy to the future.

One More Time: Reform from the Great Society to the Present Day

The most recent reform era is in many ways similar to its predecessors. Because it happened so recently, it is the most difficult to assess; indeed, it is hard to say if it is over.* Thus, no effort will be made here to review this period comprehensively. But some brief comments on continuities and differences are in order.

The unique aspect of present-day reform has been its focus on racial minorities, especially black Americans.† The situation of

---

* Although the current conventional wisdom is that the days of the Great Society ended with the 1960s, legislation such as the Youth Employment and Demonstration Projects Act of 1977 is extremely reminiscent of the social reforms of the Johnson era.

† Racial minorities were of marginal concern, at best, in earlier reform eras, barring the special short-lived case of Reconstruction. The Progressive era, for instance, came on the heels of *Plessy* v. *Ferguson*, the Supreme Court case that promulgated the doctrine of "separate but equal," and was the time of Jim Crow laws. Few Progressive reformers paid attention to the situation of blacks, and when they did, it was perfunctory. Muckraking journalist Ray Stannard Baker, for instance, described a lynching with horror but saved his heaviest criticism for city officials in Springfield, Ohio, who in the wake of the lynching "were stirred by the faintest of faint spasms of righteousness; some of the Negro saloons were closed up, but within a month, the most notorious of all the dive-keepers, Hurley, the Negro political boss, was permitted to open an establishment."[70] Somehow, it seemed, black drinking was responsible for white lawlessness.

The Public Education Association in New York did commission a study of black education in 1916, but the next study of black education in New York did not appear until 1957.[71]

minorities was at once proof that equal opportunity did not exist in America and a ready-made opportunity to dust off the tools and ideologies of equal opportunity reform. From platform after platform in the last twenty years black leaders and white supporters have declared, "All we want is simple justice; all we want are the same rights for black, brown, red, and white alike; all we are asking is that our children have the same opportunities as white children." The extension of constitutional protections, a halt to discrimination in jobs, housing, schools, and elsewhere, and a fair chance for each individual to make his or her own way have been the prime goals of the civil rights movement. These are the noblest and most basic goals of the liberal tradition.

But significant as it would be if these goals were realized, they are also in some ways limited goals. Neither the aims nor the means of the movement for interracial equality (or of the subsequent movement for equality between the sexes) have, for the most part, constituted a movement for more equality per se. They do not propose closing the gap between rich and poor by redistributing income, wealth, and power more equally among different social classes. Rather, these goals stress only the wish that the current system's benefits and its penalties should fall equally on black and white.

This would be a big step, for currently blacks are about half as "equal" as whites. If blacks achieved the same "equal opportunity" as whites, black unemployment rates would be the same as those of white, not twice as high; the same percentages of blacks would complete college as whites; the same percentages would hold professional and managerial jobs, not roughly half as many. The median family income for blacks would be the same as for whites, instead of 60 percent as much. Only 30 percent of black children would live in poverty, instead of 60 percent.

These would be mammoth improvements, yet the problem of inequality would remain. As one major study put it: "There is always far more inequality between individuals than between groups. It follows that when we compare the degree of inequality between groups to the degree of inequality between individuals, inequality between groups often seems relatively unimportant. It seems quite shocking, for example, that white workers earn fifty per cent more than black workers. But we are even more disturbed by the fact that the best-paid fifth of all white workers earn 600 per cent more than the worst-paid fifth."[72]

We certainly do not argue that racial inequality is unimportant or that the movement for racial justice should be abandoned because it is not embedded in a larger movement for social equality. The long-standing goals of the civil rights movement have great moral force, and they are essential components of any overall egalitarian policy. But the movement for racial equality is handicapped when it is not linked to a broad effort to increase equality among all persons.

Of course, many of the reform programs of the 1960s—manpower training, the Job Corps, Model Cities, compensatory education, the growth of Aid to Families with Dependent Children (generally known as welfare), Medicaid and Medicare, establishment of the Office of Economic Opportunity and such OEO programs as Head Start—were not targeted exclusively at racial minorities. Michael Harrington's book *The Other America* (New York, 1962), credited by some with inspiring the War on Poverty, dwelt at length on the poverty of urban and Appalachian whites. President Kennedy's initial interest in a national attack on poverty was apparently stimulated in large measure by the poverty he saw during the West Virginia primary. In fact, because of their relative numbers, many more whites than blacks qualified for antipoverty programs in the 1960s. But with an assist from the press, most of them became widely viewed as "black" programs (so much so that in some locales, such as New York City, Puerto Rican and other minority groups attacked the Great Society for excluding them). The rhetoric and priorities of many reformers in and out of government did little to allay this concern. In the War on Poverty, the needs of the so-called working poor—especially in white urban ethnic communities—were ignored.[73] The government adopted a poverty line that made them ineligible for assistance in many programs. Many programs likewise contained heavy penalties for even small amounts of earned income. And the popular identification of programs as "black" programs, however inaccurate, tended to perpetuate divisions along racial lines within the low-income population. Logical allies, the poor and the individually power-less, were kept apart—and sometimes at each other's throats—through the culturally and emotionally divisive issues of race.

New Versions of Individual Inadequacy

Finally, questions of racial justice aside, the reform programs of the Great Society years, with some important exceptions, rever-berated with the basic flaws of earlier reforms. They caused the revival of the hypothesis that genetically determined intelligence causes social inequality. Again they invested the child with the burden of realizing the reformers' dreams. And again they con-fused services to individuals with a strategy for equality.

It is important to understand that the need for services exists independent of issues of equality. Education, health care, child care, and other human services are needed and used by families in every income group. But low-income families, under the great strains of poverty and unemployment, may need more services than others, and because they lack both the money to purchase services privately and the power to hold market providers of services accountable, they often need publicly provided services. To argue that the provision of services is not an effective strategy to promote equality is not, obviously, to argue for cutting service budgets. It is a call to relieve service systems of the one burden—effecting greater equality—that they cannot discharge and that complicates their real mission and restricts their real capability.

These services can counter some of the injuries of inequality, but they cannot destroy inequality itself. Services are insufficient by themselves to alter the powerlessness, the limited life op-tions, and the hardships of everyday experience that are the bottom line of inequality. In the 1960s service-oriented reforms such as compensatory education, preschool programs, man-power programs, and a range of health, mental health, and coun-seling programs were promoted as egalitarian measures and packaged in the rhetoric of equal opportunity. Educational pro-grams, especially, were expected to produce gains for racial minorities and low-income whites that would translate into better employment opportunities and economic returns.

As this central tenet of liberal reform was advanced again, many of the familiar patterns that undercut egalitarian efforts in the past recurred. By the 1960s planners were not using the language of moral opprobrium, but in its place—completing the Progressive transition from moralism to pseudoscience—there grew up an extensive language of psychology, which amounted to much the same thing. A leader of the "cultural deprivation" school, which provided much of the rationale for early childhood education as a supposed "passport to equality," wrote that children who fail in school (and whom teachers expect to fail) were "children who come with the fewest aptitudes for a middle-class-life-oriented situation. They are likely to be the most poorly dressed, to have a dialect, to come to school somewhat late, and, in general, are likely not to fit naturally into the kinds of middle-class structures and constrictions that are established within the school system.[74]

Along with recourse to social science jargon in order to "blame the victim," many reformers in the 1960s revived the focus on achieving social equality through the reform of individual children. In doing so, they pushed back to earlier and earlier years the date at which intervention was regarded as necessary. In the late 1950s the preoccupation was with juvenile delinquency. Dropping out of school, reformers argued, caused delinquency and led to a life of unemployment, poverty, and even crime. The need, as former Harvard President James B. Conant maintained, was to provide more effective educational programs "appropriate" to the abilities of urban youths—particularly black youths—to hold them in school and defuse this "social dynamite." Concern about juvenile delinquency was widespread, but by the early 1960s many were arguing that high school was too late to catch problems.

Compensatory education programs and preschool ventures such as Head Start were mounted on the basis of emerging theories that early development substantially determines the rest of a child's life. Head Start produced some cognitive gains for children enrolled, but when those gains failed to hold up through the early years of school, some critics concluded that ages four and five, the Head Start years, were also too late. Commenting on discouraging assessments of early schooling programs in 1968, a leading child developmentalist argued for earlier intervention: "With any failure to demonstrate the effectiveness of compensatory experiences offered to children of any given age, one is entitled to conclude parsimoniously that perhaps the enrichment was not offered at the proper time."[75]

Many agreed, if less parsimoniously. Harvard psychologist Burton White has claimed that the critical developmental period is the first eighteen months, a point of view that has provided the rationale for publicly funded programs in which social workers and psychologists attempt to train parents in the "proper" form of child rearing from the day of birth or earlier.[76] Gerald Ford's commissioner of education, T. H. Bell, exemplified the recurrent resort to moralism in his statement to the American Association of School Administrators in 1975: "Have our increased efforts in education been negated by a decline of the home and a neglect of the education responsibilities that parents traditionally and absolutely must assume? I submit that this is precisely the situation. . . . Entirely too many of the children coming to us are emotionally disturbed and psychologically unstable. To strive to teach the child without reaching out to the source of this difficulty is to treat the symptom and ignore the basic cause." Findings that school programs are a less important determinant of pupils' achievement than family status have also fueled the rationale for earlier and earlier programs of intervention.

Another idea that has gained adherence in recent years is that of parent education. Like so many social reform programs, this one is based on a highly debatable idea. Certainly there are parents who are ill equipped for the job—in every income range. There are parents who feel insecure and want help and information. In a world of isolated and sometimes lonely nuclear families, they have few resources to turn to. Professionally run educational programs are one possible response to their needs, although existing evidence gives little reason to believe that many such programs will be effective.[77] But it is a big and illogical step from this possibility to the conclusion that parent-education programs will improve the school performance or life chances of poor children. To the extent that poor school performance reflects a parent's child-rearing style, it is by no means clear that the cause of a given approach to parenting is parents' ignorance. If a parent is clearly inadequate to the task of child rearing, exhaustion and anxiety produced by economic stress may be the cause. Or it may be that a certain style of raising children is entirely appropriate for the life situation of a given family but inappropriate to produce children tuned to the requirements of school. But it is highly compatible with historic American patterns of reform to regard parent education as a strategy for equality, so it continues to be advanced as such.

Finally, recent reforms have led to neo-Progressive refinements in school tracking, again garbed in scientific language, which have resulted in individual children—especially poor and minority-group children—getting labeled, treated with behavior-modifying drugs, and assigned to special classes, all in the name of individualizing education and equalizing opportunity.

The growth of medical explanations for a school's failure is an example. If a child is categorized as sick, the school can be confident that there is no social problem, no issue of social structure, but only an individual problem— or a whole slew of individual problems. The systematic misclassification of black children as retarded is one example of this kind of conversion, by which problems with a social origin can be perceived as individual problems and blamed on the people who suffer from them.[78] The discovery of "learning disabilities" is another, particularly exquisite case of converting a social value judgment into a medical diagnosis.

In a few short years an entire subprofession has sprung up, ready to diagnose and treat such vague and grandiloquently titled ailments as *minimum brain dysfunction* (MBD) and *hyperkinesis* (a word derived from the Greek which, freely translated, simply means "this kid won't sit still in class"). These ailments now compete with cultural deprivation theories as popular explanations for why children do poorly in school and hence miss out on opportunity.

Presumably there are learning disabilities that some children suffer. Efforts to correct them are in order. But there is more than a little debate about etiology, diagnosis, and cure,[79] and there is an enormous potential for abuse of this potentially useful concept, given our cultural predispositions. Consider the following. A paper reporting the results of a seven-year follow-up study of five hundred children screened for learning disabilities in second, fourth, and fifth grade concluded:

The data we have presented appear to confirm the notion that children who are identified early as having behavioral and learning problems are at risk for developing academic as well as social adjustment problems in adolescence. In comparison to our control group, our "hyperkinetic" children had substantially lower mean grade point averages, achievement scores and I.Q. scores.

Furthermore, the "hyperkinetic" population was much more likely than the control group to be in the slow or remedial sections in school, to exhibit poor or very poor social adjustment, and to have repeated one or more grades. In addition [note: here comes the moralism], a substantial fraction of our hyperkinetic adolescents were described as being immature, stubborn, inattentive, distractable, sneaky, lazy, easily discouraged, defiant, annoying, and/or unpredictable.[80]

The claim sounds good: neurological problems produce poor social adjustment and poor school performance. In some cases this is probably true. If children can be identified early, much agony may be saved. But the worms in this can slither into view when we ask how learning-disabled children are identified and diagnosed. For it seems that the "behavioral and learning problems" that cause these "academic as well as social adjustment problems" are diagnosed not by neurological evidence but by the existence of academic and social adjustment problems: "The method of designating children as hyperkinetic . . . consists of a questionnaire completed by the teacher which assesses social maturity, neuro-muscular development, academic performance and general attitude and behavior."[81]

So there it is: to prevent academic and social problems, identify and treat a learning disability. But to identify a learning disability, find an academic and social problem. Vicious circles, indeed. It might be funny if it were fiction, but when this fiction is taken for fact, the potential for damage to the individuals who receive this diagnosis, as others have pointed out, is great.

The ultimate danger is not simply that individual children—mostly from nonwhite or low-income families—will be mislabeled and stigmatized. It is that medical explanations of poverty, explanations that again locate the causes of inequality in individual pathology, will lead to yet another round of efforts to reduce inequality by reforming individuals.

Whatever the merits of recent reform efforts, and whatever the importance of school desegregation and other equal opportunity programs in securing racial justice, the liberal reforms that emerged from the Great Society years so far appear to be no more effective as strategies for reducing inequality than were their Jacksonian and Progressive antecedents. Study after study has suggested that the Great Society programs produced only the smallest steps toward equality for poor blacks or poor whites.

The Qualities of Liberal Reform

In all three eras of liberal reform—Jacksonian, Progressive, and Great Society—certain features have reappeared. The major tendencies they have had in common are:

1. An effort to restore society to the image of an earlier "golden age" where liberalism "worked," while simultaneously promoting a brave new world of industrial growth.

2. The translation of issues of inequality (and its chief manifestation, poverty) into the terms of equality of *opportunity*. This translation is critical since no specific degree of equality of *condition*, no desired distribution of goods, resources, power, or influence, is implied by equality of opportunity. Rather, the dream is deferred, and achieving it becomes the job of children.

3. The domination of reform movements by members of the middle or upper classes, who have tended to see economic and political issues in moral terms. Social reform in the Jacksonian era, Progressive era, and even the present day has been in-

extricably bound up with efforts to improve the morality of the poor, especially of children and their parents, with the assumption—often made explicit—that lack of morality *causes* poverty.

4. The chronic reliance of reformers on professionals in centrally governed institutions—bureaucracies—to implement reforms. While professionalism is promoted, no doubt sincerely, as the way to increase efficiency, to ensure quality of service, and to safeguard against corruption, the inevitable concomitant of this tendency has been to place the control of reform programs in the hands of the more affluent and powerful, while eroding the power and influence of the supposed beneficiaries of reform, the poor. Furthermore, putting reform in the hands of bureaucracies has fostered the development of institutions that mimic organizational modes prevailing in the economic system. The result, especially in the case of schools, has been the creation of institutions that, through their basic design and operation, socialize children to accept the norms of the very institutions that generate the original social and economic inequalities the reforms are supposed to correct.

5. The long-standing faith that childhood experience substantially determines adult capacities. This belief, which is almost as old as liberalism itself, has taken many forms, both "scientific" and popular. The idea that "the child is father of the man" has conditioned our entire understanding of childhood and our cultural interpretation of what its mission is.

6. An inevitable period of disillusionment in which assertions are made that the individuals in question are inherently inferior. With liberalism's emphasis on the individual as "master of his fate," if a program fails to "improve" an individual, liberal reformers can always argue that the individual was beyond help—too stupid, too sick, too pathological, or too genetically debased. Thus, the failure of reforms, rather than discrediting the theories on which they are based, somehow only confirms them.

The "Success" of Liberal Failure

We cannot brand all liberal reform programs as failures without some qualification. We are not suggesting that poor children would be better off with bad education or no education at all, or that efforts to provide health care to migrant workers are a waste of time and money, or that welfare is such a mess that the best thing for the government to do is stop providing any money to poor families. Nor are we arguing that discriminatory school placements are a trivial matter or that separate can long mean equal in American society. We have no quarrel with the argument that education or health care or good parents or rich early childhood experiences are important.

Furthermore, it can plausibly be argued that whatever its shortcomings, liberal reform aimed at improving equality in the society has been the only such reform that was politically feasible. Even then, it has usually not come easily. Many who have realized that the sources of inequality lie beyond the scope of individually focused liberal reforms have settled for these reforms as the best they could get. And sometimes the push for liberal reforms has given poor people and minority groups symbolic and strategic leverage that enabled them to press for more fundamental change.[82]

Finally, there have been significant changes in the reform agenda in the past decade, in good measure because of the pressure applied by activists from minority groups. Black activists and their allies have had considerable success in "piggybacking" onto traditional liberal programs structural reforms that get directly at issues of equality. One prime example is afforded by recent efforts to cut into professional power through laws requiring community participation—in the form of advisory or controlling boards—in the planning, implementation, and evaluation of a wide range of government programs and services. A second is regulatory insistence on the hiring of members of low-income or minority communities to work in programs serving those communities.

Similarly, emphasis on affirmative action in employment, community-based economic development, and job creation programs and a growing pressure to link welfare reform with tax reform in a redistributive package both contain the seeds of a direct egalitarian policy.

But when all the appropriate qualifications are made, the data still remain. Reforms posited on the ideology of equal opportunity have not produced an egalitarian society. The liberal tradition has not enabled the children of the poor to have anything like the same chance as the children of the rich for attaining economic security. It has produced a society in which the children of the poor stand a high risk of poor health and poor health care, of continued poverty and unemployment, and of systematically class- and race-biased mistreatment by the institutions that are supposed to help them. The ultimate failure of liberal reform is that in making children the preeminent objects of reform concern, it has spawned a set of ideas and institutions the inherent contradictions of which undermine their explicit goals. As our thumbnail sketch of reform history indicates, reform eras in the past 150 years have had distinctly paradoxical attributes. These paradoxes disappear only if one assumes that the tacit function of reform may have been to "cool out" protest, not actually to resolve underlying contradictions in the liberal tradition. Looked at in this light, liberal reform has been a distinct success. It *has* indeed cooled out the demands of the have-nots for equality through a set of concepts and strategies that have reinforced the power of the very class whose power was threatened. It has dampened protests by successfully promulgating a conception of equal opportunity that in essence defers the dream of equality from the present to the future, a tomorrow that never comes. In so doing, liberal reform has made children simultaneously the bearers of the dream and the excuse for its failure.

The persistent belief of liberal reformers has been that it is possible to have your cake and eat it, too; that the elimination of inequality does not depend on redistribution from rich and powerful to poor and powerless; rather, that the way to change society is to change individuals. Liberals have believed that individual reform and economic growth were made for each other, that the interests of the rich and powerful are similar to those of the poor and powerless. Whether or not they were designed as such, these beliefs have been an effective strategy for appeasement. Each time privilege, wealth, corporate power, and extremely unequal distributions of all these have emerged intact.

The ultimate measure of the "success" of these failures is not that the liberal upper-class reformers were always successful in dominating such institutions as schools (although they usually have been) or that they were always able to mold individuals into compliant and industrious workers who blamed only themselves for economic hardship (although they sometimes have). Rather, it is that the premises of liberal reform have been so deeply ingrained in basic social institutions, in the premises of social science, and in our national mythology that efforts to challenge them have trouble even gaining a foothold.

The American emphasis on individual rights and freedom appears to have had high cost—cultural blindness to the significance of social structure and the dynamics of that structure. That blindness is built deeply into the ways we think about children, from popular theories to the most thoroughly elaborated academic theories of child development.

Chapter Three

Help That Can Hurt

This is the monstruosity in love, lady; that the will is
infinite and the execution confin'd; that the desire is
boundless and the act a slave to limit.
—William Shakespeare, *Troilus and Cressida*,
    III, 2, ll. 82–84

Inequality generates hundreds of thousands of jobs in our society—for probation officers, social workers, vocational counselors, manpower trainers, therapists, drug-abuse counselors, and
paraprofessional human service workers whose clients are children, adults, and families of the poor; jobs for administrators,
planners, evaluators, consultants, clerical workers, accountants,
lawyers, custodians, and others whose work maintains the bureaucracies and agencies set up to provide services for the poor;
and jobs for academics and the research staff of groups such as
the Carnegie Council on Children who study and theorize about
inequality and its causes, effects, and "cures."

It is inaccurate to assume, as some people do, that those who
work at providing services and assistance to the poor are vultures
feeding off poverty and providing little in return. Certainly among
these hundreds of thousands of so-called poverticians, as in all
walks of life, there are swindlers, incompetents, and government
workers just putting in time and piling up pension payments. But
the great majority enter social service motivated by idealism,
empathy, commitment, and a fine edge of anger at injustice, only
to encounter frustrations that produce bitterness, disillusionment, or a sense of futility. It has often been from their encounter with these limits that social service workers have pro-

78

vided some of the starkest and most graphic analyses of the need for broader structural change.

The tradition of liberal reform embodies limits (or failures) of policy. Developmental theory embodies limits of concept. But there are still other limits to social programs that have attempted to create a more egalitarian society through assistance to individuals: social structure, in a context of social and economic inequality, gives rise to social processes that can undermine the avowed intent of social programs and even the best efforts of many who staff those programs. The ironic result is that programs designed to assist individuals often end up offering help that hurts.

Examples of this structural irony are provided by three programs aimed specifically at helping children: Aid to Families with Dependent Children (AFDC); the so-called child welfare system, which includes foster care, institutional care of children outside their homes, and the family court system that helps steer both; and the juvenile justice system. This chapter will briefly review these programs and then attempt to reveal the processes that both underlie and undermine them.

Welfare: The Price of Dependence

Aid to Families with Dependent Children (AFDC), generally known as welfare, is the central patch in the crazy quilt of programs designed to provide cash, food, and services to poor families with children. It is remarkable not only for its jerry-built structure but also because almost everyone agrees it is a "mess," yet no administration or Congress has ever got around to reforming it. This is in part because the prescriptions for reform vary widely, and in part because the politically volatile nature of the subject makes consensus and bold action difficult. But beyond the political and technical complexities, welfare and the subject of reforming it offer a prime example of the perils that surface when the liberal tradition tries to come to grips with the issue of the distribution of income in our society.

Welfare is, of course, a redistributive program, designed to give tax monies of nonwelfare recipients to low-income families in the form of cash "transfer payments" or in the form of such nonpecuniary transfers as food stamps, Medicaid, and social services. Welfare is the prime source of cash income for most AFDC families, and the redistributive effect of the program is indicated by the fact that before transfer payments, the bottom fifth of families receive about 2 percent of total family income (through earnings), while after welfare (and taxes) this fifth's share rises to just over 5 percent.

Lest this be interpreted as sheer generosity, it should be recollected that all government expenditures benefit someone, directly or indirectly. Estimates of who benefits from all local, state, and federal government grants (e.g., public schooling, highways, investment tax credits, garbage collection, and police protection) remain crude,[1] but there is evidence that the benefits are spread rather evenly across income classes.[2] Exemptions from taxation on capital gains and municipal bonds (which are government expenditures in the sense that government agrees not to collect the federal income these would represent) benefit primarily families in the top fifth of the income distribution, and these benefits, in terms of reduced tax liability, are roughly fifteen times the total federal bill for AFDC.[3] The notion that the poor get from government and everyone else gives is simply not valid.

Furthermore, if we examine what the poor actually get from welfare, the limits of this form of redistribution become clear. The benefits remain small, and the penalties and stigma associated with receiving welfare can be high.

AFDC is the only cash assistance program aimed specifically at children.* Yet, in 1977, of more than 10 million children living below the government poverty line, only 7.7 million were in families receiving AFDC at any time during the year. This figure did not include many children living below the more realistic low-income level of 50 percent of the median. (These figures reflect the exclusion of two-parent families, as well as wide variations in eligibility from state to state.)[4]

---

* Others benefit veterans, the disabled, and older persons not eligible for Social Security insurance. Only occasionally do families receiving such benefits include children.

These 7.7 million children came from 3.5 million families receiving AFDC, which represented more than 10 percent of all American families with children. AFDC has become a powerful moderator in American family life. Yet program benefits are grossly inadequate to the needs of children. Maximum benefits available from AFDC and food stamps *combined* exceed the official poverty line in only six states, and then only by a very small amount. In 1977 the average monthly welfare payment nationwide was $78.05 per recipient—$18.01 a week. (The lowest payments were in Mississippi, where families received an average of $47.42 a month—that is, only $14.54 a month per recipient. In affluent Connecticut in 1978, a family's daily food allowance was set at $1.54 per person.)[5]

In the fiscal year 1977 the federal outlay for AFDC was $6.1 billion, which represented only 2.5 percent of the $248.15 billion the government spent on income transfer programs that year and 11 percent of the meager $55.4 billion directed to persons defined as in need of cash assistance. More than 10 percent of the AFDC money went for state and local administration.[6]

It is only a slight exaggeration to say that, regardless of intent, this is money spent to degrade and harass welfare recipients. This money supports welfare bureaucracies that ensnarl both welfare workers and recipients in an ever-shifting maze of changing regulations, procedures of uncertain logic and purpose, and depersonalizing transactions the likes of which make an IRS audit seem like a picnic.* But unlike most of us, who have to deal with the IRS rarely, if at all, welfare recipients must routinely undergo the ritual processing of the system, where the message of eligibility checkups and work requirements is that you are dishonest until proved eligible and unworthy if proved eligible.

Adding insult to injury, AFDC permits caseworkers, state and federal investigators, and the court system to intervene in many of the most personal choices of the AFDC recipients' lives, to make decisions concerning food, clothing, housing, home en-

* Doubters are referred to Fred Wiseman's documentary film *Welfare* or should spend a few days visiting welfare centers and talking to workers and clients, as the author did on a recent consulting assignment for the New York State Department of Social Services.

vironment, and parent-child relationships, on the basis of criteria that are often, as anthropologist Carol Stack has shown,[7] irrelevant to and disruptive of the familial and communal networks that may sustain the very poor. Although the stereotype of the meddling caseworker may be as overdone as the stereotype of the welfare chiseler, the fact remains that "generally it is up to the caseworker to decide within very broad limits how much and in what manner she [*sic*] wants to question and investigate finances, responsible relatives and the suitability of the home, employability and the more intimate aspects of the applicant's life."[8] Whether or not that power is exercised, no other group of families lives under such a shadow.

The flaws of welfare do not end here. It remains true that in the majority of states the presence of a man (including an unemployed man) in the household destroys eligibility for welfare payments; this policy produces a fiscal incentive for families to break up, although the extent to which family breakup is caused by welfare is unclear.[9] It is also true that despite recent modifications, welfare recipients can lose up to 67 cents in welfare benefits for every dollar they earn after $30 a month (although local regulations are rarely that harsh). This creates a fiscal disincentive to work;[10] this stands in bizarre contrast with the work requirements that have recently been imposed on welfare recipients. These requirements can properly be viewed as a form of harassment. They reflect the demonstrably false belief that welfare recipients prefer the dole to work, which, along with the false notions that welfare recipients migrate to areas with high payments to enjoy the dole and that people once on welfare tend to stay forever, makes up a good portion of this country's welfare mythology.[11] Work requirements ignore the blunt fact that there are not enough jobs to go around. Such jobs as are available through the Work Incentives Program (WIN) and other efforts to employ welfare recipients tend to be low-paying jobs leading nowhere, in occupations where rapid turnover and job instability are the rule.

Ida Johnson, a welfare mother in Davenport, Iowa, described what it is like to live on AFDC to an interviewer from the Carnegie Council on Children:

Whenever you say "poor" or "people on welfare," they say, "They don't want to work." I've heard that so many times, I don't even react anymore. I'm on partial welfare; but I work forty hours a week, and I've worked now for almost five years. Most of my friends are on welfare, and they want to work; but all they can do is clean somebody's house, be a nurse's aide, work in a hotel, or cook in a kitchen, and all they're making is a dollar sixty cents an hour, maybe two dollars if they have to be paid by check. If you're paid by cash, they get you cheaper. So you're paying a bus maybe sixty cents to get to work. If she's got little kids at home, she has to pay maybe fifteen or twenty dollars a week for a baby-sitter and she may only be making fifty dollars a week as a domestic. And she goes and tells her welfare caseworker, "Okay, I'm working, I have a job." And when they get through, if she's making two dollars a week over what she's allowed, what the system has set up, they'll start cutting her check. So she's not making any more by working than if she just sat at home and drew that AFDC check every month. She doesn't have to worry about getting out in the snow and going to a job where she's not making decent wages to begin with and a job that isn't going to teach her anything, ever.[12]

When all is said and done, the only defense of the welfare system is that things might be worse without it. Some writers have argued that since welfare payments plus food stamps plus Medicaid plus housing allowances and social services can be priced out at a total benefit package above the poverty line, the system is not so bad after all. This argument, as we discussed in the Introduction, is another reflection of the notion that poverty is an absolute condition. It ignores two facts: that many who are eligible for these benefits do not receive them and that the affluent also receive similar noncash benefits.[13] This kind of defense illustrates more than the changing and fickle nature of welfare politics, however. It begins to suggest why welfare is, and remains, a mess. Beyond the surface political issues and inherently cumbersome welfare administration, the reasons for this mess can be traced to the endemic flaws of the liberal world view.

The notion that welfare benefits are not so bad after all, in addition to ignoring both the depersonalizing and debilitating effects of the welfare system on recipients and the uneven distribution of benefits, ignores the overall distributional issue—the relative nature of poverty. Only a handful of welfare families make it above the low-income line of half the median family income as a result of their benefits. Those who do appear to be brought up over the low-income line make it only because non-cash income is counted (e.g., the presumed worth of Medicaid, whose actual worth to a family, if one introduces concern for quality of health care, is questionable). But if noncash income of the poor is counted, noncash income of the affluent should also be counted to determine relative benefits. The defense of welfare, in other words, is based both on implicit use of an absolute poverty criterion and on a double standard in measuring income which makes it appear that the poor get something the rest of us do not.*

More telling, perhaps, is the implicit assumption, reflected in the regulations of welfare, that people on welfare are generally untrustworthy and have no one to blame but themselves for their lack of income. For instance, when an affluent person gets a tax break worth many times what the average welfare recipient receives, a signature at the bottom of the tax return is sufficient (subject, of course, to audit) to qualify the individual for that implicit governmental grant. In effect, the affluent are considered deserving until proved otherwise. The reverse is the case for the welfare recipient. More blatantly, the work requirements, checks on household status, moral probing, and other state interventions into the lives of welfare recipients derive their legitimacy only from the assumption that such individuals have to be pushed, prodded, double-checked, and regulated into productive citizenship.[14] Behind this assumption stand the notion that the individual is master of his or her fate and the correlative disregard of the large social, economic, and historical forces that conspire, far more often than not, to force individuals out of the mainstream of productive society into the backwaters of the welfare system. Such assumptions, part and parcel of our liberal heritage, generate a politics that turns the country's prime redistributive strategy into a shambles.

---

* For many of the affluent, for example, health care is paid for by employers and thus does not appear as income subject to taxation.

The Child Welfare System: Children
at the Mercy of the State

In most states, the child welfare system (not to be confused with
AFDC or "welfare") is a mixture of voluntary and public agencies
supposed to care for children who are without families, who
have been surrendered by their parents, or whom the courts have
removed from home on the ground that their parents are incompetent to raise them.* This difficult job falls to adoption
agencies, foster-care agencies, small group homes, residential
institutions (for handicapped children, mentally retarded children, or children with records of delinquency), and "temporary
shelters," where children may be housed while awaiting assignment to any of the others.

Tragically, disaster and breakup can and do afflict families
in all social groups, so there will always be a child welfare system
and always be an imperative to improve it. But this system exists
in good measure to handle the most severe casualties of inequality, children whose families crack under the pressure of poverty,
disease, unemployment, racism, or, for that matter, welfare. In
1972, 431,000 American children were "processed" by child welfare agencies. More than 225,000 were in foster families or
group homes, 90,000 were in institutions, and almost 70,000
were adopted in that year.[15] The great majority of these children,
in numbers far out of proportion to the population as a whole,
came from poor or minority-group families.

In 1971, 61 percent of the children in foster care homes in
Massachusetts came from families with incomes below $5,000,
then about half the median. Only 6 percent came from families
with incomes above $10,000. Sixty-seven percent came from
families whose head of household was unemployed. A review of
studies from many states shows that minority-group children
from black, Hispanic, and Native American families are, by

* Although in many instances the child welfare system and the juvenile justice
system overlap, the two are separated here for purposes of discussion. The
juvenile justice system is discussed later in this chapter.

lopsided margins, much more likely to end up in this system than white children are.[16]

Children enter the child welfare system by two routes. Some are placed in it at their parents' or guardians' initiative. The illness, death, or imprisonment of a parent may account for as many as half of all placements in the system; others are taken from their parents by juvenile or family court when the court determines that the home is inadequate. Court orders are estimated to account for 30 to 50 percent of all placements, and there is considerable evidence that many "voluntary" placements are actually the result of coercion by welfare workers, probation officers, and others who, holding the threat of court action over parents' heads (an action which, in the majority of cases, will mean removal), persuade parents to give up the care of their children. The majority of court-ordered placements, however, are for such broad and ill-defined reasons as parental "neglect" or "inadequacy."[17] No doubt there are often legitimate grounds for removing children from families, but the vagueness of statutes and the unpredictability of judicial decisions create a clear and present danger that tens of thousands of children each year will suffer the trauma of removal from their homes on grounds that are at best well-intended guesses based on amateur psychology and at worst race- and class-biased. The reality of this danger is made clear by a study that asked three judges to rule independently, in a simulated setting, on whether or not to remove certain children from their homes. In only a third of the cases did all three judges agree, and even then their rationales often differed widely.[18]

Whether they are removed for good or bad reasons, the future that awaits most children in the child welfare system is bleak. In effect, many of these children are being punished for what a court, social worker, or other authority regards as the sins of their parents. These judgments are generally imposed by middle-class whites on families whose life-style differs dramatically from their own. Ironically, the punishment generally falls most heavily on the child who is removed, when other forms of help—money, counseling, the offer of a job—might have preserved intact what every child needs most: his or her own family.

Only a minority of children removed from their homes—primarily children of unwed mothers or those who are orphaned—are classified as eligible for adoption. Adoption, when appropriate and legally permissible, is widely acknowledged as the best choice for a child needing care since it is most likely to produce a stable and enduring family setting. Even for many theoretically eligible children, adoption is unlikely—especially for those who are handicapped, over three, or nonwhite. Blacks constitute 20 percent of all children placed for adoption, but 40 percent of the backlog who have not yet been adopted, according to one national survey.[19]

For children not eligible for adoption, or not adopted, there remain two choices: life in an institution—most often the fate of the mentally or physically handicapped—or placement in foster care, which is more common than institutionalization.

Although foster care is intended as a temporary measure while the problems at home are patched up, it frequently turns into a permanent status for the child. More than 46 percent of children placed in foster homes are still there after three and a half years, although frequently not in the same ones they started in; depending on the state, anywhere from 25 to 65 percent of children in foster care are moved at least once.[20]

The aura of transience can strain both the child and the foster family, but the unpredictability of foster care looks good compared to the permanence and ghastly predictability of state institutions, which, despite exposés from the muckraking journals of the Progressive era to yesterday's newspaper, too often remain underfunded, understaffed, and grotesquely dehumanizing for residents and staff alike. A scene in one such place— unaccredited because it is so severely understaffed—was described like this:

You walk into a large barren room. In it are beds—cribs really—with people anywhere from six to twenty years old lying in them. But it's hard to tell their ages without reading the tags on the beds because they all look about the same—skinny, bones protruding, staring blankly at the ceiling, looking like the pictures of Biafran children starving. Staff sit in a glassed-in cubicle. In one corner a little room was walled off, and three children were sitting on the floor, a cold linoleum floor. The room was completely bare—no toys, no pictures on the wall.[21]

In most states it costs well over $15,000 a year to maintain one child in such an institution.

Mental retardation and physical handicaps afflict children from all social classes and backgrounds, but the children who end up in the back wards of public institutions like these are usually from poor families who can afford nothing better. The children who end up in foster care are most often those whose families have been under the immense strain of unemployment and low income.

Poor Children's Justice

The juvenile justice system, like the foster care system, is meant to benefit children. In fact, it does even less for the children it reaches than foster care does, and it reaches into the same segment of the population.

Children in the United States have their own separate system of justice, which, unlike the adult system, does not simply rule on legal and illegal acts; it has the additional function of trying to protect children from malign environmental influences (this in practice sometimes means parents whose behavior the court finds unacceptable). Premised on individualized justice, the system gives judges great discretionary power in dealing with individual cases. People under sixteen (or, in some states, eighteen) years old should not be held accountable, it is argued, to the same strict application of law as adults. They should be handled on a case-by-case basis by a wise and concerned court that makes decisions in the "best interest" of each child.

The theory sounds valid, but the very vagueness of many juvenile laws, including the standards by which children are removed from families, opens the way for abuse. The facts suggest that the juvenile justice system, from courts to detention homes, is yet another way that society penalizes the children of the poor and minority groups. For example, status offenses such as truancy, loitering, unseemly behavior, and "incorrigibility" are enforced primarily against poor and nonwhite children. Individualized justice and judicial discretion mean one thing if the defendant is poor and black (or brown or red); another if he or she is white and middle-class. As David Bazelon, chief judge of the United States Circuit Court of Appeals for Washington, D.C., has put it:

When a child from a well-to-do white family needs special attention, he and his parents are less dependent upon court facilities. His parents are likely to seek help privately . . . [and the] courts are willing to accept assurances from families that the child will receive private care and attention, even when quite serious offenses are involved. . . .

When a well-to-do child offends, particularly in a vicious or violent way, we tend immediately to think of mental illness. After all, a nice child would not do such a thing unless he "wasn't right." When a ghetto child commits the same act, however, we may . . . assume that such behavior is merely normal in view of his upbringing.[22]

Some people argue that the juvenile courts are full of the poor and minorities because the crime rate is higher in those segments of the population. But as with much data concerning criminal activity, it is always unclear whether the figures on juvenile arrests measure the behavior of police or the behavior of the population. If, for instance, police habitually let white or middle-class youths off with a warning but arrest black or poor youths for a similar offense, it is impossible to infer from police records whether or not poor or nonwhite teenagers engage in more frequent delinquent behavior. A recent study in Chicago found that the extent of "hidden" delinquency among middle-class white youths was great enough to wipe out the disparity in crime rates that most studies show between white middle-class and nonwhite or low-income youths.[23]

Differential crime rates may also reflect differential opportunities for crime. When a middle-class youth is caught stealing from a private home, the incident may be handled informally among families with no involvement of the police or courts. Low-income youths, with less access to private homes that have anything worth stealing, are more likely to be involved in crimes that are visible or violent, so their cases are more often referred to the police.*

There is overwhelming evidence that every stage of the juvenile justice system systematically treats low-income and nonwhite children more harshly than affluent white children, particularly for more minor offenses which are by far the most numerous. (When major offenses such as crimes of violence are involved, class and race do not appear to alter significantly the arrest rates, the determination of which cases are brought to court, or the rate of conviction,[24] although discrepancies in sentencing appear in a number of studies.)

When a juvenile offender comes in contact with the police, the first question is whether or not the contact will lead to arrest and a court appearance. Nationally about 75 percent of juvenile cases are handled informally. Typically, this means a youth is warned and turned back to his or her parents at the station house, without formal charges being lodged. If charges are lodged, the case may be dropped before arraignment, usually by agreement between the prosecutor and the child's parents or attorney.[25] But this kind of informality does not necessarily apply to all young people who are arrested. In Philadelphia, for example, one study showed that in the case of black youths charged with minor offenses only 22 percent are handled in this fashion, while the other 78 percent are brought to court.[26] By contrast, most white youths' cases were handled informally.

The poor and nonwhite continue to get different treatment at the next stage of the system—the disposition of cases (acquittal or conviction). The discrepancy continues through conviction, after which the judge must choose between probation and incarceration,[27] even to the final choice of what kind of incarceration is appropriate, the notoriously overcrowded "public training schools" or more favored placement in privately run shelters.[28] A glimpse of life in a training school reveals the irony of this institutional label:

---

* This is not to explain away or condone crime, whatever the race or social class background of the offender, but merely to indicate that it is a precarious leap from the data to the stereotyped conclusion, drawn by many, that poor and nonwhite youths are more prone to crime than the white middle class.

The youths go to school three hours a day, either in the morning or the afternoon, and have four classes, the same as in state vocational schools, but only a little more than half the schedule offered in standard academic programs. . . .

In one English class the other day, the teacher passed out workbooks at 8:30 a.m., indicated that two pages were to be read and that several questions at the end were to be answered on a separate sheet of paper. Then he sat back in silence. He answered two questions: What is a praying mantis and in what season is September. At 8:58 the teacher announced "quitting time" and began collecting the workbooks.[29]

How a Small Margin of Discrimination Is Multiplied

It does not take raw prejudice and gross discrimination at each step of the juvenile justice system to produce garishly unequal outcomes at the end. Policemen and judges need be no worse discriminators than the populace at large to produce cumulative injustice and inequality of substantial magnitude, because there are a number of steps to the juvenile justice process, and at each step the effect of minor discrimination at the previous stage gets multiplied.

For purposes of illustration, consider the juvenile justice system as a route with six points of decision: (1) whether or not the offender is turned in to or seized by police; (2) whether the police release the offender at the station house or make an arrest; (3) whether the case is dismissed or brought to trial; (4) whether the offender is convicted or found innocent; (5) whether the convicted offender is given a suspended sentence (released to the custody of his or her parents) or incarcerated; and (6) whether the offender is incarcerated in a group home or a training school.

Keeping these six stages in mind, we can follow 1,000 white middle-class youths and 1,000 black poor youths, all of whom committed offenses of similar magnitude, on a hypothetical road through the juvenile justice system. Assume that differences in the circumstances of their crimes (e.g., robbery of an acquaintance's home vs. robbery of a store) result in police involvement for 60 percent of the white youths and for 80 percent of the blacks. Then assume that, after this 20 percent gap, additional discrimination is minimal, accounting for only a 10 percent difference in the treatment of these two groups at each exit point.

Here is what happens on the road to the training school:

	1.	2.	3.	4.	5.	6.
						Assigned
					Sentenced	*to*
	Referred		*Brought*	*Con-*	*to be in-*	*training*
	to police	*Arrested*	*to trial*	*victed*	*carcerated*	*school*
	% No.	% No.	% No.	% No.	% No.	% No.
White	60 600	80 480	70 336	80 269	60 161	50 81
Black	80 800	90 720	80 576	90 518	70 363	60 218

These numbers are purely hypothetical, but in comparison to the rates of discrimination commonly uncovered by studies of the system, they appear to understate considerably the amount of differential treatment on the basis of race. At no step along the way could one say there is glaring discrimination; treatment is almost evenhanded. But twice as many blacks end up with a conviction, and almost three times as many end up in detention homes. With very little help from malice, the dynamics of discrimination and inequality takes a heavy toll. And while this example employs only racial differences, not class differences, the evidence shows that the lower class is also penalized in the system and that the combination of being nonwhite and lower-class is particularly lethal.

The net impact of this system of "individualized" justice on those individuals against whom it discriminates is clear and predictable. Poor and nonwhite children are most likely to accumulate police records and with them a stigma that may affect their dealings with schools and, as they reach adulthood, with employers. They also stand the greatest chance of spending time in a juvenile detention facility, where they are likely to develop a peer group from whom they learn how to be "better" criminals on the outside. Equally important, their contacts with officialdom teach a very clear lesson—that society's deck is stacked against them. This view, founded on strong evidence, makes the career choice of crime almost reasonable.

The Limits of Social Programs

The three institutions we have sketched—the welfare system, the child welfare system, and the juvenile court—have, along with other systems not considered here (such as mental health agencies), been subject to frequent scrutiny, enormous criticism, and countless, generally unsuccessful efforts at repair. Yet whatever their flaws, simply eliminating those systems would be irresponsible. Half a loaf is better than none, and it seems that each system employs individuals whose skill and dedication from time to time produce very important benefits for clients. But it is also true that by a simple standard these systems fall well short of their mark. Each represents an attempt to substitute for or patch up families that are crippled, often by the effects of unemployment and low income. But at their worst, these systems can exacerbate the problems of families or even create new ones. Aspects of these systems that try to stand in for family functions are poor substitutes for families with the resources and stability to struggle through and rear children on their own.

There are any number of fairly obvious reasons for this. For one, service systems are secondary strategies to deal, after the fact, with primary problems. That is, without a comprehensive national policy that succeeds in providing all families the basic decency, security, power, and economic resources to remain intact and healthy—physically, mentally, and socially—efforts to provide patch-up services are also trying to play catch-up, with tools that are by themselves unable to confront what is so often the source of the problem: social and economic inequality. Second, the task that is given to those who provide services—tasks such as "straightening out" a juvenile delinquent, reintegrating a family structure that has cracked under stress, finding "appropriate" foster care placement for a child who has become emotionally fragile and socially difficult—imply a human technology that simply does not exist. For instance, it is often possible to make marginal improvements in the law, the funding, the administration or the clinical follow-up required in making foster care placements, but even under the best circumstances, once the "problem" has become one of foster care, there may not be a good solution. The arrival of a new child can be traumatic enough for natural parents, most of whom have been socialized to accept as moral imperatives the kinds of adjustments and sacrifices required of good parents. No such social sanctions operate when, for instance, a family with the best intentions tries to incorporate a difficult seven-year-old into the household. It is too easy—and entirely human—to buckle under pressure and give the child back to the agency. Third, of course, simple class bias and racial prejudice can and do skew the outcome of services.

Beyond these constraints, the institutional procedures of social programs pose further limitations that both reflect and perpetuate the dynamics of an inegalitarian social structure. The example of the juvenile justice system—the multiplication of small disparities into large ones—demonstrates what can be called institutionalized discrimination; it is built into the structure of the process. Even if such systems were completely devoid of individuals with class or race bias (as no human system can be), the adoption of criteria to determine "risk" (e.g., family configuration, prior police contacts, or school status)[30] is likely to result in discriminatory outcomes, reinforcing and compounding the effects of inequality that already exist before the system intervenes.

The process of stigmatization is another risk run by children who enter social programs. The word *stigma* comes from the Greek word for a mark or tattoo. An archaic English usage found in Webster's is "a scar left by a hot iron." Today the word usually refers to a social branding the mark of which is found not in the flesh, but in the psyche, in the treatment of the stigmatized by the stigmatizers, and, in this paperwork world, in the records—educational records, criminal records, psychological records—that follow individuals from cradle to grave.

For stigmatization to occur, three conditions must be met: first, there must be an inequality that permits some to stigmatize others (peers may hate, libel, or destroy one another, but they cannot stigmatize); second, there must be a socially sanctioned way for one group to define the other; and third, there must be a set of procedures or institutions through which the more powerful stigmatizer can treat the less powerful stigmatized persons in some special or different way.

Differential treatment becomes a self-fulfilling prophecy; not only do the expectations of others limit the stigmatized individual's option, but, if the individual internalizes the stigma, he or she acts as if the other's categorization were apt.[31] For example, the more powerful and affluent members of society, acting through the state, create a special category, the welfare recipient. People in this special category are subject to rules and regulations that, as we have seen, perversely reward the recipient for behaving in ways that confirm the stereotype: creating financial incentives for family breakup and disincentives for working, etc.

The imbalance of power and the categorization that are stigmatizing structural features of the welfare system are duplicated in other systems. The power of the welfare caseworker has its parallels in the power of the family court social worker or the power of the juvenile court judge. The act of categorization is built into funding mechanisms, bureaucratic organization, and the professional lexicon of many social programs: programs for the "handicapped," the "disadvantaged," the "delinquent" (with the advent of the Law Enforcement Assistance Act), the "predelinquent" (an absurd term that is a stunning example of the self-fulfilling logic of stigma), the "underachiever," and so forth.

The point is obvious. The potential for stigma and its effects are built into any situation that gives one individual, or a group of individuals, power to define another; that gives those same individuals power over those others while making the others dependent; and that effectively defines a special group of intended beneficiaries as a "problem." This act of definition and categorization and this distribution of power are almost invariably built into the laws, the funding, and the management of systems and programs set up to "help." So long as efforts to alleviate inequality depend on such helping strategies, the risk of stigma, and the effects, seem to some extent inevitable.

The power of these effects is, of course, uncertain, and naturally it varies from place to place, program to program. Most people would probably assume that while stigmatizing effects of special programs set up to help people with this or that problem may offset the programs' effectiveness, the programs are overall beneficial. The only rigorous way to test this assumption is through an experiment in which similar individuals diagnosed as needing "help" are assigned at random to control and experimental groups and are then followed over a long period of time.

We know of only one study that has approximated this strategy.[32] It is a recent follow-up of 506 boys, aged five to thirteen, who were identified in 1942 as potential delinquents and criminals on the basis of early brushes with the law, school records, family background, and other factors. At the time these boys were randomly assigned to control and experimental groups. The experimental group and their families received visits by a social worker twice a month for five years, as well as medical, psychiatric, education, recreational, and other services. Some thirty-five years later Dr. Joan McCord succeeded in tracking down 95 percent of the youths who had participated in the study and found that in a number of dimensions, including criminal behavior, alcoholism, mental illness, physical illness, occupational status, and occupational prestige, those in the experimental group were worse off than those in the control group, who had received no services.*

* Of the individuals Dr. McCord located, 60 percent of the controls and 54 percent of the experimental group responded to detailed questionnaires, and additional information on all located subjects was gathered by examination of court records. Dr. McCord found that the controls and the experimentals were equally likely to have been convicted of a crime (168 in each group), but beyond this fact, the experimentals were worse off on a host of measures. The experimental group had more members who had committed major crimes (49 to 42), which was not statistically significant, but had significantly more repeat offenders, significantly more alcoholics, and significantly more individuals with diagnosed serious mental illness; twice as many members held less prestigious jobs and reported less job satisfaction than controls by significant margins. (Nonetheless, most reported that the services they had received were helpful.) Dr. McCord mildly concluded, "Results of this first study indicated that intervention programs risk damaging the individuals they are designed to assist."

It is not possible to infer from such data whether the negative effects of intervention resulted from stigma or from other mechanisms,* and, of course, one cannot generalize from one study to all interventions. But coupled with the known high rates of recidivism of incarcerated juvenile offenders, of addicts who have gone through treatment programs, and of mental patients and with findings on the continued poor school performance of students who are grouped, tracked, or otherwise institutionally labeled slow learners, it gives cause for thought.

The Reproduction of
Social Inequality: Schools

Many writers have recognized that stigma, institutionalized discrimination, and other varieties of differential treatment that are born of inequality undermine efforts to remedy inequality. Nonetheless, we believe that the continuing power of liberal mythology (coupled with the lack of any clear, palatable, and politically viable alternative) results in either minimization or total disregard of such factors, in the rhetoric and rationale of social reformers, and in the formation of social legislation. Concern for the individual, however genuine and warranted at root, keeps turning into individualistic theories that obscure the importance of social structure and social process. The cases we have examined in this chapter thus far illustrate that tendency. Schools, the liberal reform instrument par excellence, illustrate it in its purest form.

From Horace Mann on, with more or less enthusiasm from time to time, Americans have looked at schools as the "great equalizer," the place where individual talent could be shaped

* Dr. McCord assumes that stigma was not present since social workers had not been told which of the boys they were visiting had been diagnosed as predelinquent. She speculates that experimentals may have formed a kind of dependence on social workers—an unrealistic expectation that help would always be available to solve problems. However, if stigma follows from special treatment at the hands of professionals in circumstances of unequal power relationships, the issue of whether or not professionals had information that biased their approach toward given youths may not be relevant to the effect of stigma.

and developed to liberate individuals from social origins. Most people, when they speak of school as an equalizer, mean that advantages obtained through schooling will cancel out socially inherited disadvantages as children become adults. They are not suggesting, of course, that school will make all children come out "the same"—with identical skills, test scores, years of education, income, and occupational status—but rather that equal educational opportunity will help equalize life chances, so that a given individual is no more likely than any other to become a college graduate, a surgeon, a sales clerk, or ditchdigger simply because of class, race, or sex. The theory is that once life chances are equalized, talent will have free rein to do its work.

Most people also believe that the skills schools teach (or children learn) play a direct and critical role in preparing children for adult success, especially occupational success. Certainly a great deal of concern for high-quality education *and* parental and other pressures on children to get good grades stem directly from this belief. In fact, a rather substantial body of research suggests that academic achievement (grades and test scores) is, at best, a weak predictor of career success. For example, contrary to widespread opinion, it does not appear that college-educated employees are any more productive than employees without a college education who hold similar jobs.[33] Despite widespread popular support of vocational education programs and the new popularity of job-oriented "career education," comprehensive reviews of the research fail to show that beyond short-lived and modest differentials in entry-level pay, graduates of vocational programs fare better (or receive better ratings) in their chosen fields than graduates of general high school courses who receive no specific occupational training.[34] Efforts to correlate grades in graduate school or performance on tests for entering graduate school with earnings or other indices of success in such professions as law and medicine have not shown strong relationships.[35] Correlations between IQ scores (which are closely related to school success) and occupational status or earnings are quite low when the more significant factors of social class origin and years of education are controlled.[36] Even aptitude tests constructed specifically to predict occupational ability in one field or another end up yielding low correlations with job success.[37]

Evidence such as this must be interpreted carefully. Even low correlations, for instance, are better than no correlations for an employer trying to judge whom to hire. Even if law school grades themselves do not indicate how successful a lawyer the student will become, the law school population as a whole is made up of students who received fairly high grades in school and college. (One test maker even suggested that if employer ratings do not agree with someone's earlier test scores, there is something wrong with the employer's rating system.) But the evidence does suggest that the use of school credentials as a sorting and selecting mechanism is arbitrary and that the general credence given them is extravagant. Ironically, one career in which the evidence is most pronounced is the field of education, where literally scores of studies performed over the last sixty years have failed to establish any consistent relationship between either the years of educational training teachers receive or their academic records as students and their effectiveness as teachers.[38] This is no small irony, since almost a quarter of all college graduates work in education.

Further, the well-known conclusions of a host of recent studies have suggested that variations in factors popularly associated with educational quality, such as the length of a teacher's experience, the size of the class, the cost of education per pupil, and how modern the facilities are, make remarkably little difference in pupils' achievements.* [39]

---

* While the evidence from such studies is impressive in its consistency, it should be interpreted with caution. It is always true that a given teacher or a given school can do a better or worse job, for instance, and parents who push for improvements in their local school have no reason to believe that such improvements will not be beneficial in some degree for at least some pupils. There are studies of individual schools, much more fine-grained than the evidence produced in broad-scale survey analyses of school effectiveness, which suggest that schools with quite similar student bodies show quite different patterns of achievement, differences that seem to be attributable to some combination of administrative excellence, goal clarity, and teacher competence.[40] The studies of school effectiveness that characterize the bulk of the literature so far have also been criticized on a variety of methodological grounds, and a "second generation" of school productivity studies may, with closer analysis of determinants of effectiveness, yield different results.[41] Given all these caveats,

None of this means that schooling makes no difference in terms of career success. To the contrary, the correlations between *years* of schooling and earnings are strong. What this suggests, however, is that (within reasonable limits) neither how well students do in school nor the quality of education they receive is the critical factor. Rather, schools contribute to career success in great part through their so-called credentialing effect. That is, presumably employers screen and select employees in some significant measure on the basis of the number of years of schooling they have obtained, and once most individuals have entered full-time employment, their occupational mobility patterns are fairly well set.[42] Indeed, in a world where by law, as well as custom, twenty years of schooling are required to enter the highest-paid occupational rank (medicine),* and where most of the highest-paying jobs require at least a college education before one can even apply for consideration, there is an inevitable correlation between income and educational "attainment" (years of education as opposed to achievement measures such as test scores or grades).[43]

If the equalizing potential of schooling, then, rests heavily on its power as a credentialing institution,[44] this lends added urgency to a traditional goal of the civil rights movement, the closing of the gap between white and black school attainment.[45]

But credentialing is a double-edged sword: a credentialing

---

however, it remains true that on the evidence so far, school characteristics appear to play a limited role in producing variations in pupil achievements, by contrast with social-class characteristics, and it seems entirely reasonable to conclude that when an occasional school does produce remarkable results, it is because of special circumstances (e.g., a remarkable staff) which are not likely to be replicated on any wide-scale basis. (Indeed, the remarkable staff might have less success with a different set of pupils at a different time or place.)

* The rationale for educational requirements is, of course, that they help assure the quality and competence of professional services. To be sure, it is difficult to find anyone willing to submit to brain surgery by an untrained knife wielder. But the issue here is whether there may not be a superfluity of educational requirements, on the one hand, and an excessive emphasis placed on education as *the* prerequisite, on the other. Both suspicions are raised by the remarkable failure of most studies to show strong connections between school performance and job performance and the apparent increase and expansion in the use of educational prerequisites for employment, both throughout government and in many parts of the private sector.

system rations opportunity, selecting some and excluding others. The result is a kind of paradox, familiar to economists, in which rational behavior on the part of an individual (e.g., obtaining a credential) becomes irrational if all individuals pursue the same course (if everyone obtains a credential, selection must be based on some other factor). A similar phenomenon has been called "educational inflation" by some; as educational attainment rises for all, it is necessary to get more and more schooling to obtain the same competitive advantage in the labor market. Further, the evidence suggests, when all is said and done, that while the education system's function as an access route to employment opportunity may make it the best hope for a given individual to achieve upward mobility, schooling by itself cannot produce interclass or interracial equality. On the contrary, the rules of the educational credentialing game seem rigged to ensure that outcomes will be related to class. As one scholar, reviewing both European and American evidence, has put it: "To paraphrase Orwell: those who at the outset are more equal than others will take more advantage. That is the lesson learned from equalization programs at all levels of education."[46] It may always have been so. At any rate, the historical record is now beginning to make it clear that immigrant groups that in the past have made it up from poverty did *not* do so, as legend has had it, through the schools. If anything, causality has run the other way: after establishing economic footholds by dint of sweat, ingenuity, crime, politics, unions, or any other route, immigrant groups, like all the others who preceded them, began to insist that their children go to school. Earlier on, the children were valuable assets who were put to work helping the families "make it."[47]

None of this is surprising if we stop looking at education as an individual attainment and consider instead the social process at work in and through schools. Schools themselves, of course, are institutions embedded in a larger social structure, and the same mechanisms that undercut the effectiveness of other social programs are at work in the schooling enterprise. For a number of reasons, the effort to create greater social equality through focusing programs on individuals in schools is just as likely as other social programs to help transmit inequality from generation to generation. One reason is that school performance—grades and test scores—substantially correlate with the socio-economic status of a student's family. (This correlation is il-lustrated by the accompanying table.) The higher the student's

The Relationship of College Board Scores (SATs) and Family Incomes (1973–74)[48]

(Mean family income of students scoring in each range)

Students' Scores	Students' Mean Family Income
750–800	$24,124.00
700–749	$21,980.00
650–699	$21,292.00
600–649	$20,330.30
550–599	$19,481.00
500–549	$18,824.00
450–499	$18,122.00
400–449	$17,387.00
350–399	$16,182.00
300–349	$14,355.00
250–299	$11,428.00
200–249	$ 8,639.00

Average Score: 462

Number of Students: 647,031

social status, the higher the probability that he or she will get high grades. Similarly, the higher the grades and test scores, the more likely an individual from any socioeconomic status is to get more schooling. This is in part because higher education admits students on the basis of grades and test scores and in part because those who do well in school develop a taste for more schooling.[49] However one feels about the emphasis schools put on grades and test scores, this makes it inevitable that a higher proportion of the most desirable credentials will go to the children of the affluent. Given the relatively weak correlations between grades or test scores and job performance, the pervasiveness of educational requirements suggests a certain arbitrariness, a rigged game that is class biased. Indeed, the more that schools play the quasi-monopolistic role of personnel office for the corporate economy, the more rigged the game seems. As one writer has put it: "The ideology of academic standards brilliantly reconciles two conflicting values: equality and equality of opportunity. Through the system of public education, everyone is exposed to academic standards, yet only those who succeed in meeting them advance in our competitive system. Everyone enters the educational contest, and the rules are usually applied without conscious bias. But since the affluent tend to be most successful, the net result of the game is to perpetuate intergenerational inequality. Thus, academic standards help make acceptable something which runs against the American grain: the inheritance of status."[50] Educational tests and academic standards are by no means the sole cause of class-related inequalities in educational or occupational outcomes. In fact, class-related differences in test scores are less pronounced than class-related differences in educational attainment.[51] To put it another way, even when academic achievement is comparable, children like Jimmy, from lower-income families, are likely to get substantially less education than children like Bobby, from high-income families. For instance, a recent major study followed 9,000 Wisconsin students through high school. It found that high-ability students from the top quartile in socioeconomic status were twice as likely to enroll in college as students who also had high ability but came from families whose social status placed them in the bottom quartile. They were twice as likely again to graduate from college and 3.5 times as likely to enter graduate school. These disparities increased as ability decreased. The same study found that men were also more likely to proceed with education than women. The author concluded: "In their opportunities for higher education, the members of the sample cohort seldom escape the influence of their social origins. The selective influences of socioeconomic background and sex operate independently of academic ability at every stage in the process of educational attainment."[52]

Unless one adopts the genetic hypothesis (which, as the next chapter argues, is a shaky hypothesis indeed), correlations between test scores and social status can be explained only on the grounds that tests measure something about socially determined background and experience, not innate individual capacities. But a number of possible and mutually compatible explanations exist for class-related inequalities in educational attainment even when test scores are comparable. Money is behind most of them. Despite considerable scholarship and loan assistance, supporting a college student strains the resources of many families. Furthermore, going to college or graduate school not only means laying out money but also means forgoing immediate earnings —presumably in anticipation of greater earnings later. Students from low-income families are less able, by definition, to afford those opportunity costs. Family tradition may be another explanation. All other things being equal, students from families in which parents have received a lot of education are more likely to continue education themselves; history here affects the individual, whether in the form of encouragement to continue schooling or discouragement.[53]

Whatever the reasons, the data force us beyond liberal ideology to a consideration of the social structure itself. Educational attainment and the occupational and financial advantage conferred by it are not simply matters of individual ability and diligence; they are in good measure a function of where one starts in the socioeconomic structure. The issue is no small matter: the average child from a family whose income is in the top fourth (more than \$22,300 in 1976) gets four years more schooling than the average child whose family income is in the bottom fourth (below \$8,700).[54]

Differential Treatment and the Transmission of Inequality

The kinds of data reviewed above reveal a lot about the dynamics of educational attainment in a class-stratified society. They suggest that apparently "fair" standards and treatment can have substantially unequal and "unfair" outcomes, in which the lottery of birth exercises great influence on a child's probable future. But they give little glimpse of what happens in schools: the subtle and not-so-subtle, deeply institutionalized practices that result in unequal treatment, stigma, and the "preparation" of children to assume adult roles that perpetuate their inherited social status.

The most blatant form of differential treatment is that given the many children who are—deliberately or through neglect—partially or wholly excluded from school. This group includes early dropouts, students who are suspended, expelled, or otherwise kept out of school (by language barriers, for instance), plus handicapped children for whom no programs exist, despite a growing body of law and policy mandating such programs.

Reports of the Children's Defense Fund estimate that approximately 2.4 million school-age children or 5 *percent* of all school-age children in the country are not enrolled in a school at all.[55] Close to another 5 percent miss forty-five or more days a year, a quarter of the school year. Children in these categories are overwhelmingly nonwhite or poor. The Children's Defense Fund found that combinations of active exclusions (such as suspension) and sheer neglect on the part of school officials account for many of these cases. Being excluded from education forces children into the streets of a society that offers children not in school few opportunities except drugs, vandalism, and petty crime. If society prepares school dropouts for any kinds of adult futures, they are futures of chronic dependence, unemployment, drudge work, institutionalization, or the Byzantine pathways of the criminal justice system.

To children who are temporarily or permanently excluded from school can be added those children who are classified or, more to the point, misclassified as capable of no more than minimal learning and placed in classes that teach accordingly. It is incongruous that at the same time the United States is making belated efforts to provide appropriate classes for children with physical handicaps, severe retardation, or organic brain damage, some children whose main "problem" is poverty are misclassified as having emotional or mental disorders and placed in special classes that are not designed to give any more than a minimal education and that stigmatize the children placed in them.

Any kind of labeling is worrisome, for, as Nicholas Hobbs's

monumental study on the classification of children concludes, what starts out as a useful, even necessary diagnostic label tends to stick with a child and may, over time, change from a basis for help to a stigmatizing judgment or self-fulfilling prophecy.[56] It is not possible to determine the extent of misclassification of children in American school systems, although some small studies in various cities and locales have suggested it may be a major problem. The risk of misclassification appears to be greatest by far for poor and minority-group children, whose parents lack the resources to fight back.[57]

Even though we cannot estimate how much misclassification goes on, it is not difficult to explain why it happens. For one thing, the categories by which children are classified are often fuzzy, and diagnosis may rely entirely or partly on observed behavior rather than on any demonstrated organic or neurological problem. This is especially true in the burgeoning new field of learning disabilities. For instance, according to the President's Committee on Mental Retardation, about 90 percent of all children diagnosed as retarded have no known organic difficulty but suffer from so-called socioeconomic retardation.[58] Similarly, a recent review of the literature on minimum brain dysfunction concluded that despite widespread acceptance that such a disability exists, the evidence that it does is circular, based on the assumption that "behaviors such as hyperactivity were signs of brain damage independent of neurologic indexes, and therefore that many behavior problem children had brain damage."[59]

In the face of such reasoning, learning disabilities and socioeconomic retardation sometimes sound curiously like drapetomania—a disease identified by a renowned nineteenth-century physician as an odd affliction that caused slaves to run away.

No doubt learning disabilities are not simply a medical label that distracts us from socioeconomic inequities; they do affect many children, from all classes. But given vague etiology, the social nature of many symptoms, and the use of inadequate or inappropriate diagnostic procedures, there is an enormous danger that class or race bias will slip into classification procedures, just as it almost inevitably does when middle-class family court judges decide to remove poor children from their homes because aspects of the parents' life-styles do not seem to the judge to be proper behavior for parents. In the assembly-line world of mass education, the reassuring rhetoric of science—without the rigors of science—provides a handy way of writing off some children or of turning them over to special programs for help that cannot be delivered because they do not have the ailment for which the help is designed. Sometimes inadequate diagnostic procedures may be the problem, whether these are a reflection of professional incompetence or of understaffed, underfinanced, and overloaded departments. The President's Committee on Mental Retardation found evidence that contrary to widely known canons of good practice, children are often labeled retarded on the basis of marginal scores on *one* IQ test, a completely inadequate and inappropriate diagnostic procedure.[60] In other instances, the very vagueness of categories may permit systematic abuse, whatever the motives of school personnel. A citizen task force in Boston concluded that in some schools there was a regular practice of labeling children whom teachers found disruptive "retarded" to get them out of the classroom, and the U.S. Civil Rights Commission reached the same conclusion about Chicago.[61]

Whatever the reason, placement in "labeled" classes creates a strong possibility that children will absorb those labels, receive minimal education, and face adult futures not much rosier than those faced by children who are totally excluded from school.

Adding together the number of children excluded wholly from school, the number excluded partially, the number who are misclassified, and the smaller number who are "educated" in the juvenile justice system, a rough estimate is that somewhere between 10 and 15 percent of American children are getting either no schooling or schooling that prepares them for nothing.

This situation cries out for change. Some of that change has to come from within schools themselves, and nothing short of public overseeing, pressure, and vigilance seems likely to produce it.

Discrimination by Expectation

Such children represent the extreme. But the most pervasive, institutionalized, and entrenched forms of differential educational treatment for low-income and nonwhite children appear in regular classrooms, as part of the daily routine and mundane transactions between students and teachers. These are differences hard to detect through survey research and hard to check by administrative fiat or policy manipulation, differences between the experiences of middle-class students and the experiences of low-income students that do not show in such measurable school "inputs" as how many dollars are spent per pupil, how large classes are, or how much experience teachers have. These latter are differences that researchers can detect and that administrators, if given the wherewithal and the motivation, can correct. The most insidious differences in many cases are beyond the reach of either of these.

Abundant journalistic and scholarly studies suggest, on the basis of intensive classroom observation, that many teachers behave differently toward children from different socioeconomic and racial backgrounds and adjust educational goals, teach different material, and reward or punish behavior differently by class and race as well.[62] Typically, such studies have found that teachers of low-income children minimize cognitive discussion and interaction with children while emphasizing pure rote learning. When low-income children ask questions that are tangential to the point, they are rebuked or ignored. Middle-class children, on the other hand, receive answers; their questions are taken seriously. Teachers ridicule students frequently in classrooms with predominantly low-income children.[63] One study found that when lower- and middle-class children were mixed in one first-grade classroom, they were divided within the class into ability groups ("Cardinals" and "Tigers") that reflected social class differences perfectly, and treatment differed accordingly.[64] Another found that when teachers of low-income children were asked about their educational goals, the ones they put first were behavior control and adjustment of children to the norms of the school, and sometimes academic goals were not mentioned at all.[65] By contrast, teachers of predominantly middle-class children stressed cognitive growth and students' satisfaction in learning as their major goals. Small wonder, then, if test scores differ!

One study, in fact, found that teachers were most positive in their attitudes toward middle-class children with high IQs and most *negative* toward poor black children with high IQs.[66] The author suggests that this is because the latter were more outspoken and less docile than most of their classmates and thus presented obstacles, as the teachers saw it, to control and order in the classroom.

There are often fewer opportunities for schoolchildren in low-income neighborhoods to exercise initiative and independence in curricular matters. Eleanor Leacock, for instance, found that differential treatment extended not simply to formal classroom work but also to other activities. In a middle-class school, she found a variety of student committees and tasks for students, such as leading class discussions. There were substantially fewer such opportunities in the lower-class schools she studied. Even in a classroom where there was "considerable latitude for independence and initiative it was primarily in relation to handling materials and supplies and not the *content of the work itself.*" As Leacock observes: "The lesson in socialization for [the middle-class] pupils, many of whom would be moving into the ranks of 'organization men,' should be considered. The organizational goal is to move into successful positions of increasing independence and responsibility, and the taking of each step necessitates being able to appraise and handle competently the problems that arise from sharing responsibilities with a supervisor. . . . This is coordinate with the classroom structure as we have described."[67]

By contrast, even in the lower-class classrooms where there is some latitude for initiative, the kinds of tasks permitted are more congruent with the work of blue-collar workers. This, Leacock concluded, reflected the attitude of the teacher who accepted as "socially defined [that] the optimal goal for most of these children is the achievement of steady employment and minimal economic and social security."

The point, it should be stressed, is *not* that teachers are overtly racist or class biased. Rather, teachers typically adopt the assumptions of the society to which they belong—and how could they do otherwise? Given the way our society works, it can be argued that teachers who treat children differently on the basis of social class or racial background are performing a good job of helping their students make a "social adjustment."

Nor is it sufficient to argue that socially derived assumptions of teachers are the cause of differential treatment. Rather, as we saw in reviewing Progressive era education, the institutional apparatus of schools is explicitly designed to provide differential treatment in performing its occupational screening and selection funtions, and such differentiation is broadly legitimized by the rationale of "individualized instruction." If one considers a typical school system in total, the structure of differentiation is apparent. For instance, in one large urban system,[68] the elite track consists of special academic high schools in which admission is by tests and grades. Within those schools there are accelerated courses (called star classes in one school), the enrollees of which automatically have five points added to their grades by virtue of admission to the class! Then there are regular high schools, divided into a number of curriculum tracks (college preparatory, general education, various vocational and trade courses) with ability groupings within grades and within classrooms.[69] There are vocational schools, which traditionally have been dumping grounds but which have recently, for some courses, adopted admissions standards and become desired placements. Finally, there are schools for the retarded and schools for students with combined academic and disciplinary problems (including established "remedial disciplinary" schools and, more recently, so-called alternative schools). The point is that teachers who have differential expectations for students, and who treat students accordingly, are merely reflecting practice built into the basic institutional fabric of the system they work in. It would be improbable for them to do otherwise. It is unlikely that these patterns will alter within schools unless they first change in the broader society.

The Consequences of Differential Treatment

The preceding examples—from exclusion and misclassification to subtle differences in expectations and classroom experience —all exhibit, in greater or lesser degree, the characteristics of the process of stigma. In many cases, we would speculate, individual children accept and internalize the stigma, coming to view themselves and their own potential much as society and its agent, the schools, view them. Certainly the early judgments of the school, as represented by grades, test scores, and curriculum placements (into fast and slow groups, for instance), hold up remarkably firmly over time. Grades and test scores achieved in the third grade are highly correlated with those received in subsequent years.[70] By the ninth or tenth grade most students have formed aspirations for career and further education that predict rather well what they will actually do.[71] As they enter formal curriculum tracks in the beginning of senior high school, their educational future begins to look less like a track than a tunnel.[72]

The school system, like the juvenile justice system, has multiple exit points—in this case points at which the individual student must choose whether to drop out or proceed. Again, small differences in the treatment of students from different class or racial backgrounds may accumulate into large differences in outcome.[73]

Neither in the school's relationship to the occupational structure as a credentialing mechanism nor in its internal operations (which, in mirroring the social relations and values of the larger society, breed stigma) is schooling well adapted to serve the goal of creating greater social equality. A more plausible view, instead, is that, as Jencks, among others, has concluded, it serves "primarily to legitimize inequality,"[74] or perhaps—a stronger point—to reproduce it.[75]

The final dilemma is, as the French sociologist Raymond Boudon has argued, that even if it were possible to equalize educational attainment, greater social equality might not result.[76] To the contrary, Boudon has suggested that if schooling were equalized among all classes, class-related correlations in achieved social and economic status might grow even stronger. For if education were equal, selection would be made directly on the basis of something else—and social class origin would be a likely contender.

This little paradox suggests that there is no getting away from social class. The dynamics of inequality, embedded in the political and economic structure of the society, partially define and delimit the futures of children, whatever their individual traits. The structures of institutions through which children pass all but inevitably reflect and transmit those dynamics, producing differential treatment and differential outcomes, whether overt bias is present or not. If U.S. social policy is to be egalitarian, if it is to eliminate the insults, injuries, and small futures ordained by inequality, it must confront this fact head on, for no amount of individual "help," whether delivered by schools, judges, or social workers, can make changes that are needed. It is the original inequality of social class (or race, or sex) that must be changed.

Chapter Four

Child Development:
American Theories on the
Sources of Inequality

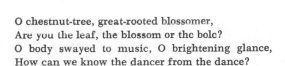

O chestnut-tree, great-rooted blossomer,
Are you the leaf, the blossom or the bole?
O body swayed to music, O brightening glance,
How can we know the dancer from the dance?

—W. B. Yeats, "Among School Children"

A set of beliefs, hovering somewhere in the ground between popular theory and academic precept, between psychological hypothesis and social creed, have governed at one and the same time our understanding of childhood and our creation of social policy in the United States: the belief that individual adult characteristics determine social status, the belief that those adult characteristics are substantially determined by characteristics developed in childhood, and, finally, the belief that the "micro" environment of the family, without reference to the society, or "macro" environment in which it is embedded, is what substantially determines the way children develop. None of these is entirely accurate. They have distorted our understanding of development—that is, the child's experience—and they have misled us as to the requirements of egalitarian reform.

To state the case so baldly is to overstate it, to ignore the conflict and diversity of thought that characterize developmental theory, and to ignore the caution with which many psychologists and researchers advance views that are inflated in popular theory from tentative, circumscribed hypotheses to "truths." But our interest is in how child development theory has fed popular social theory, serving as a field of assumptions in which political action (the framing and implementation of social policy) occurs. In this field fine distinctions are often lost, and flaws in theory are magnified into flawed prescriptions and policies that can have large consequences.

Liberal Reform and Developmental Theory

In its origins, liberal social theory was closely tied to psychological theory. John Locke's fertile mind was the progenitor both of liberal political theory and of what can be broadly considered the behaviorist school of psychology—the empiricist's view that the child is a highly plastic organism whose qualities are shaped over time by the imprint of environment. Likewise, Enlightenment thought, typified by Pope's "Essay on Man," developed a view of society as a drama whose plot consisted of thousands of individual contests of reason and desire, pleasure and pain, seeking harmonious equilibrium. This picture is closely mirrored by the view of the market in classic economic theory.

The interweaving of psychological and social theory produced an atomistic view of the political economy: society became the sum of individual actions and decisions, a notion apparent in the Lockean concept of the social contract and in Adam Smith's view of the free market as well, in which the "unseen hand" of the marketplace is actually the end result of untold numbers of individual decisions—reasoned choice in the pursuit of desire. It is a short, if not entirely logical, step from that atomistic view to the notion that each individual is master of his fate and but another short step to the idea that society can be reformed through shaping the child since, as the Lockean tradition of psychology suggests, the attributes children develop (abilities, personality, morality) prepare them to become signatories to the social contract, free and rational adults, the makers of their own fates.

These origins are worth noting because in the course of this century, particularly, the liberal world view and psychological theories about child development have been locked in a dance that often makes it hard to distinguish one from another. Liberal theories of reality—including social reality—have shaped psychological theory, and conversely, psychological theory has helped shape (or reinforce) social theory. In particular, egalitarian reform movements, with their focus on the child, have almost required a theory of individual development, and theories of individual development have in turn shaped the strategies of reformers.

There is a clear and present danger, psychologist William Kessen has written, that "our conclusions about the development of human knowledge may derive in large measure from the preconceptions of the nature of man and the nature of reality that we have stuffed—or, worse, let slip—into our initial conception of the psychological task."[1]

While preconceptions of social reality may influence developmental theory, the converse is also true: theories of child development may influence our understanding of social reality. Both dangers have been especially "clear and present" because the history of child development theory has been closely linked to the history of social reform.

For instance, G. Stanley Hall, sometimes called the father of child study, was a social reformer who influenced late-nineteenth-century and Progressive-era educational practice. The early behaviorists such as John Broadus Watson, learning theorists such as John Dewey and Edward Lee Thorndike, and the father of American intelligence testing, Lewis Terman, were deeply involved in the Progressive effort to make education more scientific and efficient. Likewise, in the past fifteen years, the child development literature has multiplied enormously under the stimulus of government grants associated with various Great Society efforts in the early-childhood education movement such as Head Start, Follow Through, Parent-Child Centers, and Home Start. Theories of cultural deprivation, which attempted to explain supposed deficiencies in a child's cognitive development by blaming "impoverished" early parent-child interactions, are perhaps the best-known output of this recent flurry. Efforts to adapt Piagetian stage theories of development, Skinnerian behaviorism, and medical-biological theories of development (from the role of nutrition to the role of the genes) have been prominent as well.

A significant example of social theory informing developmental theory (in this case, that branch concerned with learning) is provided by John Dewey's work. In his early book *The School and Society* (1899) Dewey codified the Progressive belief that the switch from a rural, agrarian to an urban, industrial society had profoundly altered the conditions of a child's development. Assuming that the "organic" world of the farm was the optimal learning situation, because experience was the teacher and a child could directly perceive the connections between present activities and subsequent experience, Dewey developed a theory of experience to re-create that situation scientifically in school settings. Echoes of these ideas are still alive, particularly among advocates of the open classroom. The cultural deprivationists of the 1960s worked with an implicit social theory of nuclear families in which the father was seen as the breadwinner and the mother as the nurturer of the child. Study after study, accordingly, focused on mother-child interaction, working up correlations between certain kinds of mother-child interaction and such measures as IQ or other standardized tests and rating scales.* Not only did this focus leave the question of fathers' contribution a blank, but it had to disregard the increasingly difficult-to-ignore realization that mothers were entering the labor force in droves. The social norm on which this model depends (a norm that never described the reality of many families) is now controverted by social reality, and there is much scholarly debate about the impact of mothers' working on their children's development. Conversely, the cultural deprivationists'

---

* The overwhelming emphasis in recent child development literature on mother-child interaction, and the relative paucity of studies looking at father-child interaction, is documented in *Child Care in the Family: A Review of Research and Some Propositions for Policy,* a Carnegie Council on Children monograph by Alison Clarke-Stewart (New York, 1977).

theory of cognitive development reinforced liberal social theory about inequality. In crude outline, this process can be seen taking shape with the assumption that inequality in social standing reflects inequality of individual capability—the natural outcome of liberalism's emphasis on the individual. The next step was to examine what shapes individual development and, drawing on earlier human and animal research and theory, to codify the notion that the early years of childhood are critical to development.[2]

This belief reached its strongest and perhaps most influential assertion in Benjamin Bloom's *Stability and Change in Human Characteristics* (New York, 1964), which asserted that "the stability of measured intelligence increases with age . . . in terms of intelligence measured at age 17, about 50 percent of the development takes place between conception and age 4, about 30 percent between ages 4 and 8, and about 20 percent between ages 8 and 17."[3] His statement—based primarily on erroneous inference from a review of studies that administered IQ tests to different population samples over a period of years—helped give rise to a plethora of studies of the determinants of early intellectual development,* focusing on the "richness" of early childhood environment as measured by observing mother-child interactions. Out of these studies came the notion of cultural deprivation—the belief that some children did not receive enough verbal and other stimulation in the home and, because of this, developed low verbal ability and did poorly in school.

The next step was the development of various strategies for "intervention" in early childhood to "enrich" the child's environment, of which the Head Start program was the most famous.[4] There have been many incidental benefits to Head Start: sometimes Head Start programs have provided a focus for parent organization that led to the increased involvement of parents in community and school affairs; in some communities Head Start programs have provided a locus for delivering preventive health care and other important services; Head Start's emphasis on hiring paraprofessionals from the community served has created

---

* Studies on the impact of early experience on animals' development also gave impetus to this movement, as discussed later.

jobs for countless thousands of low-income individuals who might otherwise have been out of work. Head Start programs did, often, briefly raise the test performance of children (for the duration of Head Start), and current follow-up studies suggest that eight or ten years later there have been some benefits in terms of school performance for Head Start youngsters, although the benefits appear modest and the still-incomplete evidence appears somewhat contradictory.[5] Other early intervention programs also compiled an ambiguous record; they generally failed to create or sustain improvements in IQ and other test scores, and an explanation for this failure had to be found. One, expounded by the American experimental psychologist Arthur Jensen, was that more or less immutable genetic factors explain intelligence.[6] Another, typified by the line of research that leads from Coleman to Jencks, was that school is unable to compensate for the effects of family.[7] Both views hold that the family as an institution inevitably transmits inequality, either through the environment or through the genes. A third explanation, closely allied to the second, was the theory of the "pathology" of black families.[8] Here the depressed status of black Americans in the social system was seen as a result of the intrinsic pathology of the black family caused by its historically depressed position in American society.[9] Minus the overt emphasis on ethnic-group pathology, which rapidly became political anathema, the general theory of family inadequacy is still in circulation among proponents of parent education and early childhood education.

The historic interrelationship of liberal social theory, liberal reform movements, and developmental psychology is not simply an intellectual curio; it has become an integral part of the knot that binds children's policy to egalitarian policy, to the detriment of both. For if it is in fact true that inequalities in adult capabilities explain social inequalities, that those adult capabilities are determined by childhood experience, and that either genetic inheritance or characteristics of that microenvironment the family are the prime determinants of development, then any society that believes that social and economic status and rewards should be assigned on the basis of individual achievement, as liberal society does, has little choice but to promote equality through children, deferring the dream of equality to the next generation.

There is in fact not much evidence to support any of these contentions. Rather, there is increasing evidence that disputes all three and an increasing tendency on the part of child developmentalists to submit their conclusions to agonizing reappraisal. The balance of this chapter will review some of the evidence that casts doubt on the developmental assumptions and will argue that liberal social theory and much of the conventional wisdom of developmental theory have shared flaws that must be corrected before it is possible to consider an egalitarian children's policy that is more than a delusion.

In so doing, we must point out that we are not attempting any comprehensive review of developmental theory, which is a complex, multidimensional field of inquiry. We are concerned solely with theories that have emerged out of psychological research and theory into the mainstream of social thought and social theory, where they have had such an immense impact on the formation of public policy. More specifically, we are concerned with psychological theories that have emerged as both cause and effect of the liberal emphasis on the "naked individual" as master of his fate. These theories, sharing the conventional disregard of how social structure affects individual development, see that structure itself as the sum of individual characteristics. Thus, they explain social inequalities as the inevitable result of individual differences. In our economy, which operates substantially on brain power, alleged differences in cognitive ability have often been singled out to "explain" differences in social status.

Three broad theories or points of view are particularly salient. One is the view that inherited genetic factors explain differences in individual capacity which create social inequalities. This view departs, of course, from the environmentalism that has dominated American psychological thought in the last generation, but it is easily assimilated into the liberal view that individual differences are what counts.

We will also consider a second view: the belief that family characteristics, especially parenting style, determine how a child develops. This view is in the mainstream of behaviorism and of the optimistic liberal theory that each of us is born a *tabula rasa*, a blank slate upon which the experiences of childhood are written. It contrasts strongly, of course, with the genetic theories, but both wind up ignoring the effects of social structure in favor of finding the fault in either the individual child or the child's family.

Finally, we will examine the validity of the axiom, common to liberal social theory and child development alike, that "the child is father of the man." This notion embraces diverse fields of child development theory and, especially, its application to social policy.

Differences in IQ and Social Standing

In our society, the most common form of the argument that blames social inequalities on genetic differences concerns the development of cognitive abilities—the brainpower or intelligence that so many aspects of our social system, beginning with school, stress so heavily. A prime example is the periodically recurring claim that the poor educational achievement and depressed socioeconomic status of blacks results from lower "intelligence" as recorded in IQ tests.

When Alfred Binet, the French psychologist, developed the first IQ tests in 1905, he warned that they should not be used as proof of genetic inferiority, and he cautioned against the "brutal pessimism" of those who believed intelligence was a fixed endowment. But his followers often ignored him, and in the popular imagination since then, IQ has often been vested with a heavy significance that it simply will not bear. The history of IQ testing and its social and cultural uses (or abuses) is quite bizarre.

On its face, it seems comical that a paper-and-pencil test should become a point of such recurring academic and social controversy, stirring rhetoric and emotions as few other subjects have; that parents should swell with pride when they learn their child has a "high IQ" (like Molière's *bourgeois gentilhomme* upon discovering that he speaks prose); that millions of dollars should be spent every year on programmatic interventions the aim of which is to increase IQ scores, while millions of dollars' worth of other programs should be evaluated by students' performance on IQ tests.

The passions that IQ arouses from time to time, including the recent outbreak of controversy following Jensen's extremist assertion that well-known average differences in black and white IQ scores reflect genetic differences, occur because it is widely assumed that:

1. IQ tests measure an innate, underlying, universal ability factor called intelligence.

2. At least some proportion of intelligence is genetically determined and fixed at birth.

3. Differences in IQ "determine" not simply how well an individual is likely to do in school, but how well he or she will later do in life.*

Without our replowing the well-worked soil of the IQ controversy, it is worth briefly reviewing these contentions because they contain commonly made (if well-known) errors of fact which are themselves symptomatic of larger inadequacies in the way development is popularly conceived and even to some extent in the way it is professionally conceived.

What Does an IQ Test Measure?

The common belief that the intelligence quotient measures some ability called intelligence is a misperception on several counts. For one, the IQ is a norm-referenced test. This means the test has been constructed so that if a random sample of the population takes the test, the scores will be distributed along a bell-shaped curve, with a few scores at the bottom, a lot in the middle, and a few at the top.

In other words, such scores provide rankings, but they tell little about what a person can *do*—or even what or how much a person knows.[10] Further, because individual scores can vary on successive administrations of reliable tests, it is dangerous to infer anything about a given individual from one IQ test score.

---

* This belief accounts for the concept of an *overachiever*, a term sometimes applied to schoolchildren whose grades are higher than test scores lead one to believe they will be, which carries the extraordinary implication that a child is doing better than he or she has the ability to do.

The IQ issue confronts us with a classic—almost tragic—question of what is in a name. The one thing IQ tests are fairly good at doing is predicting the kinds of grades and other scores students are likely to get in school. If instead of calling test scores intelligence quotients we had named them "school performance quotients," much mischief might have been avoided. For the kinds of mental operations IQ tests attempt to gauge are essentially the same as those that schools presumably try to develop. Indeed, if it turned out that individuals who did badly in school were routinely performing well on the IQ tests, the test would be presumed to be invalid.[11]

Misconceptions of what an IQ test actually is would perhaps be a trivial concern if they were not frequently wrapped in the larger ones outlined above, specifically in the belief that differences in ability explain social inequalities. This is how psychological theories get inflated into social theories, leading, on the one hand, to public policy based on fallacies and, on the other, to apologies for inequalities in the status quo.

The first belief, that differences in ability, however measured, predict or explain adult social status, is not surprising given the meritocratic ideology that most industrial societies have inherited from their liberal tradition. The idea is that society does and should reward individuals economically and otherwise on the basis of "merit." The word *meritocracy* was coined in a satirical novel that derided the notion that merit (defined as "IQ plus effort") would establish an aristocracy any more just or decent than an aristocracy of bloodlines.[12]

Despite the term's origins, it is hardly surprising that meritocracy should have become such a prized concept since it harmonizes so well with the basic precepts of the liberal tradition. But precious little evidence supports the notion that this society is a meritocracy. As the example of Bobby and Jimmy reminded us, adult prospects have a lot more to do with social status at birth than they do with an individual's ability—at least, any of the abilities we presume to be able to measure.[13] For instance, economists Samuel Bowles and Herbert Gintis have shown that once social class and amount of education are taken into account, individuals whose IQ scores place them in the top 10 percent of IQs are only 1.5 times as likely to end up in the top tenth economically as individuals whose IQ scores are in the bottom 10 percent.[14] Such data suggest that IQ plays a very modest role in explaining adult inequalities. By contrast, we might remember that on the basis of social class alone, Bobby was twenty-seven times as likely as Jimmy to end up in the top tenth of incomes, although their IQ scores were the same. Similarly, correlations between a host of aptitude tests and the professions or jobs they are designed to relate to are usually weak. Differences in scores on such tests rarely explain as much as one-tenth of the variance between individuals in actual job performance, although they, like IQ tests, are somewhat stronger in predicting grades in professional schools or performance in other training settings.[15]

Given the limited nature of IQ tests and their limited predictive power, the notion that the difference in average IQ usually found in comparing white and black samples[16] *explains* the oppressed social and economic status of blacks in America is clearly nonsense. However, the more limited claim—actually the claim made by Arthur Jensen—is that black-white IQ test score differences indicate that blacks do less well in school than whites because of genetically transmitted differences in intelligence. One has only to remember that at the turn of the century Jews were declared by early IQ testers to be innately feebleminded (quite the reverse of current stereotypes) to be skeptical of such claims. But one can go farther, examining the evidence on which claims of genetic black inferiority are based, and find evidence that when environmental circumstances are similar, blacks do as well on IQ tests as whites.

With few exceptions, researchers agree that some of the variance in individual IQ scores reflects genetic differences—a conclusion based largely on studies that find that when identical twins are reared in different environments, their IQ scores are more similar than one would expect if inheritance made no difference at all. However, it is unclear whether heritability explains a large or small portion of variance, for, as a thorough and careful review of the literature has shown, studies that have addressed this question are riddled with methodological problems and inadequacies of data.[17]

To conclude that genetic inheritance is significant is not to conclude that intelligence is fixed and determined at birth. On the contrary, differences produced by genes can be wholly or partially eradicated by the environment.[18] And more to the point, proof that heredity explains some portion of the variance in IQ scores among individuals does not, as any biologist knows, mean that test score differences between races are genetically determined—most obviously not when the social and economic conditions in which average black and white children in America are raised are so widely disparate. The glaring error made by Jensen and others is the false inference that the same factors that "explain" IQ variance between white twins must explain variance between races—an apples-and-oranges comparison.[19] The existing evidence, if anything, refutes rather than confirms the hypothesis that racial differences in IQ test scores result from genetic factors.

Logic requires that to demonstrate a genetically based racial difference in IQ scores, one of two broad research strategies must be followed: either there must be biological evidence that isolates some genetic property responsible for intelligence and shows that property to be more common in one race than in another, or there must be an experimental design that isolates the racial factor. The biological evidence is nonexistent since it exceeds present knowledge. There have been experiments trying to isolate the racial factor, conducted along two main lines. One examines children of mixed parentage. The assumption here is that if white genes are "smarter," children of racially mixed parentage will do better on IQ tests than those of all-black parents. A second line that tries to isolate race as an experimental factor is the study of adopted black children reared in white homes or white and black children reared in identical environments.

There have been relatively few studies of either type, but what recent evidence does exist comes down squarely on the side of the environmentalist hypothesis. In a comprehensive review of evidence, John C. Loehlin, G. Lindzey, and J. N. Spuhler cite two mixed-parentage studies. One study tried to determine whether children with racially mixed parents were more likely than those of all-black parents to be in the highest IQ bracket (over 140). The answer was no.[20] A second studied a large sample of illegitimate children born in Germany after World War II. It contrasted those having white mothers and black GI fathers to those having all-white parents. There was no difference in IQ test scores.[21]

Sandra Scarr has studied black children adopted by whites and found an average IQ of 106—slightly above the white norm—and Tizard compared blacks and whites raised in institutional environments and found no significant IQ differences.[22] The overwhelming preponderance of available evidence from these studies, then, leaves the genetic explanation of interracial IQ differences way out on a very frail limb.

This conclusion is stronger than that drawn by Loehlin, Lindzey, and Spuhler. Their caution can be justified on grounds that none of these studies is exempt from methodological or data disputes—a drawback shared by literally every other study on the subject. In addition, Loehlin cites two studies of mixed parentage performed in the 1930s that reached different conclusions. However, both studies as discussed were so weak on methodological grounds that there seems no compelling reason to weigh them in the balance against more recent and more sophisticated studies. The canons of social science, which is rarely a definitive discipline, hold that some evidence is better than none and that the preponderance of evidence should be accepted until disproved. What applies to scads of other subjects should certainly be applied to the race and IQ controversy—unless there is a double standard at work.

The social significance of whatever variance does exist in IQ scores is unclear, the definition of intelligence from which IQ tests depend is in dispute, and the contribution of IQ to achieved adult status is difficult to demonstrate.

When all this is said, it is hard to understand the fuss that has been made over IQ ever since the Progressive era except as the product of a tradition in psychological and social thought that attempts to explain social outcomes by individual traits. The misperceptions—and misuses—of IQ tests not only stem from the flaws inherent in that tradition but also, like other aspects of developmental theory, help perpetuate them.

Blaming the Family for Inequality

Genetic determinism that attributes social differences to genetic differences such as variations in IQ scores, although it reflects liberalism's individualistic bias, is itself not a characteristically liberal argument. Environmentalism, by contrast, *is*. From Locke on, the predominant liberal psychological stance has been behavioral: development is viewed as the consequence of interaction between the environment and a highly plastic and impressionable organism, the child—born "equal" because born a blank slate.

The broad statement that development occurs through the interaction of organism and environment is unassailable. But in centuries of popular thought and a scant century of formal psychological study of the child, both the nature of that interaction and the environment have been defined quite narrowly. The child has been regarded, more often than not, as an almost passive recipient of environmental influences, and environment has been, more often than not, defined primarily as "the family."

Under these definitions issues of development are often interpreted as issues of "good" or "bad" parenting. And just as low IQ scores have been seized upon to explain social inequality, inadequate parenting or bad family environments have sometimes been used to explain why whole groups of children do badly in school, or grow up to commit crimes, to experience poverty and unemployment, or to become emotionally and mentally unstable. Ironically, while adherents of the genetic hypothesis and the environmental hypothesis often dispute each other, their theories of individual development, when blown up into social theories, look alike. Both explain societal outcomes by individual traits. Both ignore the effect of broad social structure (including historical setting) on individual development, focusing instead on the narrow variables of genes or parenting styles.

From colonial days on, a great deal of public policy explicitly concerned with children has been framed as an effort to correct parents' shortcomings. The Old Deluder Satan Act, passed in 1647, established the first public schools in part to "save" children from immoral or inadequate parents. Subsequent educational reformers, as we have seen, drew on a similar rationale. At the turn of this century juvenile and family courts were given the power to remove children from their families on similar grounds, a power they still possess. Today it is common to hear educators assert that certain children are unteachable because of their family environment. Proposals and programs for parent education are widespread, and occasionally one even reads a letter to the editor suggesting that to ensure against ineptness, parents should be licensed by the state. Over the years the explanations for what constitutes "bad" parenting have shifted from moral to psychological terms, but the basic formula remains the same. In recent years social scientists square in the middle of the liberal tradition have argued one or more of the following variations on this theme:

—Poor children grow up in intellectually and verbally barren, "culturally deprived" homes, where they fail to receive enough stimulus from their parents to develop the cognitive skills necessary to succeed in school and adulthood.

—Poor and working-class parents have rigid and authoritarian child-rearing styles, which limit the stimulation their children receive and suppress the playfulness and natural curiosity that full cognitive development requires.

—Poverty creates its own culture, a culture of instant gratification, sexual promiscuity, and disorder, and the social and emotional development of children who grow up in this culture equips them poorly for success in school or adulthood.

—The black family is inherently unstable because of a tradition of matriarchy, which results in broken homes, economic instability, and, for male children, a lack of good role models.

—Minority children belong to subcultures the norms, values, and styles of which differ from those of the dominant society, and this difference makes it hard for them to cope with the schools or ultimately the work requirements of the dominant society.

Each of these theories is from time to time advanced as part of the more general theory of early childhood determinism—the belief that adult intelligence and social and emotional competence are critically shaped during the early years.

These beliefs add new strength to the liberal reform tradition since they all but dictate intervention in childhood as the way to break the so-called cycle of poverty. But there is no strong empirical evidence to support all these theories or the broader theory of early childhood determinism on which they are founded, and their conceptual framework suffers from the same kind of poor logic and blind spots that beset liberal social theory.

Consider, for example, recent efforts to explain inequalities in the status of blacks and whites in the society on the basis of supposed inadequacies or differences in the black family. A typical argument is that black families are traditionally matriarchal. As Warren Ten Houten has shown, anthropological evidence suggests that few matriarchies exist anywhere on the globe, and the black American family does not fit the formal definition of any of them.[23] Yet the broader notion that for one reason or another the black family is a weak institution, unstable and hence incapable of providing children the right psychological nourishment, persists. In reality, evidence indicates that there is only one significant difference between black families and white: black families bear a disproportionate share of the social and economic inequality characteristic of the society. As some scholars have pointed out, inferences about the inherent weakness of black families have typically been drawn from data that mistake social class differences for racial differences, perpetuating stereotypes and bad analysis in the process.[24]

The importance of the distinction between class and racial factors is illustrated by John F. Kantner and Melvin Zelnik's studies of teenage sexual experience.[25] Their data confront the widespread stereotyped belief that black teenagers, as a result of their racial identity, tend to be sexually promiscuous and prone to unwed pregnancy. Although it is true that a disproportionate number of teenage pregnancies are found among black teenagers, Kantner and Zelnik's data suggest that social class standing, not race, explains this fact. Indeed, they found that middle-class black teenagers were more likely to use contraceptive devices than any other sexually active teenagers; this suggests that the disproportionate number of black teenage pregnancies reflects the disproportionate number of black teenagers from low-income families, not any racial characteristic as such.

The same can be said for the higher rates of family breakup among blacks. Heather Ross and Isabel Sawhill, for instance, present impressive evidence that factors of unemployment and low income explain almost entirely the difference between white and black rates of family dissolution.[26] The monumental historical research of Herbert Gutman has made it clear that far from being unstable, the family has traditionally been a source of remarkable strength for blacks, during slavery and since.[27] Other studies have demonstrated the continued existence of extended families and quasi-familial networks of friends and relatives that compensate for the breakup of families under stress of low income, unemployment, or the welfare system.

In short, a higher incidence of poverty and unemployment, not of any inherent weakness or pathology, is what sets the black family apart. Accordingly, programs, policies, or rationalizations of inequality posited on theories of the inherent weakness of the black family are at best wide of the mark. At worst they perpetuate the tendency to try to correct through individuals (or their families) conditions that are the result, not the cause, of social inequalities.

The argument that blacks and other minority groups are culturally different is somewhat different from the theory that the black family is inherently unstable. Advocates of the cultural difference theory typically place no value judgments on those differences; indeed, they tend to argue that the problem is the inability or unwillingness of the dominant society and its institutions to honor and adapt to those differences.[28] But there are serious flaws to this theory, too. The evidence pointing to the existence of a distinct subculture that can be called black is itself uncertain. Charles A. Valentine, for instance, has argued that any rigorous analysis would have to reject the idea of a black subculture in favor of as many as fourteen different Afro-American subgroups with "more or less distinct cultures" grouped under three linguistic types: Afro-English, Afro-French, and Afro-Spanish.[29] And even if a convincing argument could be made for the existence of one or more black subcultures, the sharper question, as anthropologist John Ogbu has stressed, is:[30] why should subcultural membership constitute a liability for blacks?

The idea that a cultural difference represents a deficit on either side is treacherous. The statement is meaningless unless adherence to a subculture hinders a person's ability to cope with the dominant culture.

For some groups, subcultural membership or a strong sense of ethnic identity appears to be an asset, not a liability, for making it in America. Chinese Americans, Japanese Americans, and West Indians, for instance, have sustained strong cultural traditions that do not seem to impede their academic achievement.[31] Andrew W. Greeley found that the most successful Roman Catholics with European ethnic roots (e.g., Italians, Poles, Irish), who on the average do as well as or better than native American Protestants on such indices as median income and years of schooling, fall into two categories—those who retain strong ethnic and religious ties and those who reject them in favor of full assimilation.[32] The least successful group was composed of those caught between the two modes.

In recent years the theory that to differ culturally from the dominant majority is a liability has been advanced primarily with regard to black Americans. Most observers blame black English. Yet why should black English be any more of an obstacle to success—or to learning standard English—than regional dialects or the foreign languages spoken in the homes of immigrant children? The interesting question, indeed, is why so many black children grow up learning and using the language spoken in their homes rather than the language of the mainstream, which children of many accented or foreign-language-speaking parents seem to acquire with great ease. The answer is not likely to be found in Afro-American culture but rather in the dominant white society's oppression of blacks. One possible explanation is that racial isolation (segregation) promotes linguistic isolation. Another is that language provides a kind of protective covering for the oppressed. In either case, the "problem" of black English is a problem created by white society, not by black culture.

If differences between groups exist, the question becomes whether these differences really indicate a subculture. That is, does the group transmit from generation to generation a pattern of values and behavior that has a symbolic life of its own? Or is the apparent subculture not an independent entity but an *adaptive response* to the group's position in the main culture? For instance, the stereotype of the good-natured, childlike, foot-shuffling "darkie" was obviously not a legacy of the African heritage but an adaptive response to slavery, not simplemindedness but a creative and skillful way to appease and sometimes manipulate members of an oppressor class.

In short, efforts to explain social outcomes by intrinsic characteristics of individuals or the groups to which they belong seem to put the cart before the horse. So do theories that attribute certain kinds of inadequate child-rearing habits to members of given classes or to the existence of a self-perpetuating culture of poverty. Whether the argument is that a culture of poverty socializes children to instant gratification or that poor parents adopt rigid and authoritarian child-rearing styles that thwart creative intellectual growth, it is hard to find clear empirical support. Both assertions are gross generalizations made on the basis of survey evidence or of laboratory studies, which offer incomplete evidence of what families actually do. Contrary evidence exists from similar sources, casting further doubt on the validity of these generalizations. For instance, a major recent study found no evidence that corporal punishment was more common in one class than another.[33]

Reviewing the evidence, some scholars have concluded that there is no such thing as a generic class-bound parenting style but rather that in all classes there are fashions and trends that change over time, with changes in lower-class styles sometimes lagging a generation behind the middle class and vice versa. An alternative theory, advanced by Melvin Kohn and supported by his massive longitudinal study of 10,000 families, is that parental child-rearing philosophies tend to reflect the parents' experience in the workplace.[34] Parents who work in tightly supervised jobs in which there is little room for personal initiative and in which the exhibition of playful curiosity would be likely to get them fired tend to adopt authoritarian approaches to child rearing. Parents whose jobs reward creativity and individual initiative are likely to encourage these same things in their children.

If analysis such as Kohn's is correct, the point is clear enough: social trends and social structure (specifically, the occupational structure) determine—as much as anything determines—child-rearing practices. If so, it is erroneous and misleading to attribute social class standing to child-rearing practices, and approaches such as parent-education programs that aim to narrow the gap in opportunity between Bobby and Jimmy by providing every child a middle-class environment are pursuing a chimera.

Cultural Deprivation Theory

Even those who hold that all these sociological theories of development are inconclusive or wrong can still argue that for whatever reason, many low-income and nonwhite children grow up in family environments that stunt their development. Here the argument moves from sociological to psychological grounds, and it has two parts: first, the contention that many lower-class home environments fail to provide the necessary stimulation for optimal development and, second, the contention that early childhood development is the critical period, setting a foundation that determines subsequent adult traits and capabilities, cognitive and emotional.

The notion that parental "inputs"—love, play, verbal and physical interaction—are crucial to early development is widespread and promoted by a large body of literature.[35] Less widely known, perhaps, is that the literature generally fails to establish how much interaction is "required," and in fact, the evidence seems to be that the quality of interaction is far more important than the quantity. This tends to counter the fears that families with working parents—that is, no parent at home all day—will produce emotionally or cognitively stunted children.

But it is a far leap from saying that parent-child interaction is an important component of early development to saying that children from low-income families systematically receive inadequate parental attention or that by an early age many children from low-income families have, as a result of inadequate parenting, accumulated developmental deficits that they can never overcome. These two assertions form the core of cultural deprivation theories, which have been frequently advanced in recent years by psychologists and educators to explain why "disadvantaged" children do badly in schools and subsequently run a high risk of adult poverty and unemployment or worse.

It is probably true that the enormous stresses on families who have little income, who bear the psychological as well as the fiscal burdens of unemployment, and whose energies go to the battle to make ends meet have a hard time giving their children the time and sometimes even the affection that any child should have, although millions manage, heroically, to do so. But it is far from clear that even under such conditions early childhood experiences "determine" adult outcomes. And it is surely wrong to credit such shortcomings in the everyday lives of children to characteristics inherent in their families. Rather, the problems are inherent in their situation. Yet it is still a commonplace to blame the family for social inequalities.

In fact, there is very little empirical evidence to support the notion that the familial environments of low-income children are developmentally deficient. As a leading developmentalist, Urie Bronfenbrenner, has observed, the overwhelming body of developmental literature has suffered from a common flaw so gigantic as to call it all in doubt. Influenced by his firsthand observations of children in other cultures (where patterns of development and patterns of child-adult interaction often appear to differ dramatically from those in the United States), Bronfenbrenner argues that development must be understood "ecologically"—that is, the child's growth can be understood only in the context of interaction with a larger environment. But most child development literature relies overwhelmingly on laboratory situations such as a child's performing a test under the eye of an observer in a strange room or a mother and child observed by a researcher who is a stranger. Most studies, Bronfenbrenner says, "have almost invariably involved situations that are unfamiliar, artificial, and short-lived and call for unusual behaviors that are difficult to generalize to the real world. From this perspective, it can be said that much of developmental psychology is *the science of the strange behavior of children in strange situations with strange adults for the briefest possible periods of time.*"[36] Studies with this frail a connection to the real world hardly provide grounds for concluding that the parents of low-income or nonwhite children do not give their children enough verbal or other stimulation.

The notion that low-income black children, specifically, come from verbally deficient homes, causing them to lag behind white children on standard tests of reading achievement and verbal ability, has been particularly widespread. But some studies by linguists have refuted both the conclusion that black children receive less verbal interaction and the conclusion that they have less verbal ability than whites.

To be sure, the average low-income black child does not perform as well as the average white child on tests using "standard" (i.e., white) English, but he or she does compare favorably to whites in frequency of speech, richness of expression, complexity of sentence structure, and quantity of vocabulary used— all in what some have called black English.[37]

Of course, it can still be argued that in white America it is a liability to speak black English. But the issue, as suggested above, shifts from one of family adequacy or the verbal ability of individuals to the question of why black linguistic traditions are so strong.

Early Childhood Determinism

The chief reason that social scientists and policymakers focus on early childhood environments is their assumption that development in the early years of childhood is the critical determinant of adult characteristics. If this contention is not supportable, if the child is *not* father of the man, a considerable amount of developmental theory and a wide body of social policies and programs based on that belief need to be critically reexamined.

Since the theory of early childhood determinism was refurbished in the 1960s, the overriding concern of child developmentalists has been with cognitive development. Perhaps this reflects the popular belief that the nature of our economy makes "brainpower" the prime determinant of adult status. Even though the evidence to support this contention is weak, it can still be argued that optimal development of intelligence is desirable. Some would argue that intelligence *should* be a prime determinant of adult status. In any event, it remains valuable to know what influences the development of intelligence and whether it is true that the developmental experience of the early years determines subsequent adult competence.

Two notable books helped codify the early childhood determinism of the 1960s. Joseph McVicker Hunt's *Intelligence and Experience* (New York, 1961) drew heavily on research with animals, and Benjamin Bloom's *Stability and Change in Human Characteristics* (New York, 1964) placed particular stress on longitudinal studies showing that IQ scores in childhood were highly correlated with adult IQ scores. This fact led Bloom to conclude—improperly—that 50 percent of human intellectual capacity was developed and fixed by the age of eight. Hunt's and Bloom's books, combined with John Bowlby's studies of institutionalized children who were deprived of maternal care, Harry Harlow's studies of the effects of maternal deprivation on monkeys, and a few other seminal works, encouraged a widespread belief that while in the early years children were highly plastic and amenable to environmental influences in both cognitive and emotional development, the period of plasticity was brief.[38] By the early years of schooling, it was believed, a child's developmental path was more or less fixed. Hence such studies provided a major rationale for the Great Society programs that emphasized early childhood education as the way to break the cycle of poverty; they also spawned thousands of studies of parent-child interaction to determine what kinds of parental behavior caused healthy development—most of these the kinds of laboratory studies that Bronfenbrenner has criticized. Yet the viewpoint they represent has had a lingering influence on both professional and popular concepts of child development. As an example, a 1978 advertisement for a government-funded parent-education program on Philadelphia radio stations warned listeners: "Your child's experience today will determine his prospects in the future."

Recent work has cast considerable doubt on the theory of early childhood determinism.[39] New animal studies, for instance, have eroded the belief that early developmental periods are critical. Reviewing the evidence in a thorough study, Harvard psychologist Sheldon White concluded that while early periods of growth are "sensitive," they are not critical or irreversible in effect, at least for cognitive development. He wrote that the evidence showing early development to be critical "is clear only for socio-emotional and physiological development. This is not true for intellectual development; here the evidence does not support the sensitive period hypothesis in early development. Even for socio-emotional development, precise time periods are difficult to identify (if not impossible) and may vary within members of a species, although ranges can be determined with some accuracy."[40]

Furthermore, Benjamin Bloom's famous conclusion that 50 percent of adult intellectual capacity is determined by age four proved to be simply an incorrect inference. Bloom based his conclusion on longitudinal studies, such as Bayley's, which showed that, for instance, IQ scores at age four correlated with IQ scores at age seventeen at the .71 level. (A perfect correlation —everyone's having the same score at the age of seventeen as at the age of four—would be 1.0. No relationship at all between early and late IQ scores would be o.) In statistical terms, such findings mean that the score at age four "explains" 50 percent of the variance in scores at age seventeen. However, it is an error to leap from the mathematical meaning of "explained variance" to everyday inferences of causality. First of all, in the everyday meaning of causality, it is clearly absurd to say that a test score at age four "causes" a given test score at age seventeen (although the same factors may cause both scores). Second, as we discussed previously, IQ tests are norm referenced. They tell us how people rank in relationship to others, but not how much they know or what they can do. Therefore, it is clearly specious to argue that strong correlations between rank at age four and rank at age seventeen on tests that themselves vary substantially in form and content mean that 50 percent of intelligence has been developed at age four. (What is entirely amazing is that such a blatant error should have received such uncritical acceptance and still be cited today as "fact.")

However, it remains striking that the correlations between the IQ scores of four-year-olds and those of teenagers, and between children's marks in the third grade and in high school, are fairly high.[41] It is true, furthermore, that knowing a few facts—parents' occupation, parents' income, parents' education, a student's test scores, a student's race—lets us predict with reasonable accuracy the probabilities of a given child's ending up in any particular social class as an adult, as we did with Bobby and Jimmy. The question is: what explains this predictability?

Both liberal social theory and liberal psychological theory, as we have seen, predispose many people to think that these predictable continuities are explained by basic (if acquired) characteristics of the individual that determine fairly early the future he or she is likely to face as an adult. But another possibility is equally plausible. That is that the social structure, an environment far broader than the family, works to ensure that, over time, stabilities of experience perpetuate developed differences among individuals. In the former case, the predictable continuity is "inside" the individual, lodged in cognitive, emotional, and behavioral patterns that are formed and solidified in the early years. In the latter, the continuity is a sameness in the experiences "outside" the individual, or a sameness in the individual's perception of possible futures, which are derived from the predictable, stable sequence of experiences and possibilities characteristic of a given social class or racial situation.

The evidence cited to support the theory that childhood experience is predictive is, at best, ambiguous. Furthermore, there are a number of studies that have followed children over a considerable period of time—some from infancy to adulthood—and have cast considerable doubt on the premise that early childhood experience is predictive of either cognitive or emotional development.[42] Some of these studies have investigated correlations between infant characteristics and characteristics through childhood and adulthood, and they have generally failed to show significant correlations, suggesting, as one psychologist concluded after reviewing the evidence, that "parents simply do not have that much control over their children's development; too many other factors are influencing it."[43] Fairly stable correlations between childhood and subsequent characteristics do not begin to appear until the early school years—well beyond the early childhood period—and even so, considerable variability remains.[44] Other studies have shown that children three or older, after dramatic changes in environment, undergo dramatic developmental changes. Such studies have included recent studies of wartime orphans adopted by American families[45] and a classic study performed by H. M. Skeels some forty years ago. In Skeels's experiment, thirteen children aged three with an average infant IQ of 64 were selected at random from an orphanage and transferred to an institution for the mentally retarded. There they were placed under the care of female retardates. Within three years the average IQ of these children had improved by 26 points, while the comparison group, which remained at the orphanage, dropped 27 points. Adult follow-up studies showed continued dramatic disparities, with the thirteen experimental children becoming self-supporting and receiving an average of 11.7 years of schooling (then above the norm), while those in the comparison group received less than four years of schooling and one-third remained institutionalized.[46] The stunning point of this study, of course, is not only the developmental surge that the

experimental children went through but the fact that it oc-
curred in an environment one would hardly consider ideal.

What are we to make of such evidence? Since much of the information challenging the assumption that early experiences are
critical is "based on relatively crude methods," as Jerome Kagan
has observed, "it is proper to retain a cautious attitude toward
the new information. Nevertheless, it is reasonable that we at
least begin to question our cherished assumption."[47] Certainly
the early years are important, a "sensitive," if not a "critical,"
period. Infant deprivation may not have irreversible effects, but
of course, it is far more desirable not to have deprivation to deal
with, or, as somebody put it, "I've tried both rich and poor, and
I like rich better." The organism is vulnerable in infancy; nu-
tritional and physiological impairment in the early years can
have lifelong effects that may also in turn be transmitted from
generation to generation through mothers. The state of social
science is not such that one can say evidence supports defini-
tively the proposition that either early childhood *or* social continuities of experience are the critical determinants of development in its many aspects. But certainly there are grounds for
suggesting that American laymen, psychologists, and social
planners have adopted the early childhood determinist position
far too avidly. One can also suggest that a culture so imbued with
liberal social theory has been strongly predisposed to this position—despite the shortcomings and contradictions in the empirical evidence that liberalism, with its emphasis on rationality,
also embraces.

To go on basing social policy and egalitarian reform strategies
on such shaky theory is to run the high risk of continued in-
effectiveness. The more prudent course is to move beyond an individualistic psychology to one that embraces wholly the interplay of social structure and individual.

Chapter Five

Toward a Situational Theory
of Child Development

> I don't know, you see, what *your* children go dreaming,
> but *my* children know all about poverty: the dying,
> the hunger, the illness. That's what's in their dreams.
> Real things, real problems are what they have running
> around in their heads. Ain't no telling how and when
> those things are going to be coming back out, but that's
> the real stuff they fear. I can tell you that. They got
> politics in their dreams. . . . That's the way it is with
> all God's children. They take in everything and no one
> can say for sure when they'll jump down from where
> they were setting.
>
> —A mother quoted by Thomas J. Cottle in
>   *Black Children, White Dreams*

A theory of child development that takes account of social structure as an influence in shaping individual growth, besides telling us something about the stages and conditions through which the child moves to adulthood (as Piaget's stage theory attempts for cognitive development), would at a minimum take account of:

1. the significance of diverse social structures (including social class, racial group membership, and the occupational system);

2. the role of the individual as an active participant in his or her own development;

3. the importance of history, both personal and social, as the medium within which development occurs.

It is a massive task, however, to move toward formulating—or even sketching out—a theory of development that meets these tests and also illuminates all the various aspects of development into which the study of the developing child has been divided, such as cognitive development, social development, emotional development, and personality development. Here we can only sketch the broad outlines of such a theory, drawing on the work of others who have already begun the task. A good place to start is with a prime concern of many parents and the field of inquiry of most recent developmental studies: cognition.

Adapting to the Situation

Abundant anthropological and cross-cultural studies already exist to demonstrate how the large sociocultural environment shapes cognition, showing that patterns of thought develop differently given distinct cultural requirements having no relation to the cognitive capabilities of the individuals involved. Claude Lévi-Strauss has argued, for instance, that so-called primitive and so-called civilized societies *both* engage in a high level of abstract thought (problem solving) but that the processes used vary because of different systems of categorization.[1] "Primitive" classification systems, Lévi-Strauss argues, consist of minute, discrete categorizations of objects that are familiar to primitive people in the natural world on which they so directly depend. "Civilized" classifications, while including taxonomies, are typically more abstract; they rely on generalizations from the observed reality, which are used in efforts to go beyond immediate experience. (This effort is central to the idea of progress and the conquest of nature.) He illustrates the difference through his famous example of the *bricoleur,* or jack-of-all-trades, whom he views as the generic "primitive" problem solver. The *bricoleur* assembles a set of tools or a "treasury," which he uses for many different purposes and problems, but the set remains more or less constant. The engineer, whom Lévi-Strauss contrasts with the *bricoleur,* characteristically attempts to find a new tool that will perform the specific function demanded by his concept. The distinction is summarized as follows: "The engineer is always trying to make his way out of and go beyond the constraints imposed by a particular state of civilization, while the *bricoleur* by inclination or necessity always remains within them."[2] The point is not, of course, that one mode of problem solving is superior to the other. Rather, both are equally functional in very different kinds of societies.

Less theoretically, Michael Cole and his co-authors present evidence indicating different styles of thinking and variations in the use of different cognitive abilities in a study contrasting American children with Kpelle children (and adults) in Liberia.[3] Kpelle adults' and children's responses to a series of "riddles" these writers posed—riddles that to us seem simple—showed an apparent lack of Western logic. For example: "Flumo and Yakpalo always drink cane juice [rum] together. Flumo is drinking cane juice. Is Yakpalo drinking cane juice?" The overwhelming majority of Kpelles raised in traditional environments gave "wrong" answers to this and similar questions. A typical response was: "Flumo and Yakpalo drink cane juice together, but the time Flumo was drinking the first one, Yakpalo was not there on that day." Or to a similar question: "But I was not there. How can I answer such a question?"[4]

Apparently, most of the time, most traditional Kpelles "processed" these questions not by rules of logic, but by reference to experience. ("I was not there.") One cannot conclude that their answers were wrong; rather, their selection of problem-solving modes differed from those that Westerners use. This does not mean that Kpelles lack logical abilities. Kpelles who had received four or more years of Western schooling answered the riddles as we would. Even the traditional Kpelles generally gave the correct answer when the experimenters provided answers to the riddles and asked whether they were true or false. Furthermore, in situations more natural to their lives, Kpelles used various logical processes, such as plotting strategy in traditional games, debating at tribal divorce proceedings, etc. And in a variety of tests comparing Kpelle and American children, such as tests of classification and tests of the speed with which learning occurs, Kpelle and American children exhibited similar cognitive processes. (Not surprisingly, in tests where the task was more familiar to members of Kpelle culture, such as measuring rice or sorting leaves, Kpelles outperformed Americans.) But the interesting difference was that while American children almost always sought to apply conceptual rules to tasks, the circumstances under which Kpelles used conceptual vs. concrete (memorizing) approaches varied. The main conclusion Cole and his associates reached was that "cultural differences in cognition reside *more in the situations to which particular cognitive processes are applied than in the existence of a process in one cultural group and its absence in another* [emphasis added]."[5]

In our thinking about cognitive development, it is common to distinguish between the development of the capacity to use underlying cognitive processes (e.g., the ability to think abstractly, the ability to classify information, the ability to recall information) and the content of cognition (e.g., the kind and extent of information possessed, the modes of classification used). The significance of the distinction can be simply illustrated. One individual may be an excellent chess player but know little about the game of bridge. A second individual may be an excellent bridge player but not know a knight from a rook. We do not conclude that the first is stupid if he fails to bid a bridge hand correctly any more than we conclude that the second is slow-witted if he moves a knight in a straight line. Rather, we conclude that both have an underlying capability that makes each "smart"—a capability demonstrated through games the rules and play of which each has experienced. Similarly, we do not consider a Frenchman stupid if he cannot speak English. The search for "culture-free" tests of ability is built on this kind of distinction; it is a search for tests to measure what are presumed to be underlying, generic abilities that exist regardless of the particular content of an individual's experience. This distinction is made by those who argue, for instance, that tests of verbal ability conducted in "standard" English fail to measure the linguistic ability of minority groups who use black English or other nonstandard forms.

This distinction between the process and content of cognition is clearly important. We can scarcely expect an individual who has never been exposed to physics to be a good physicist, for instance, regardless of ability or "aptitude" for physics. Hence, we create schools and other forms of training that are vehicles for broadening experience and familiarity with one or more content areas, some very basic and some quite specialized. This simple fact has clear implications for policy since some individuals or groups have been systematically excluded from opportunities, whether in school or in the workplace, to gain certain kinds of experience and the knowledge that goes with it and since a lack of such experience is sometimes taken, however absurdly, as proof of a lack of capacity. An extreme example reported in the press concerned a woman who joined a previously all-male work force in a warehouse on a job that involved heavy loading. The men on the crew watched while she tried to lift a heavy object by hand instead of using a forklift, and when she sprained her back, the union objected to management that this was proof that women should not be hired for such jobs.

At a deeper level, the distinction between process and content may be misleading, recapitulating the false dichotomy between individual and environment. Some psychologists have long held that the development of certain capabilities comes through interaction with the environment, as when a child responds to a parent in play. Further, since our assumptions about the existence of an "underlying" capacity or process are always inferences from behavior that has an explicit content, the possibility of confusing experience with capacity is omnipresent. But the concept of situation that Cole has advanced goes even further in eroding this distinction. It implies that cognitive process and cognitive content are bound together in an eternal embrace, that any effort to measure cognitive capacity, as opposed to content or knowledge, by inference from observed behavior (whether the behavior is a test, a task, or any other observable form), commits a fallacy. For if the differences that the measurement detects "reside more in the situations to which particular cognitive processes are applied than in the existence of a process in one cultural group and its absence in another," what is actually being measured is what we can call a situational code, a code that (unconsciously) determines the cognitive process used in a given circumstance, making process and content, capacity and experience inseparable. The possibility is raised that differences in apparent capacities of individuals *within the same culture* may, like the more obvious differences between individuals from contrasting cultures, in fact be manifestations of different situational codes. For the differences between settings within a given culture or society (right down to the level of differences within the same family) may create very fine-grained differences in situation which produce nearly infinite numbers of situational codes.

The concept of situation is an important one that has just begun to be recognized. Cognition is only one example. Erving Goffman, for instance, has demonstrated how the norms and structure of mental institutions (and other settings) influence the behavior and attitudes of both caretakers and mental patients.[6] Fred Wiseman's film *The Titicut Follies*, a documentary about Bridgewater State Hospital in Massachusetts, showed one side of this influence vividly—the gradual descent into "insanity" of a middle-aged man who was committed in a case of mistaken identity. All his protestations were taken as evidence of insanity, and he ended up naked in a cell, screaming and banging his head against a wall. David H. Rosenhan, a Stanford professor, had his graduate students voluntarily commit themselves to mental hospitals as part of a research project.[7] The students made no effort to fake mental illness, but almost all were diagnosed by the professional staff as having various disorders. (In this case the situation influenced the observers, not the observed.) Similarly, Roger Barker and associates, in a number of studies, have investigated the way spatial arrangements such as the placement of the different parties in a courtroom or the height of a speaker's dais influence patterns of behavior, inspiring deference or reinforcing authority.[8] John Gliedman and William Roth* have attempted a thorough analysis of the way "the situation of handicap" influences the behavior and attitudes of both handicapped and able-bodied persons in interactions. They argue, in essence, that handicap is as much a social construction as it is a

* John Gliedman and William Roth, *The Unexpected Minority,* a Carnegie Council on Children monograph, 1979 (forthcoming).

biological reality, and they attempt to show how that construction affects the psychological and cognitive development of handicapped children.

Closer to the subject at hand, Frederick Erickson and his .associates at Harvard have been attempting to understand how children learn (and apply) different sociolinguistic codes in different social situations.[9] As one part of their research strategy, they videotaped a child in different settings: at home, in the classroom with a teacher present, in the classroom with only peers present, in the playground, etc. The resulting tapes reveal stunning differences. In the presence of the teacher, for instance, the child appears reticent, inarticulate, and puzzled, leading the teacher to conclude that the child has limited verbal ability or leadership potential. But at home a completely different child seems to emerge: talkative, witty, and extroverted, dominating the family's conversation at the dinner table.

Similar kinds of changes in children when they move from one situation to another are suggested by the work of William Labov, who has demonstrated that black children whose IQ test scores seem to indicate that they lack certain cognitive abilities exhibit those same abilities in natural settings.[10]

All these examples suggest that situation is a concept with important implications for understanding development.

Defining "Situation"

Situations obviously come in many shapes and sizes. For the purposes of a working definition, however, a developmental situation can be said to begin with the following elements:

1. a *setting* (a culture, an institution, a place, a room)

2. a set of *norms* (formal, informal, or cultural "rules" associated with a given setting)

3. *actors* (people performing different roles in that setting in accordance with those rules)*

Obviously, these general definitions can be applied to a wide

* *Actors* should be distinguished from the individual participant, as described immediately below.

range of circumstances. For instance, something as discrete as a schoolroom, a home, a playground, or a block, or as large and diffuse as a social class or a culture, may be defined as a setting, with each containing different subsettings. Yet none of these features has meaning for development without the person who experiences them—the person who is developing. So another element is needed to define what we are calling a developmental "situation":

4. the *individual* who takes information from and gives meaning and perceptual definition to the elements listed above

Just as inkblots become a Rorschach test only when a subject reacts to them, so a situation assumes definition only through the participation of an individual. Situations, of course, almost always include more than one individual. In that sense, when the anthropologist meets the Kpelle child, two situations are occurring in the same space at the same time.

Finally, a situation exists at a particular moment or during a given interval of time. The setting, norms, and actors are each part of a history that exists regardless of any participating individual, and participating individuals bring a history of their own development to each situation, a history that shapes the meaning they give to the information presented in any situation and in turn is itself reshaped by it. Thus, we close the list of characteristics for a situation with:

5. the *history* of the situation itself and, individually, of the people participating in it

The broad implications of the concept of situation for a theory of human development are fairly clear. The child's environment (or, to use a more dynamic word, experience) can be thought of as a more or less continuous series of situations, which has two distinct effects on development. First, the series of situations determines what is available for a child to learn from, in terms of facts, behavior, and emotional and cognitive processes. So, in a fixed, invariant environment barren of stimulus, no creature will learn much of anything by way of social response, emotional repertoire, information, or cognitive process. A second effect, analogous to that discerned by Cole and others in their study of Kpelle children, is that situations will, in some poorly under-

stood fashion, have an influence on when a child—or an adult
—uses a particular ability or process in his or her repertoire.

The work of the British sociologist Basil Bernstein has perhaps gone farthest toward elaborating a theory of how the different situations of social class constitute different learning
environments.[11] Bernstein argues that with the division of labor
in industrial societies goes a division of cognitive styles. Some
work tasks require symbolic organization and individual decision making, in which the worker (i.e., a manager) manipu-
lates abstract concepts that transcend a particular time and
place. Most tasks, however, require only "context-tied operations." Such differences, Bernstein argues, are transmitted from
the workplace through the family to the child, and they result
in distinct sociolinguistic codes, by which Bernstein does not
mean so much syntactical differences but differences in how individuals realize different meanings in similar circumstances
(even when overt linguistic patterns are similar).

The fact that situations influence what aspect of knowledge
or behavior an individual brings to bear at a particular moment
poses a problem. It becomes extremely difficult to measure any
particular ability since one cannot be sure whether the measure
describes a characteristic of the child or a characteristic of the
situation to which the child responds. For one thing, present
methods are not designed to look at the problem this way. In fact,
this second possibility may mean that apparent differences in
sociolinguistic codes such as Bernstein records are nothing more
than differences in situational response, although the two effects
are not mutually exclusive: out in the world the consequences
may be the same whether differences in behavior were caused by
variations in ability or simply by different responses to the situation; someone who "freezes" on a test will fail to get a civil
service promotion as surely as someone who simply doesn't
know the answer.

The Cole hypothesis—that differences in cognition reside more
in the *situation* than in the cultural group—should be viewed
simply as that—a hypothesis that is richly suggestive but not
strictly proved. Furthermore, it is in some ways hard to grasp.
Everyday explanations do exist for understanding why a child may

appear to be a "very different person" in different circumstances; the child Erickson videotaped, for instance, may have been more comfortable and secure at home. But the notion that many kinds of cognitive (or other) abilities exist latent in everyone's repertoire and are realized only in certain situations is less easily explained. It runs hard against our cultural tendency to quantify ability and assume that some people have more of it than others, and it needs a lot more testing before one can say it is proved. However, it is not difficult to grasp the range of elements that enter into the situations a child learns from, nor is it hard to see that the elements of such situations derive from a far larger "environment" or context than the family itself. This argument, a familiar one to anthropologists,[12] certainly presents a coherent alternative to the view that development is primarily the effect of genes and family environment on a malleable and curiously passive organism.

Situations Within Situations

It is certainly true that genes have something to do with differences in individual development, although the extent to which those differences explain social outcomes is somewhere between unclear and limited. And it would be silly to suggest that families do not play an important role in a child's development as well. The demands of rearing a child and how the parents respond to them are important for all children. What is important here, however, is to place the influence of genes and parents in a broader context and to indicate the dimensions of development over which neither holds sway and the considerable extent to which their influences depend on the broader context. Specifically, we are concerned with what can be called social development, the acquisition of an admixture of skills, attitudes, behaviors, and the situational codes that tie them together, which are developed and manifested in such social settings as schools and workplaces.

For purposes of illustration, the developmental context for any given child may be thought of as a series of overlapping circles with the child in the middle of them all. Each of these circles, which we might call elements of social structure, constitutes an environmental context or setting for development. The nature of inner circles such as family and school is affected by the shape of the outer circles such as social class or race, which could be defined as "master settings." Conversely, the child's experience and perception of those outer circles is influenced by the nature of the inner circles. For example, the degree of industrialization in a society will shape the experiences broadly characteristic of each social class and its members. But growing up in a family of semiskilled workers may mean one thing for the child of immigrants for whom even a low-paying American job is better than what they left behind, and it may mean quite another thing for a child whose parents have grown up in a shrinking urban economy and view their work as a dead end. Finally, these elements of social structure are dynamic, changing over the course of a child's development.

The outer ring, the broadest context for development, is the social order and especially its economic structure, from which are derived the kinds of adult roles available in the society, roles for which children are "prepared" and from which we derive the developmental desiderata for children. Any culture, and any economic system, contains a set of characteristic "problems" whose solutions require different cognitive skills and, one should add, attitudinal and affective skills as well. The skills that are most generally valued—hence, those aspects of development of greatest concern to a given society—are those that are presumed to be most functional to the economy of a given society at a given time, whether they are described in the language of the layman or the language of the psychologist; whether we speak of a "self-starter" or an "achievement-motivated individual," a "quick study" or someone deft in "relational and symbolic thinking."

In the writings of Horace Mann and his contemporaries, two dominant pedagogic themes were the development of physical health and the development of internalized self-discipline. Both were important for the emerging industrial economy: the factories of the time were labor intensive, and individuals who were physically weak or missed work because of poor health, or who showed up irregularly, were a major source of productive inefficiency. Today, while these early concerns linger, psychologists and laymen alike tend to place much more emphasis on the development of cognitive skills, "human relations" skills, and, a concept that hovers between these two, "communications skills." These concerns reflect the growth of an economy that is increasingly "knowledge based" and organized in complex public and corporate bureaucracies in which breakdowns in communication or human relations are more common sources of inefficiency than a lack of muscle power.

In all societies the economic structure appears to be the dominant influence on developmental desiderata, but it is presumably not the only influence. Cultural traditions and social values from society to society or among subgroups within a society no doubt have their influence as well. It seems reasonable to conclude that culture, the collective expression of a social aesthetic, is to some extent a force independent of economic structure. For instance, not all industrial societies place the same cultural premium on individual freedom. But there is also a considerable extent to which cultural traditions and social values are derived from the technostructure, either as direct manifestations of it or as reactions to it. The ideal of competing for jobs, the related value put on individual effort, and the not-infrequent assumption that poor people are lazy or in some other way defective, for instance, are derived straightforwardly from the nature of liberal capitalism. Likewise, when we travel to a country such as India, few of us assume that individual deficiencies are causing the poverty there; rather, we attribute it to structural factors—the nature of the Indian economy.

Social Class as a Master Setting

It has been suggested by many writers that the spread of mass communications and the growth of national and multinational industries created an increasingly homogeneous culture in the United States and in other industrialized nations. Not only do children from Florida and Alaska watch cartoons produced in Hollywood, but children from Maine to Hawaii are measured against standards developed by a test maker in Princeton, New

Jersey. In this sense the existence of a broad, common social context for development is clear.

Yet tremendous differences remain to characterize the location of individual children within that broad context. Two of particular importance for our concerns are social class and race, and these intersecting circles constitute a next layer of developmental context.

Social class is generally measured by such factors as occupational category, occupational prestige, years of education attained, income, and other status symbols. Of these, occupational status is the most powerful factor. But the significance of class as a developmental context does not lie in these trappings; rather, it lies in experience typical of members of each class and in the meaning each individual attaches to that experience. Social class is not simply the classification of the job one's parent holds, but, for instance, the content of the job: the kinds of skills and behavior the job requires and rewards; the authority it bestows; the deference to others it imposes or commands; how much control the parent has over the job, including control over a company's investment decisions and the means and organization of its production, as well as over how his or her own time is allocated. Class as defined by the jobs parents hold depends also on the variety, latitude, and freedom they have in their work and the possibilities for growth that it implies. A child's as well as a parent's understanding of how the world works is formed through these differences in experience. In other words, the human and, therefore, the developmental significance of class must be understood in terms of experience itself—experience such as how much power and control one can exercise in everyday life, in social settings, and over subsequent events; the array and variety of experiences that are available or potentially available and through which one learns, develops, applies knowledge, and receives rewards; the probable futures that, given the dynamics of social structure, one can expect; and the amenities and pleasures that are available through one's control of such resources as time and money.

In most contemporary societies the lines that separate social classes are not sharp.[13] Class is better conceived as an array along a continuum than a series of discrete steps. Yet while a line between, say, lower middle class and middle class is arbitrary, the relative differences between the two are clear enough, and it remains useful for analytic purposes to speak of distinct classes.

The situations of different classes, like those of different cultures, present different characteristic "problems" to be "solved" through development. With those differences, we may speculate, are variations in situational code. In this sense, different social classes and different races constitute different developmental contexts within a given society. Further, in our society class status and racial status combine to form a developmental context.

Caste as a Master Setting

If the lines that separate classes in American society are fuzzy, the lines that separate racial groups are hard and clear. (Consider, for instance, that children of mixed racial parentage are considered, by themselves and others, as black.) The clarity of this distinction is one clue that America has been—and remains —a caste society, and caste provides a particularly vivid example of the influence of social structure on development.

Caste is not a popular word. Just as many Americans prefer to believe that this society is classless—or at least that class origin is a trivial matter—so most Americans, we suspect, think of caste as something that exists only in faraway places such as India. Yet the facts in the United States fit the standard definition of caste.[14]

It can be argued that at least four distinct groups occupy a lower caste position in the United States: blacks, Mexican Americans, Puerto Rican Americans, and Native Americans. The depressed socioeconomic status of these groups, the historic discrimination, once rooted in law (as opposed to mere prejudice), and the experience of conquest or forcible subjugation that each group suffered at the hands of white Americans are marks they bear in common. If we focus on the caste status of black Americans, that is because they are the largest minority group and the group whose caste oppression is most widely known and thoroughly documented.

The caste status of blacks, as distinct from slave status, was willfully imposed after Emancipation and the Reconstruction era. Its imposition proceeded on three broad fronts: through political disenfranchisement;[15] through the perpetuation of segregated school systems; and, perhaps most important, through the creation of a double-track employment system in which blacks were systematically excluded from the most desirable occupations and subjected to a "job ceiling" that limited their prospects for advancement in occupations they *were* permitted to enter.[16]

Since World War II the legal basis for caste has been steadily obliterated by a variety of laws and court actions. But the principles of caste remain and are perhaps all the harder to eradicate because they are more subtle and less easy to attack, rooted in discriminatory attitudes and the social inertia of history as it affects both blacks and whites. For example, instead of being barred from occupational adancement on the basis of their color, blacks are now excluded from many jobs on the basis of inadequate training, lack of experience, or "low aptitude." The rationale changes, but the marks of caste remain. They appear in housing patterns, in income statistics, in the dramatic under-representation of blacks in elective offices, and, above all, in employment.

The facts are well known: black unemployment is twice that of white unemployment, a ratio that has remained more or less constant since World War II. The median family income of blacks relative to whites has improved only slightly since 1900,[17] and the modest increases of the past few years are attributable almost entirely to increased welfare payments or the greater number of two-or-more-earner families among blacks. Whites enjoy higher rates of upward mobility than blacks, both inter-generational and intragenerational.[18] Federal efforts to reduce unemployment work better for whites than for blacks; manpower training programs and public employment programs, for instance, produce lower returns for the average black participant (who remains likely, because of seniority rules, to be "last hired, first fired") than for whites.[19] The issue is more fundamental than a matter of social class (although a smaller percentage of blacks are middle-class than are whites), for caste status affects those of all social class standings within the subordinate caste group. A recent Department of Labor study, while reporting on modest increases in the numbers of black professional, managerial, and technical workers in the late 1960s, concluded that even they experienced the presence of a job ceiling:

Three of five of the surveyed men felt that they, as black professionals, did not have the same opportunities as whites in their firm. Their comments indicated that the basis for this view was expectations concerning the future. The men felt there was a ceiling on how far they could go, and that the ceiling was rather low. The fact that so few of the surveyed group had attained supervisory or managerial positions and that average salaries did not increase beyond the ninth year of service, though some of the men had worked for the same firm more than 25 years, suggests that the respondents' evaluation of their situation was based on observation and experience. If the future were to mirror the past, their attitudes were realistic.[20]

If the future were to mirror the past*—the phrase captures the basic principle of caste as a historic mode of social organization, and it is laden with implications for children and their development. Implicit in the notion of development are growth and expansion into a future of increasing possibility. Implicit in the notion of caste is a constricted, limited, and unchanging future —a constraint whose objective corollary can be found in the historical rigidity of black social statistics, in the limited opportunities for mobility, in the presence of job ceilings. This conflict between growth and containment, between self and caste, is one of the dominant themes of black literature, from W. E. B. Du

---

* To be sure, there have been real changes in the past twenty years. Integrated education is the law of the land, and there has been progress toward actual desegregation. We have civil rights acts outlawing discrimination in jobs, housing, and education, and the number of black elected officials has grown. But the question is whether these changes have been nearly sufficient in scope or in scale to alter significantly the developmental setting of caste. The evidence overwhelmingly suggests that they have not.

Bois's famous account of his childhood awareness of a "double-self" in *The Souls of Black Folk* to Alex Haley's effort in *Roots* to escape the culturally defined identity of caste through his long journey, both literal and metaphoric, back to his pre-American African roots.

The intersection of a reality imposed by social structure—the structure of caste—with individual development is dramatically captured in James Weldon Johnson's remarkable 1912 novel *The Autobiography of an Ex-Coloured Man.* The narrator, the son of a white man and a black woman, describes the day when, at age eleven, he learned he was black through the actions of a teacher: "And so I have often lived through that hour, that day, that week, in which was wrought the miracle of my transition from one world into another, for I did indeed pass into another world. From that time I looked out through other eyes, my thoughts were coloured, my words dictated my actions limited by one dominating, all-pervading idea which constantly increased in force and weight until I finally realized in it a great tangible fact."

The sense of double identity, one a "true" self and the other a self derived from the caste imposed by the dominant society, is not found only in black literature. A 1976 survey conducted by the *New York Times*, for instance, found that twoness was the "single most consistent pattern" in the lives of black Americans today.[21]

The implications of this for black child development are subtle and profound, we would argue, for the ultimate impact of caste is that it constitutes a developmental master setting, differentiating the situation of subordinate caste members from that of dominant caste members (i.e., blacks from whites) almost as sharply as the situation of Kpelle children differs from that of American children.

As a master setting, caste contains a set of messages about the futures black children can expect and the tasks and abilities appropriate to and rewarded by those futures. Insofar as these differ from those of other children, patterns of development—both surface manifestations that we may measure or observe and underlying situational codes that we may infer—will also differ.

The existence of a job ceiling for black adults, for instance, creates on its face a clear disincentive for black children to go on with school, whatever the hopes and urgings of their parents. For example, anthropologist John Ogbu, drawing on both his own field studies and a review of literature, has argued that much of what seem to be bad study habits, disruptive behavior, or poor school performance among black children in the United States can be better understood as perfectly accurate indications of the unimportance of school performance by the subordinate caste since career opportunities remain limited and prescribed. He bolsters the argument with a review of cross-cultural studies that show similar patterns in caste societies around the world.[22]

Suggestive as well are data showing that blacks who migrated from the rural South to the North in the 1950s and 1960s tended to gain somewhat better-paying jobs and to experience less unemployment than urban-born blacks.[23] These data contradict the once-popular theory that many so-called urban problems were caused by an influx of rural blacks who were ill prepared to cope with city life. The second-generation migrants, however, did not sustain the advantage of their parents; growing up in the city appears to be a disadvantage.[24] One reason, we suspect, is that for first-generation migrants, for whom the South was a reference point, as the homeland often is for immigrants, the move north represents a new situation, a break with historical continuities of experience, a cause for optimism. But by the second generation, that effect—like the effect of most Head Start programs—wore off in the face of a more intransigent reality: the existence of caste as a principle in American society without geographic bounds.

Inferences from broad examples like these gain in plausibility if they are congruent with what we know from extensive, in-depth observation of individual children. Few studies of this sort, as we have noted, exist; that is one reason why black literature provides an important source for gaining insight into black child development. But one, Thomas Cottle's *Black Children, White Dreams*, a moving document based on extensive conversations between a white sociologist and two black children and their families in Boston in 1972,[25] provides graphic examples of how an "environment" as broad as society, and as long as history, shapes development. In Cottle's words, these children have "transposed gossip, classroom discussions, newspapers and television reports and conversations into attitudes and even into political stances on certain issues"; they "size up the political fortune of their people, keep their ears and eyes open, gather their information, make their calculations." Cottle found great ambivalence, another reflection of twoness; they "fear the punishment, lack of protection, abandonment, mistreatment they and their families have always experienced." Yet " to speak of change in the society is to arouse in them the experiences of hurt and death that regularly accompanied any attempt at change or personal and family improvement they have ever known about. It is not necessarily that they are cynical; they are doubtful, intelligent, self-protective, knowledgeable of the histories of their parents, grandparents and often great-grandparents as well. . . ."[26] Or, as the mother of one child put it, "They have politics in their dreams."

The "they" of these sentences, an eleven-year-old boy and a twelve-year-old girl, reveal in their conversation a perceptive sense of politics and history, uneven as the content of their knowledge is. They live in homes where hardworking mothers encourage and support children to do well in school, to "better themselves" in the great American tradition. But they experience every day in their immediate lives examples of futility and oppression which are reinforced by their knowledge of history, their assessment of the society around them, and the words of their parents. "We know exactly what is coming to us and most especially what is never *ever* going to be coming to us," says one mother, echoing the basic principle of caste.

To the large developmental contexts of class and caste one must add more intimate ones of which school, neighborhood, and family are clearly among the most important. For young children, especially, it is through these intimate contexts that contact with the broader dimensions of class, race, and the social and economic order is made. Again, it is important to stress that all these smaller contexts and the larger ones surrounding them interact and affect each other. The nature of a society at a given time shapes the structure of social classes; social class influences the nature of family life and experience; racial membership influences likely occupation; through income, occupation helps determine neighborhood. Neighborhood determines where one goes to school, and not only is family background associated with how a child does in school, but it may influence how the school treats a child and the ability of the child and family to manipulate the institutional ropes of a school. Schooling in turn influences subsequent social class standing, and to some extent the skills that the population as a whole develops influence the contours of economic activity,[27] and so on in a series of permutations, combinations, and feedback loops. In the midst of this complex, breathing organism called social structure is the child.

The implications of these multiple contexts for development are best grasped if the objective dimensions of social structure, the dynamic relationships among them, and the child's own experience—an experience shaped by class, racial, and sexual membership—all are viewed as "messages" that help structure and define the situations of development.

The full range of mechanisms by which a child takes in all these messages is well beyond our ability to understand or describe here. But the crucial point—if these suggestions are correct—is that at their source these messages derive from the social structure itself.

These messages are, of course, transmitted in greater or lesser degree through those mediating institutions which, serving as a kind of filter, constitute a child's intimate and immediate environment. At school, class-differentiated criteria of the occupational system are often reflected in the training, sorting, and selecting of children. Through the neighborhood, in our class- and income-stratified residential settings, children, we hypothesize, get their first glimpse of what adulthood will be like for "people like me." In addition to their direct and idiosyncratic influence (that is, characteristics not clearly related in any way to class or occupational or racial status), parents tend to reflect and transmit in various aspects of their behavior, including their child-rearing practices, the social, emotional, and cognitive attributes required by their occupational status.

It would obviously be a mistake to discount the importance of these mediating institutions, especially of the family, to a child's development but it is also possible to overemphasize it. Inasmuch as the family (or the school or another institution) plays an intermediary role, one cannot logically identify it as the "cause" of this or that pattern of development. It is merely the medium through which such causality passes. What it filters and how it filters it are both determined to a considerable degree by the larger social structure it is part of and by its location in that structure. Just as it has become conventional wisdom that one cannot effect major changes in schooling or the class-related outcomes of schooling without making accompanying changes in the economic system that the school serves, so it seems unlikely that one can effect major changes in most families or in parenting styles without changes in the socioeconomic situation of families.

We have begun to meet one of the criteria set forth for a developmental theory: that it illuminate the significance of diverse social structures as developmental environments. But defining environment in broader spatial terms than the family still ignores one critical ingredient in any situation. The individual actor, the child, must be considered if we are to avoid the error of determinism. Without the individual there is nothing to develop, so a theory of how development occurs must take account of how the individual perceives each situation and thereby also affects it.

The Child's Theory of Social Reality

As we have seen, popular conceptions of prevailing behavioral theories of development describe the child as a strangely passive creature, the product of genes and environment, with little active, autonomous participation in his or her own development.[28] The child is, in fact, an important actor, who processes information from situations and history and in that processing introduces a crucial new variable into the developmental equation: his or her own theory of social reality.

A child's theory of social reality (constructed by a process that is far from clear and that occurs without the child's "knowing" it) provides a kind of diagram of the social universe, including his or her location in it, as well as a kind of map of his or her likely future, a map constructed out of inference from personal, family, group, and social history as the child becomes aware of it through various media, including family and school.

Some of the messages the child takes in may be explicit pieces of information or data directly communicated or observed and absorbed by the child—e.g., his or her knowledge of occupations or the kinds of things one may do when one is grown up. Some may be inferences the child makes about the way the world works, such as the probabilities of obtaining a certain social status through good school performance, a concept that may be part of the child's tacit understanding of social class dynamics, whether or not he or she can articulate it clearly. Some are implicit in the content of experience itself; for instance, the different cultural tasks that we, with Cole, have suggested may produce different situational codes governing the use of specific cognitive modes. That is, some messages may have an open and manifest effect on the child's conscious, articulable beliefs and attitudes. Others may do their work underground or tacitly, influencing modes of cognition and linguistic patterns, which, like breathing, are not learned consciously.

We are suggesting that the experiences characteristic of different social class and racial situations, plus the history of the group to which an individual belongs, come together and realize their developmental impact in the child's theory of social reality. The material of situations and histories provides the child with information that is a given beyond the child's control. These givens vary substantially from child to child, although certain crude similarities in information will exist for those whose social situations and historical moments are similar. But the child, rather than being simply a passive recipient of that information, transforms it into a theory of social reality through abilities that may be as universal as the ability to speak, much as Piaget has argued that the child interacting with the immediate physical environment forms certain cognitive constructs—in what may be a universal sequence—that come to define spatial and causal "reality." We are not suggesting that the child can consciously articulate his or her theory of social reality any more than the Piagetian child can articulate the theory of conservation.[29] It is at the tacit level that the child constructs his or her theory. Thereafter that social theory in turn helps guide the child's own development, serving as a kind of feedback loop in a self-steering process. In each developmental situation, large and small, the encounter between the child's theory of the world and the situation leads to a new configuration within the child, a slightly altered and elaborated theory, which will govern the child's understanding and approach to the next situation.

The child's map would seem to have particularly important implications for development, for it seems plain that no one will try to become what he or she believes intuitively to be impossible or useless. This seems true whether "becoming" is defined in simple terms (becoming a lawyer), in terms of personality (one who defers gratification), or in more abstruse terms (one who uses associative logic to solve problems that arise in managerial situations). Popular psychological theory suggests that children learn to be like their "role models." Our speculation suggests that children learn to be like a "role model" only if their theory of the future—derived from their theory of social reality—tells them that the characteristics of the "role" fit the part *they* are to play. "Time past and time present are both perhaps present in time future," T. S. Eliot wrote. So the child's experience of social reality and sense of historical trends (both "stored" in the tacit dimension of the child's mind)* may create a theory of the future toward which he or she "becomes."

* The phrase *tacit dimension* is borrowed from the philosopher Michael Polanyi, whose theory of tacit knowledge is pertinent here.[30] "We know more than we can tell," Polanyi states, arguing that it is in the tacit dimension of the mind that we are able (instantaneously and without being conscious of it) to integrate knowledge of particulars into an understanding of the whole. This tacit act occurs again and again in each individual, with each new act building on the old, to structure our perception and understanding of experience. "Meaning," Polanyi argues, is the result of this tacit process—the outcome of "an active shaping of experience performed in the pursuit of knowledge." Polanyi illustrates the existence of the tacit dimension by citing the paradox, first suggested by Plato, of the importance for pure research of selecting a "good" problem. He writes: "Research can be successful only if the problem is good; it can be

For a crude anecdotal example of how such theories may work, we can turn to interviews with two real children.* Both are eight-year-old second graders. One, Sally, lives in California and is the daughter of an urban school superintendent. The other, Joseph, lives in Hempstead, Long Island, with his mother, who works in the lunchroom of a public school. Sally is white; Joseph is black. They are almost as far apart in the social system as Bobby and Jimmy, the hypothetical children described in the opening pages of this book. Both, in conversation with the interviewer, appeared lively, responsive, and intelligent.

A portion of each conversation follows.

Interview 1. *Sally*

> Sally: We had tests today.
> Int.: Did you like them?
> Sally: Hmmm. [noncommittal] It was scary.
> Int.: Why?
> Sally: I don't know. It just was.
> Int.: Do you hope you did well on them?
> Sally: Oh, yeah!
> Int.: Why?
> Sally: Well, 'cause . . . it's important.
> Int.: Why?
> Sally: Well, 'cause . . . it goes all the way up to college.
> Int.: Why is college important?
> Sally: Hmm. I guess so you can get [sic] different people and things, and jobs and things.

---

original only if the problem is original. But how can one see a problem, any problem, let alone a good and original problem? For to see a problem is to see something that is hidden. It is to have an intimation of the coherence of hitherto not comprehended particulars. The problem is good if this intimation is true." The process by which a child constructs a theory of social reality and "uses" it to interpret experience, to develop a situational code, and to guide subsequent development is analogous, we are suggesting, to the process by which the philosopher or researcher selects a good problem.

* Sally was interviewed at her home, where the interviewer was a guest. Joseph, returning from a visit to his grandmother, was interviewed on a bus when he shared a seat with the interviewer. Both are interviews collected by the author as part of an ongoing project, interviewing children between the ages of five and nine about their views of school, the future, and work (investigating, essentially, that classic question "What do you want to be when you grow up?"). All interviews are being conducted in natural settings—that is, when the author comes in casual and unplanned contact with a child.

[Subsequently the interviewer changes the topic to work.]

Int.: Do you know what your father does?

Sally: Sort of. He bosses other people around. Not really bosses, but he tells them how to run the schools.

Int.: Would you like to have that job when you grow up?

Sally: No.

Int.: Why?

Sally: You have to do too much work at home.

Int.: What other jobs are there?

Sally: Well . . . doctors, lawyers, nurses. People who make new things.

Int.: People who make new things?

Sally: Yeah, like inventors.

Int.: Would you like to do any of those things?

Sally: Yeah, I guess so. I don't really know.

Int.: What job would you like best?

Sally: Maybe . . . maybe a nurse or a doctor. I don't really know.

Int.: Can you think of any other jobs?

Sally: Hmmm. People in the supermarket when you pay. But I don't think I could do that. My fingers aren't fast enough.

Interview 2. *Joseph*

Int.: Do you like school?

Joseph: It's OK.

Int.: Do you like the teacher?

[Joseph shrugs and smiles noncommittally]

Int.: Do they give tests at your school?

Joseph: Yeah.

Int.: Are they hard?

Joseph: Yeah.

Int.: Do you try to do well on the tests?

Joseph: Yeah.

Int.: Why?

Joseph: 'Cause if you don't, you don't move on up.

Int.: Why is it important to move on up?

[Joseph squirms in his seat, folds his hands, doesn't answer.]

Int.: Why do you think it's important?

Joseph: So you can get out of school.

Int.: And what happens when you get out of school?

Joseph: Then you go to work.
    Int.: What kind of work do people do?
Joseph: They do different kinds.
    Int.: Can you tell me some kinds?
Joseph: Some people work in gas stations.
    Int.: Anything else?
Joseph: Some people sell candy in the candy store.
    Int.: What kind of work would you like to do?
Joseph: I might be working in the candy store. Or maybe go in the army.
    Int.: Can you think of any other kind of work you might do?
Joseph [thinks for a moment]: What work do you do?

Tricky as it is to interpret interviews of children, several things stand out in these excerpts. First, both children give examples of adult work that are class bound. But subsequent conversation with both revealed that they in fact had knowledge of a far broader range of occupations than those cited in the interviews. (When the interviewer mentioned other kinds of work and asked them what such workers did, they were able to provide rudimentary information about many jobs.) Possibly this means their situational code yields one set of answers when they are asked to describe work in relationship to themselves and another when the topic is presented in a different frame.

Second, these excerpts suggest that both children have at least a crude theory of social reality with several components: an explicit sense of how the world works (indicated in their under-standing of what tests mean), a sense of their own possible futures (expressed in terms of subsequent schooling and career), and, implicitly, a sense of their future selves in relation to that world (i.e., the kind of process they must undergo to get to a job and the kind of job they will—or will not—take). If we simply take their words at face value, some important distinctions seems to characterize their respective theories.

Sally assumes that doing well on tests and getting through college will lead to a job. The kinds of jobs she is primarily aware of (the kinds of jobs most of her family's friends hold) are professional jobs, which in fact require at least a college education. She rules out, albeit for idiosyncratic reasons, the only manual work that comes to mind. It is rather striking that at the age of eight she is aware of beginning a process of competition that goes "all the way up to college." She has already internalized some of the values of that process: the tests are "scary," it is reasonable to conclude because some of her self-esteem (and her sense of future possibilities) is bound up in how she performs on them. While she has no clear idea of "what I want to be when I grow up," she does see a future that includes college, a professional job, and an appropriate time at which career will be her choice.

Joseph, on the other hand, while hoping to do well in school, does not articulate any clear awareness of how school performance may affect his future life chances. He seems to view school less as a means to his future than as an obstacle—something he must move through to "get out." In his words (as in his bearing during the interview) he seems less emotionally bound up with school performance—and also less tolerant of the pupil role; he wants to ask some of the questions.

One might conclude that Sally has a more sophisticated theory of social reality, reflecting superior innate intelligence or a richer home learning environment. But a quite different conclusion seems preferable: both Sally and Joseph have concocted adequate and realistic theories relative to their group and family situations in American society. If Sally could read the statistics, for instance, she would know that her chances of getting a college degree and landing a professional job are quite good (although not as good as her older brother's). If Joseph could read the statistics, he would know that his chances for a professional job are slim; indeed, the army is a fairly high career aspiration, given the history of his race and the odds facing the child of a single parent whose own earnings are limited.

So Sally's social theory may lead to an emphasis on certain kinds of cognitive development that will be useful to her in turning school into a valued instrument. Joseph may place less stress on those abilities—or use them primarily in settings other than school—simply learning to play the system well enough to get out since his map of the future suggests little use for school skills.

History, Time, and Development

As the child grows older, the environment from which he or she receives messages expands to include more and more time and space. An infant's environment is immediate, spatially limited to the people and objects with which the baby is in direct contact and temporally limited to what he or she has experienced directly. An older child not only has a broader range of direct contacts but can infer a great deal about the society that exists beyond those contacts; the capacity to build theories permits the child to construct a world beyond his or her experiences. Equally important, the temporal dimension of environment has expanded. In early childhood, the sense of time, like the spatial sense of environment, is bounded by personal experience, and any contact with history is indirect, mediated through the family. As the child grows older, however, personal time folds outward into historical time. There are a sense of future and a sense of past, which, while partly constructed on actual historical information (such as the history of a family or the history of a race), are also based on an ability to construct a sense of time future and time past. We construct a world that goes beyond experience but whose construction gives meaning to our subsequent experience. Caste again provides a clear example: it is the historical fact of job ceilings, we have suggested, that plays a critical role in defining a child's sense of the future and thus in shaping the child's developmental situation.

As the child's theory of social reality becomes more sophisticated, it plays an increasingly powerful role in filtering and interpreting the messages received from a setting. By the same token, both the aspects of the child's theory that are manifested in words and behavior and those that remain tacit as situational codes play an increasingly strong role not only in shaping the child's participation in a given situation but in guiding subsequent development. Thus, the element of history has a cumulative force in individual development.

Predictability and Variability

Public policy has long assumed that early childhood is the critical developmental stage and that family is the most critical influence in shaping what a child will become. In light of our analysis of what may constitute a "situation" for child development, it becomes possible to rephrase the importance of family as an influence and early childhood as a period. On the one hand, the issue becomes not so much the content of the familial environment as it is one of congruence and continuity. If the "messages" of family, school, neighborhood, class, race, gender, and history agree, so to speak, family influence may appear to explain development. And if the successive situations in which the individual develops are predictable and continuous, then early experience may appear to be critical, and those predictable continuities in the child's experience may be interpreted (incorrectly) as characteristic of the developing child.

The essential characteristic of social class as a developmental context is that it does provide messages that constitute a more or less congruent, continuous series of situations through family, school, and the child's direct experience of the larger social structure. Thus, development occurs in response to situations, and social class (or race or sex or other grouping) constitutes a master setting within which family and other institutions occupy a subordinate and mediating status.

Early intervention programs such as Head Start or parent education may succeed briefly in making apparent changes in the child's developmental path or in the situational code that determines when he or she exhibits a given ability because in the early years experience is temporally and spatially limited, and thus the intervention, which constitutes a significant portion of the child's environment, is able to affect a developmental course not yet steered by a powerful theory of social reality. But early intervention programs usually lack the historical scope to sustain the changes they induce. As direct contact with and knowledge of the broader social and historical environment expand, the child's theory may alter to conform with the perceived realities of situations. In the process, the "effects" of Head Start wash out[31]—not because the child was reached too late, not necessarily because parents relapsed or even because schools failed, but because the intervention lacked sufficient historical scope.

By the same token, as a child's theory of social reality becomes more powerful and more entrenched, development may appear to be less plastic (thus the correlations between school grades in third and ninth grade, for instance). But appearances can be deceptive. These continuities, as we suggested earlier, may be continuities of experience, mirrored by continuities in the child's theory of social reality and the child's situational code, but they need not indicate any inherent inability to alter theories, codes, and manifest patterns of development. Rather, if experience is sharply discontinuous, one can argue that at some point an individual's situation has changed, and with it manifest development may change, too.[32]

It follows from the argument sketched out in this chapter that the predictable continuities of experience within a culture and within a social class, which we call master settings since they exist quite independently of a child or any given individual, are important elements in the developmental situation. For instance, we expect to observe generally different developmental manifestations among the Kpelle from those we observe among American children, granting that there will also be differences within those groups. Their cultures contain histories and structures that are quite distinct. Similarly, within any class-stratified society, including ours, different classes constitute different fields of experience. Indeed, in considering the relationship between social class and development, the relevant concern is not the "inputs" characteristic of families of a given class but, rather, the extent to which it is probable that an individual's experience will be bounded by the historical requirements of a class. As our discussion of the odds facing Jimmy and Bobby and of the continuities in American class structure suggest, the issue is one of probability grounded in the stability of the class structure.

But there is a major difference between what is probable and what is strictly determined. In few, if any, cultures—and certainly not in ours—are the boundaries between classes absolutely fixed and clear, and a wide range of developmental outcomes can be expected among children born in quite comparable settings. (One has only to consider the differences between siblings.) Likewise, the large number of influences that enter into the developmental situation and the complex dynamic interrelations between them lead one to expect diversity, not predetermined outcomes. If human development were simply a matter of molding, of writing on the *tabula rasa,* it would remain theoretically possible to develop a deterministic theory sufficiently detailed and fine grained to account for all such differences. However, since development is not simply a matter of molding and we must admit the child to the developmental situation as active theory builder and autonomous participant in his or her own development, the potential developmental significance of any given experience is highly variable.

Chapter Six

Changing the Situation: Steps Toward an Egalitarian Family Policy

> . . . to criticize inequality and to desire equality is not, as is sometimes suggested, to cherish the romantic illusion that men are equal in character and intelligence. It is to hold that, while their natural endowments differ profoundly, it is the mark of a civilized society to aim at eliminating such inequalities as have their source not in individual differences . . . which are a source of social energy, [and] are more likely to ripen and find expression if social inequalities are, as far as practicable, diminished.
>
> —R. H. Tawney, *Equality*

The argument of this book has been following a great circle. It began by briefly describing the dimensions of a problem that has long, if sporadically, been a subject of public policy concern. It presented data showing that the probabilities governing the life chances—the futures—of children are deeply bound up with social class standing at birth. It described briefly the impact of inequality—the insults, injuries, and obstacles that await the "children of less." These include both the direct impact of poverty on children and the effects that reach them through their families, in the form of higher risks of family disintegration or parental mental illness or disease associated with low income and unemployment. And it reviewed data suggesting that inequality has been a significant and stable feature of our social structure, changing only modestly over long periods of time and scarcely changing at all in the last thirty years, despite the War on Poverty, periods of dramatic economic growth, and increasing expenditures for social welfare and such social services as health and education. Political concern for inequality has fluctuated, but the data have stayed remarkably constant.

Without questioning whether there is the political will to achieve a more egalitarian society (and many would argue it has been relatively weak), we have argued that the failure to alter significantly the calculus of inequality or its effects on children and families has been rooted in a series of culturally enshrined misconceptions.

A central misconception has been that poverty is the result of individual inadequacies, not the distributional mechanisms of the economic structure of our society. This viewpoint, reflected in the concept of absolute poverty and enshrined in the government's poverty line, disregards the prime issue of social equality, distribution—distribution not only of money and material goods but of power, experience, employment options, and even dignity and self-esteem. This disregard is reinforced by the venerable cultural myth that each individual is master of his fate, a concomitant of the notion that poverty results from individual flaws, which obscures the importance of social structure—including the distributive mechanisms of that structure—in shaping individual development and life chances.

The roots of all these misconceptions, we suggested, are intertwined with the political, economic, and even religious origins of liberalism, a product of the Enlightenment world view that has provided the dominant social ideology of this country from the days of the Revolution on. Liberalism is the intellectual heritage from which we have derived—and through which we interpret—many of our institutions and some of our most cherished values, including the ideals of justice, individual freedom, and equality. But there is a tension between the political and the economic aspects of our heritage. Our political tradition has a deeply egalitarian strand, stressing individual rights; our economic canons stress the prerogatives of property, which lead to inequality. This tension between two faces of the liberal tradition occurs in efforts to achieve liberty and justice as well, but its effects are most apparent in pursuit of the ideal of equality, where the tensions and even the contradictions within liberal theory make it hard to agree on the meaning of an egalitarian society, much less to achieve it.

Still circling, we have shown that in the last 150 years there have been periods when enough people perceived or suffered from the gap between the ideal of equality and the actual conditions in the society to create protest and social instability, which in turn inspired reform efforts to resolve the liberal tradition's tension: to honor the equal political rights of individuals while still protecting the economic prerogatives which lead to inequality. In each of these reform eras a common pattern has unfolded. Reformers, primarily members of the upper middle class and typically moved by good intentions, have responded to protest and upheaval with a perverse tautology by attempting to apply liberal precepts to solving flaws or contradictions in the liberal world view. In the process, the notion of equality of opportunity has emerged as the guiding ideology of reform.

The principle of equal opportunity has not only failed to help us produce greater equality of distribution (which is not necessarily even implied in the principle); but has failed in its own terms, as the differential odds that face children born in different social circumstances reveal. Equal opportunity as a principle has encouraged the marriage between children's policy and egalitarian policy. Specifically it has encouraged reformers to rely on strategies of individual assistance to children (and sometimes their families) as the antidotes to social inequality.

Implicit in attempts to solve inequality by helping individuals is the belief that social inequalities are caused by individual differences. This is a more sophisticated version of the notion that we are all masters of our fates and it is a natural companion of market economic theory. What this view, in both its cruder and its more sophisticated versions, fails to consider sufficiently is that causality also runs the other way, that social structure influences development. Accordingly, reformers' efforts to change social structure and its dynamics through changing individuals are often attempts to battle against the tides.

The disregard of Americans for social structure and the distributive mechanisms of society is a logical result of our atomistic social theory of liberal culture. The whole process—from disregarding the influence of structure to blaming individuals for inequality—has been recapitulated in the operations of various helping institutions which, in their own structure, in their interaction with the larger social structure (such as the interaction of schooling with the occupational structure) or in the ways they mirror and re-create characteristics of that larger structure have too often produced help that also hurts. Whether in the "helping" institutions or the society at large, structure in a variety of forms undermines good intentions.

The marriage of children's policy with egalitarian policy, rather than resolving the tensions inherent in liberalism, has simply shifted them from the society to the nursery and the classroom. In a sense, liberalism's focus on the individual has resulted in a betrayal of liberalism's concern for the individual; by ignoring or dismissing the extent to which social class, social dynamics, and institutional structures affect individuals and their options, social policy has implicitly helped stack the deck against some individuals, consigning them to small futures from childhood onward.

The dominant American view of childhood and its mission, as well as formal theories of development, mirror and refract axioms of liberal social thought framed in periods of social reform. The image in the mirror has changed over time, as social and economic contours of the society have changed, but at root the central axioms have remained similar for hundreds of years: that early childhood experiences determine adult characteristics; that the environmental field shaping the child is more or less coterminous with "family"; and that the child is a passive piece of putty that picks up the imprints of early experience and hardens into a set mold. At the seams where psychological theory and social theory meet, it has been widely held that characteristics developed in childhood substantially determine an individual's social and economic future and that differences among individuals, accordingly, explain our society's inequalities in social status. At this point, psychological theory and social theory merge to serve equally well as a basis for public policies (programs of individual assistance) or as an apologia for the status quo ("people are inherently unequal"). In this respect, social policy has used children.

Our overemphasis on developmental differences in explaining social differences is a manifestation of our tendency to "psychologize" everything, which is just another way to locate the cause within individuals. Factors that have nothing whatsoever to do with individual development contribute to the extent of inequality in the society. Just a few of the more obvious ones include tax laws, characteristics of the occupational hierarchy (such as the total supply of jobs and the nature of those jobs), and discrimination; public policy (for instance the level at which Social Security payments are set); "structural unemployment," which results when demography and investment patterns are out of step (when, for instance, a large urban population and a declining employment base coincide); the role of custom in determining wage levels associated with different occupations or positions within an occupational hierarchy; and luck. Similarly, the impersonal dynamics of an unequal social structure work to perpetuate inequality regardless of individual "ability," as the odds facing Jimmy and Bobby or the differences in educational attainment explained by class differences demonstrate.

But to the extent that developmental patterns are correlated with achieved social status, there is another flaw in the axioms generated by the liberal tradition. The assumption that public policy can alter individual patterns of development through programs to help individuals is dubious in the extreme. For one thing, the social and structural dynamics of public programs, as illustrated by the operation of the juvenile justice system, the welfare system, and differential socialization in schools, risk producing help that hurts. But more important, efforts to achieve social reform through individual reform are posited on a theory of development that scrambles causality.

If, as we have speculated, the individual is an active participant in his or her development, and if development proceeds not through "inputs" but through situations, efforts to enhance development by aiming programs at individuals are misconceived. These include almost all service-based strategies. Services are essential, and some important changes in services will help alter the structure of children's situations. But at the risk of repetition it must be emphasized that services cannot substantially affect social inequality through "improving" individuals. Nor does it help to wish that we could improve their families.

To the extent that families help transmit inequality, they are scarcely more than intermediate mechanisms shaped by structural inequalities. To put the matter most simply, families do not breed inequality—they reflect it. In constructing a guiding theory of social reality, the child derives in part from what his or her family *is* a sense of what he or she *will become*. Thus, efforts to change what families "do" to children will have little effect on children's futures, at least with respect to social equality. But efforts to alter what families "are," specifically with reference to their social and economic status, may affect them in two ways. First, an equalization of the distribution of social benefits will by definition affect the social status of adults and of children as they become adults; second, it will alter the settings that influence children directly and through their families—in short, it will change the whole developmental context. Changing the circumstances of families changes the situations of development.

This is not, we should stress, to suggest that family services are unimportant. Education, health care, child care, and many other services are vital to rich children and poor children alike, and for the same reasons. Furthermore, poor children and their families depend a great deal on the public provision of services that more affluent families purchase on the market, and efforts to extend the coverage of public services, improve their quality, or halt abuses are important to families. Sometimes services can temporarily alleviate some of the insults and injuries of inequality. But the importance of services in their own right should not be confused with an egalitarian strategy that promotes greater equality of life chances among children.

Individually aimed service programs that seek to promote equality by "improving" individuals rely on a deterministic philosophy that takes no account of the individual's autonomous participation (as theory builder) in his or her own development. They miss the essential equilibrium of the developmental situation: the balance between development and social structure. To put it another way, an intervention must be extremely powerful to alter that equilibrium—sufficient in scope to influence both the life chances and the theory of social reality that a child constructs out of the continuity and congruity of messages provided by social structure and history.

We can scarcely define the requirements for such a powerful intervention. Nor would we rule out the possibility that an extraordinarily influential individual (a teacher, a counselor, a peer) or an exceptional subsetting—a school, a family—can effect one. But common sense suggests that such interventions are likely to be the exception, not the rule. Neither our understanding nor our social technology is sophisticated enough to produce interventions like this willfully and systematically. Indeed, the basic notion that one class, the "helpers" who man and control service systems, can shape the destinies of another contains a contradiction, for it implies not only that one group has extraordinary power over the other but also that members of that group will easily give that power away.

If social programs cannot alter the developmental situation from "within" the child—that is, if programs of individual or family assistance cannot alter significantly and systematically the process by which an individual constructs a social theory of reality and participates in his or her own development—social policy can, at least in theory, alter the social structure from which a child derives information for that theory. To provide a crude example, the situation of racial discrimination is not affected by our providing services or counseling to black children or their families, nor is racial discrimination likely to be eliminated by our trying to change the attitudes and capabilities of individual black children. But if the "tangible facts" of the employment barriers and inequalities of social and economic status that now exist for blacks were, by the wave of some magic wand, removed, we would expect the developmental patterns of black and white children to be similar.

So we come around full circle to argue not, finally, that the marriage between egalitarian policy and children's policy be dissolved, but that the marriage contract be renegotiated: instead of trying to reduce inequality by helping children, we may be able to help children by reducing inequality.

To put the case more strongly, we believe that a necessary condition for equalizing the circumstances of development, for providing every child with a potentially full future, and for eliminating the insults and injuries of inequality is the changing of some of the basic patterns of society, including its mechanisms for distributing income, opportunity, power, and experience. The creation of a more equal society is synonymous, in our view, with the creation of a more egalitarian setting for development.

Objections to Equality

Given the shibboleths of the liberal tradition, flags begin to wave and alarms to sound when it is proposed that equality, which sounds so fine in theory, begin to be translated into reality by the reduction of inequality itself—the gap between top and bottom—in the here and now. Equality cannot be achieved by this route, it is argued, without treading on other deeply honored values in the liberal tradition, such as freedom, diversity, and economic efficiency.

The argument that equality clashes with *freedom* is rarely made by those who suffer deprivation. In its vulgar form, this argument often seems to equate freedom with the rights of property. Its proponents sometimes seem to confuse egalitarian social policy with the practices of totalitarian socialist states and see any attempts to equalize social and economic conditions as an infringement of the rights of people to own, accumulate, and control property and other resources. The absurdity of this definition lies in the realization that in the real world of finite resources, one man's freedom is another's deprivation. As economist Arthur Okun has pointed out, "That line of reasoning follows from John Locke's conception of physical property as an extension of the individual—an instrument that broadens his or her scope for action. Such a conception may have seemed natural in a world of yeomen farmers; but it loses meaning in a modern industrial society that rests heavily on wealth in the form of paper claims to assets that owners do not use directly. . . ."[1]

Underlying the argument that equality may tamper with freedom is the traditional liberal (or, in terms of American politics, "conservative") view favoring minimalist government and a separation of the economic and political spheres. The argument rests on liberalism's veneration of the "naked individual," which, as this book has been at great pains to point out, is a misplaced faith. The assumed separation of the public (state) and private (economic) sectors is a distinction hard enough to draw in the theoretical writings of conservatives such as F. A. Hayek,[2] and our actual situation is far from matching any such theory. As Robert Heilbroner and other economists have stressed, the political apparatus of government has become more and more involved in the workings of the economic sphere, not to meddle with but to preserve that sphere.[3] Far from being arbitrary, state intervention has been the almost inevitable result of industrialism. The theoretical constructs of liberal capitalism, however, have increasing difficulty accommodating this reality, a difficulty that sometimes inspires almost comical contradictions. In the name of efficiency, for instance, some firms call for less government regulation, while others call for more (variations on the theme of Teddy Roosevelt vs. Woodrow Wilson). Automobile and chemical manufacturers resist environmental regulations while airline companies plead for continued regulations, and the oil industry asks for depletion allowances at the same time that it decries price controls. Liberal ideology can no longer make sense of these contradictory ad hoc demands. The conceptual paradigm in which public and private spheres are separated has crumbled.

The argument that equality diminishes *diversity* is often based on the notion that *equality* means "sameness" and assumes that equality would require massive state action that might lead to a harshly regulated uniform populace like that envisioned in the nightmare scenario of George Orwell's *1984*.

But inequality and diversity are not synonymous, as this fear implies. Consider the diversity of tastes, beliefs, wit, values, personalities, consumption patterns, styles, thought processes—the aesthetic dimension of diversity that is the vital dimension—among individuals of the same sex and race who live on similar incomes, enjoy jobs of equivalent status and power, and share the same religion, political party affiliation, and social class origin.

It has often been argued that inequality is necessary to promote efficient economic growth because the formation of capital requires savings (which are then invested in new production) or because a big payoff is needed as an incentive to stimulate individuals to the diligence and creativity needed for maximum productivity.

The first point has lost much of its force, for private savings —the capital of the rich—are no longer the main lubricant of investment and growth; corporate earnings, institutional investors (e.g., pension plans and insurance companies), and, increasingly, government policy—such as investment tax credits—are the major sources of investment capital. In each of these instances, again, the boundaries between public and private spheres are blurred. Corporations are creatures of the state to begin with. They are formed under state charters, governed by state laws, and, increasingly, the level of their earnings (hence the amount available to reinvest) is influenced by government regulation, tax policy, and government contracts. Pension plans are likewise governed and supported by state and federal laws and policy. Furthermore, the great bulk of money in pension plans and insurance companies is derived, ultimately, from the wages of average citizens, not from the savings of the affluent.

The argument about incentives, however, still has strong adherents, and it is not easily dismissed. Material gain may not be the only motivator, but it is a reliable one. Okun and others argue that pecuniary (and power and status) incentives are necessary motivators to efficient production and that these incentives, the psychic infrastructure of capitalist theory, require inequality. The argument has two elements. On the one hand, it is argued, those with high productive potential will not use it if they get inadequate rewards, so society will lose their potential and its benefits. On the other hand, those who are poor or unproductive will not work if they are handed a livelihood on a silver platter—a form of the common belief, strongly disputed by empirical evidence,[4] that welfare payments breed and reward laziness.

The key idea in all this is, of course, that we have the optimal amount of inequality and that it is in the social interest. For, the argument goes, if public policy monkeys around too much with the distribution of income or wealth and takes the strength out of the incentive system, overall productivity will decline. If so, there will be less to go around, and at some point everyone—rich, poor, and in between—will suffer an absolute loss of welfare. This idea, which links the welfare of the poor to the welfare of the rich, the well-being of labor to the well-being of capital, has a long intellectual history, for it is a cornerstone of liberal capitalist social theory. Looked at from another perspective, it is a logical product of the axioms of market theory: in a smoothly functioning market society the degree of inequality should reflect perfect equilibrium, an optimal distribution of income and wealth to stimulate the highest degree of efficiency and reward each person commensurate with his or her productivity.

Some economists have suggested that this is a very bad description of the way society actually works since custom and structural factors, not market values and contributions to productivity, determine traditional differences in wage levels.[5] Examples of these factors include traditional wage relationships among craft unions and salary scales in public employment. In many school systems, for instance, a formula sets administrative salaries at a fixed multiple of teachers' salaries. Another departure from the idealized picture of society with "optimal distribution" is our quasi-monopolistic restrictions on entrance into the professions, which, while advanced in the name of quality control (one does not want brain surgery performed by an amateur), have also been forwarded, historical evidence suggests, to keep the supply of professionals short and the price of their services up.[6] Or we could find another exception in the structure of major industries, where a handful of firms controls markets and prices, hence wages.[7]

Moreover, the "efficiency" side of the equality-efficiency debate presumes that individuals are able to obtain jobs commensurate with their "merit"—that is, their ability and industriousness—so that they can realize their full productive potential and be rewarded for it. The concept of "merit" is extremely dubious. It begs the ultimately political question of who decides what is meritorious, and it raises all the questions that surround liberalism's emphasis on the naked individual and disregard for social structure, in a world where interdependence makes it hard to pinpoint where one person's contributions begin and another's end. As we have seen, individual "merit" in no way accounts for where many people end up in the occupational structure, in substantial part because of the inequalities intrinsic to and sustained by the class and caste structure of our society. Structural inequalities, that is, may result in underemployment, forfeited productivity, and an overall social loss of efficiency—even in the lowest-common-denominator terms of gross national product.

The argument that inequality is in the social interest has not gone undisputed. Marxists, without having any concrete theory of distribution to replace the optimal distribution notion of market theory, attack it as a rationalization for class oppression. John Rawls, with his influential theory of justice, has challenged one of the basic axioms—both ethical and economic in nature—of market theory on which this concept rests. Welfare economists from the early-nineteenth-century utilitarians on have held that the greatest good for the greatest number means progression from a given economic distribution to a subsequent distribution in which, minimally, no one was worse off than before and at least someone was better off. This postulate, of course, ignores the relative nature of poverty. Rawls stirred up an academic hornet's nest by arguing that distributional justice requires a different proposition: justice, Rawls concluded after an elaborate set of arguments, requires that a society judge any policy by the criterion of whether or not it benefits the least well-off members of that society.[8]

Clearly, the equality-efficiency "trade-off" is not as simple as it seems at first. There is no reason to believe that, in any absolute sense, the current extent of inequality is optimal, even if one believes there is a trade-off. Rather, if one views the insults and injuries of inequality and discrimination as social costs, there is a prima facie case to be made that more equality would be more efficient. (How much more becomes an ethical question, the answer to which depends upon how much one values equality.)

When the issue of redistribution is debated in political forums, it rarely involves such basic conceptual issues as fairness and efficiency. Rather, the common objection to increasing the incomes of the poor through the most direct means available, cash transfer payments (or welfare), is that if such payments go up, the work effort of recipients will go down. The opposite objection is also raised: that the work effort of the rich will decrease if their earnings are redistributed to the poor through transfer payments.

Transfer payments are not the only way to raise the income of the poor, but these objections cannot be casually dismissed. As far as the second proposition is concerned, the best available evidence suggests that higher tax rates do *not* diminish the work efforts of the rich. If anything, the reverse is true. As taxes increase, high earners seem to work harder to substitute for their lost incomes.[9] Short of total expropriation of additional earnings, no one knows with certainty where this "substitution" effect stops, but presumably it is beyond the 70 percent marginal tax rate at the top of our current federal tax structure (down from the 90 percent rate in force after World War II).

On the other hand, the best available evidence suggests that increasing transfer payments to low-income families will result in some reduction of work effort, with the amount of reduction varying by family type. This evidence, drawn from a series of income maintenance experiments conducted by the federal government in recent years, shows that when income maintenance payments are reduced fifty cents for every dollar earned, husbands in two-parent families will reduce work effort by about 6 percent; their wives will reduce work effort by about 17 percent; and single-parent female heads of household will reduce work effort by about 12 percent. (These figures are averages, of course, and the results vary somewhat in different experimental sites.)[10] In addition, these experiments found that families who received higher income maintenance payments were much more likely to break up than a "control group" of families eligible for regular welfare payments.

Some have concluded from these results that more generous income maintenance payments are a bad idea. But this conclusion seems to us a rather strained interpretation of the evidence —and an interpretation that is based on selective disregard of some findings of the experiments. To begin with, of course, these findings are totally irrelevant to the needs of families whose head cannot work or can work only by giving up the care of young children. Second, the reduction in work effort is actually quite modest, and the figures are susceptible to multiple interpretations. Consider that:

—The reduction in work effort for the average husband amounted to one hour per week.

—The reduction for the average wife was two hours per week.

—The reduction for a female household head was approximately an hour and forty minutes per week.

—The higher their income before participation in the experiment, the lower was reduction in work effort for heads of household.

From these facts we may infer that heads of households with the least remunerative (and perhaps least desirable) jobs were most willing to withdraw slightly from the labor force and to choose increased leisure or to be more selective about the kind of work accepted. This increase of options, while not captured in monetary terms, can be interpreted as an increase in individual power and well-being. The higher withdrawal rates of women may be partially explained as a preference to devote more time to children—hardly a socially undesirable result. None of these withdrawals from the labor force necessarily translates into a loss of gross national productivity since other workers may perform the same tasks. And even the higher rates of family breakup are susceptible to many interpretations. For one, this finding was not uniform at all income levels: increased income was associated with higher breakup rates only for families at the lower end of the income range prior to program participation. This may simply mean that couples who were locked into bad marriages only by economic necessity (two *do* live more cheaply than one) were able, like more affluent members of society, to exit from those bad relationships, given the cushion of modest income security. In any event, it is hard to stomach the notion that poverty should be maintained as an antidote to divorce.

A particularly important finding from these experiments— one ignored by those who use the evidence to disparage income maintenance strategies as an instrument of economic justice— is that when income maintenance is combined with improved job opportunities, work effort will *increase*. This conclusion, based on study of the labor supply response of individuals in the experiment to gains or losses of earned income, is a strong argument for the kind of approach we discuss later—an egalitarian family policy that blends welfare reform and increased levels of income maintenance with a full employment strategy.*

Premises of an Egalitarian Policy

As the basic argument of this book should make clear, a policy that aims to equalize the life chances and developmental situations of children must meet two primary conceptual tests. First, it must both acknowledge and come to grips with the inegalitarian premises of the economic side of liberalism. Second, it must promote changes in the situations of development through alterations in social structure. These two conceptual tasks are closely allied operations, if our basic argument is correct, since inequalities in the economic structure, manifest in the class and caste systems, are the framework of the master settings of development. Together, they imply the need to equalize the actual conditions of adults as the prerequisite for creating parity (not sameness) in the developmental situations of children and to achieve a new equilibrium between development and social structure. No other kind of intervention seems likely to be of

* In general form, the Carter administration's proposed Better Jobs and Incomes Program, which is about to be tested experimentally as this is being written, also represents this kind of approach, although the benefit levels being tested are lower than what we recommend.

sufficient scope to alter the historically rooted probabilities, social dynamics, and developmental mechanisms that lead children from different classes or caste groups to such divergent
adult futures.

From the vantage point of the individual child, an egalitarian
policy should aim for greater equality in the conditions of experience in the present—both quantitative (e.g., material welfare
of the family) and qualitative (e.g., the class- or caste-bound
nature of experience as reflected, for instance, in cognitive
requirements). Further, it should eradicate class- and caste-
linked probabilities governing life chances. To make this last
point another way, it should lead to an equalization of options
and realized opportunities among classes and castes (and, with
specific reference to occupational opportunity, sexes). Essentially
this means reducing to insignificance in fact the caste and class
lines which Americans have long held insignificant in rhetoric.
These two broad aims—equalizing the conditions of experience
and equalizing life chances—are, of course, closely related since
the dynamics of a society in which there is serious inequality of
condition lead inexorably to inequality of life chances through
the differential situations of development.

The key to a strategy for policy that meets these conceptual
tests and that meets these criteria for individual empowerment
can be captured in a single word: *redistribution*. This means redistribution not only of income and other basic resources, based
on an acknowledgment of the relative nature of deprivation, but
also of power—a concept that is often thought of as "political"
but that clearly has economic dimensions as well. To be relatively poor, for instance, is to have severe limits on one's ability
to influence the decisions of officials in publicly funded service
systems, some of which the poor are far more likely than the
more affluent to come in contact with (such as the courts) and
others of which they are far more likely to be excluded from (such
as the schools). This powerlessness of the poor is evident at the
level of policy (for instance, the basis on which eligibility for a
welfare program is determined or the mode of pupil classification in school) and at the level of individual decision makers (for

instance, the vice-principal who issues a suspension, the family court judge who separates a child from parents). In a world where public services are a substantial adjunct to families, this is no small issue for children. Likewise, to be poor is by definition to have little influence in the economic decisions of a society and to barter in the political marketplace from a position of weakness, trading votes for promises with little recourse when they are broken. (This issue helps explain correlations between voting frequency and income.)

As these examples suggest, the issues of redistributing power and redistributing resources are intertwined and mutually dependent. To break this circle, the classic separation of economic and political spheres in liberal social theory must be abandoned. Indeed, in many respects it has been, as the erosion of distinctions between public and private spheres in the conduct of the economy illustrate. The area where it remains, a strong and significant anachronism, is in the laissez-faire stance of public policy toward the distribution of social benefits, including occupational status and rewards, to individuals and families.

What can public policy do to confront such a basic and deeply entrenched problem? We believe the rights traditionally defined by liberalism as limited to the political sphere must be extended into the economic sphere through the political and legislative processes. The prerogatives of the marketplace and the so-called private sector must be constrained to serve the public purpose of equality. In abstract terms, the human and social costs of inequality are what economists call externalities. They do not appear on the balance sheets of any firm, and they need not, as a result, be considered in the making of investment and marketing decisions or in the setting of wages and prices, decisions governed simply by profit. The rules and rewards of the marketplace must be altered, whether through carrots or through sticks, so that economic activity occurs within a framework that makes increased equality as important an objective as profit.

In less abstract terms, public policy must attempt to reduce the economic and experiential distance between classes through policies of full employment, targeted economic development and investment policies, affirmative action, and income redistribution. These policies are by nature unlikely to be effectively pursued without federal leadership.

As the Carnegie Council has argued elsewhere and as the data in this book suggest, full employment is a crucial condition for full family welfare. Joblessness is associated with a host of palpable harms to individuals and families that affect children. Mental illness, family breakup, alcoholism, and child abuse, to name some strong examples, may each result in throwing children upon the mercy of the child welfare system. Unemployment or underemployment (a situation in which employees hold jobs below their capabilities and training) also produces low incomes, of course, and a full employment economy by itself should improve the distribution of income somewhat, both by providing earnings for the jobless and by bidding up the price of labor at the lower end of the labor queue.

Equally important, participation in and contribution to the process of production are an indispensable condition of social membership. This is still true, we believe, despite the growth of leisure time, the evidence of widespread worker alienation, and the increasingly consumerist nature of our society. To a substantial degree it is through their "works" that people are connected, for better or for worse, to the society at large and also substantially through work that people judge and assign prestige to others and esteem to themselves. That classic question of adult to child, "What do you want to be when you grow up?" is no trivial one, for both a child's sense of the future and, we have speculated, a child's situational code are tied to the answer.

Full Employment

It is easy to call for full employment; political office seekers do it all the time. Yet it is far harder to obtain it, and this country has yet to adopt it as a forthright goal with real force.[11] Keynesian manipulation of the economy is certainly an important aspect of a full employment strategy, but the record of recent years leaves no one with much confidence that it is sufficient unless *full employment* is defined, in doublethink fashion, as an unemployment rate of 6 percent or higher.* Public service employment is another important component of such a strategy, but the record in this respect has been discouraging. Perhaps because of the widespread disparagement of present public service employment (derided as "leaf-raking jobs" and "makework"), this country has yet to evolve more than a patchwork and inadequate system of public service employment. Jobs are targeted to counter high unemployment rates caused by structural or cyclical factors in the economy, but not explicitly as a step toward full employment (a step that might mean, for instance, guaranteeing all Americans willing and able to work the right to a job, with the government as the employer of last resort). The scandal-racked Comprehensive Employment and Training Act system—testimony in part to a lack of local political integrity or administrative concern—has further undermined the credibility of public service employment.[12] Overhauling this system is clearly an important priority for political leaders and citizens' groups at the local level as well as for any national administration, for it is doubtful if the federal government can do the job itself.

Improving the quality of public service jobs and expanding their numbers are important components of a full employment policy, but neither these nor economic stimulus appear likely in themselves to lead to full employment. There are probable limits to a public jobs strategy besides the administrative and political difficulties of developing good public service employment jobs in sufficient numbers with minimum corruption.[13] For instance, in the "underdeveloped" areas of America—urban ghettos and rural poverty areas where unemployment is most severe—or

---

* For the benefit of children, the relevant definition of full employment is the existence of enough decent jobs to eliminate all but "frictional" unemployment caused as workers quit to find better jobs or are temporarily out of work when a firm goes out of business. Achieving such an economy requires a concerted attack on so-called structural unemployment—a problem that is inseparable from improving the perpetually depressed economies of older urban areas—as well as on the cyclical unemployment which economic stimulus policies typically address.

among minority groups wherever they reside, the development of an economy dependent on federally funded jobs might, over the long run, create the same kinds of stigmas as a welfare economy; it would place the livelihood of millions directly and visibly in the hands of voters elsewhere, and it would create economic colonies shut off from the mainstream of the national (and international) markets of the society, to cite just two problems.

It is in these same areas that traditional economic stimulus programs fall short of the mark since the local economies are slowest to respond to stimulus, are fastest to recede in an economic downturn, and experience a considerable degree of so-called structural unemployment (that is, unemployment problems not associated with macroeconomic cycles). In addition, with the trade-off between employment and inflation apparently growing worse, so that many economists now believe unemployment rates below 6 percent will trigger unacceptable inflation, economic stimulus programs have less and less power to produce full employment anywhere, least of all in the older inner cities.[14]

Except for its impact on those with fixed incomes, inflation does not necessarily have an impact on inequality. It is an economic disease from which all income classes suffer. But the usual "cure" for inflation, a recession induced by governmental policies or by the cyclic constriction of the economy, does induce inequality, for unemployment goes with recession, and those hit hardest by unemployment are unskilled and semiskilled workers, who in the best of times hover at the brink of poverty. Thus, inflation appears to be a barrier to full employment, and recently some economists have begun to define full employment as the "nonaccelerating inflation rate of unemployment," which is far from the classic definition of full employment as a condition in which there are more jobs than job seekers.

Not all economists agree that there is an inevitable trade-off between full employment and inflation. For one thing, there are causes of inflation (such as high energy prices) which have nothing to do with the upward pressure on wages exerted when labor is in short supply. Further, creating more jobs for the "structurally unemployed"—especially the young and inner-city residents—creates major inflationary pressure only if they compete in the primary labor market with existing job holders, and many economists argue that they do not.

What these facts suggest is that a full employment strategy, as one component of egalitarian policy, must find ways to intervene in the private labor market, which accounts for more than 80 percent of the jobs in the United States. To be fully effective, intervention must occur on several fronts: first, in the decisions that private sector firms make about investments and about where to locate, so that these decisions can be targeted at areas of structural unemployment; second, in the hiring, training, and promoting practices of firms, which must be influenced so that low-income and minority-group individuals reap the employment benefits of that targeting. Currently, economic development programs, manpower programs, and affirmative action enforcement are the policy initiatives for accomplishing these aims. The main tools in the policy kit bag include a variety of tax and fiscal incentives to influence firms' decisions about location and investment; government investment in infrastructure (streets, sewers, transportation, etc.) to facilitate industrial development; geographic targeting of federal contracts and installations; manpower training programs run by public, community-based, or private organizations; affirmative action compliance procedures built into government contracts; and court enforcement of equal opportunity and civil rights legislation. Unfortunately the records of any of these approaches, singly or in combination, are less than glowing, despite sporadic progress and occasional exemplary efforts. Tax incentives do not seem strong enough to have much influence on where firms decide to locate or what they decide to invest in, and even when they do, the result may be a zero sum with different places simply competing with each other for firms, winning some and losing some.[15] Nor have tax credits had much impact on private firms' hiring policies, although the potential to affect hiring practices through tax credits or other subsidies appears substantial.[16] The impact of manpower training programs is inherently limited by the demand for workers, and even within this limited scope, problems of poor implementation, conflicting goals, red tape, and discrimination have left a sloppy record.[17] Government has rarely withheld contracts for failure to meet affirmative action requirements, and procedures for enforcing affirmative action through the courts are cumbersome, slow, and limited in impact.[18] It is extremely rare to see instances in which these three related arms of policy—economic development, manpower training, and affirmative action—are woven into a coherent, coordinated whole. For instance, a firm may locate in a central city but draw on employees from the suburbs or elsewhere. Fragmentation prevails from the federal level down, and the net results can be read clearly in the unemployment rates of older cities, underdeveloped rural areas, and minority-group members wherever they live.

There are ways for policy to improve the records and coordination of economic development, manpower development, and affirmative action programs. One approach is to try to increase the effectiveness of current efforts, through adequate funding, more effective administration, and better coordination of efforts. In the short run, this appears to be the only feasible approach, and with our attempting to enter the maze of issues involved, it is apparent that there is much to be done.

In the longer run, however, one must wonder whether any policies that rely on fiscal carrots, interagency and intergovernmental collaboration, and the goodwill or voluntary collaboration of the private sector with the public will have more than marginal impact. The record does not justify great optimism. If they will not work, direct political and legislative intervention may be required to ensure, in simple but strictly enforced requirements, that social investment and employment goals are met as a precondition for doing business; these requirements must alter the structure of rules, rewards, and incentives around which market activity is organized without eliminating the desirable properties of market economics—incentives and allocative mechanisms—within those structural constraints.*

* Illustrative examples of this type of activity are wage policies, as discussed later, or requirements that a certain percentage of a firm's investment capital be invested in the support of labor-intensive activities in urban areas.

Income Redistribution

A full employment economy by itself should result in some improvement in the distribution of income, but even under full employment, income will not be redistributed sufficiently to eliminate relative poverty as we have defined it, so that no family in the country has to live on an income of less than half the median for a family its size. Even with full employment there would remain the substantial problem of the working poor, and there would remain individuals who are unable to work and single parents with small children for whom the choice of child care in lieu of wage labor is, in our view, as valid a contribution to real social productivity as is cleaning houses, typing letters, working an assembly line, or practicing law. Public policy should honor that choice for individuals with children under school age by instituting a decent income floor—half the median. (Additionally, as children grow older, public and employer policies to stimulate flexible working hours, part-time employment, job sharing, and even the growth of latter-day cottage industry, work that can be done at home, can and should be promoted to increase the compatibility of workplace requirements with family requirements.)[19]

Again, public policy has a number of potential tools available for redistributing income. These include wage policy and wage (or earnings) subsidies, the redistributional effect of which is limited to those who are employed, and income transfers through the tax system, of which the AFDC program is a not-very-inspiring example.[20]

Currently, the prime example of wage policy is the minimum wage—a policy the benefits and beneficiaries of which, according to some economists, are unclear; there is evidence that an increase in the minimum wage, although it does raise the earnings of some low-income workers, may result in a reduction of jobs and barriers to employment for others. A different concept of wage policy has been suggested by economists Lester Thurow and Robert E. R. Lucas, who argue that wage policy could become a redistributive measure if tax incentives or stronger measures were introduced to equalize the distribution of earnings within firms. For example, a firm might receive a considerable tax break if the ratio of earnings of the highest-paid workers to the lowest-paid workers were kept within some given limit, thus narrowing inequality at least within the firm.[21] The authors of this proposal base it on the argument that wage differentials and resulting inequalities of income distribution are the result of custom and structural properties of the occupational system, not the contribution of individual workers to productivity. They argue that structural problems require a structural solution and note that even with such a policy, markets can still function since markets will adjust to any structure of rewards. While one may dispute their underlying premises about the major causes of wage differentials, their approach has conceptual appeal since it does go directly to the heart of the distributional mechanisms of the economy. But it is also a proposal that represents such a radical departure from custom and ideology that few have picked up on the idea.

A wage or earnings *subsidy,* as opposed to a wage policy, is a form of transfer payment tied to work, in which government subsidizes the wages of workers whose pay is insufficient to bring them above the low-income line. This concept, the subject of a number of studies, is essentially a withholding tax in reverse; below a certain wage level, workers receive additions to their wages instead of deductions from them. The concept has some political appeal since it does particular justice to the working poor and ties transfer payments to work. But any such program may prove costly and cumbersome to administer, and it still leaves in limbo those who, because of disability or child care responsibilities, cannot work.

In any case, achieving greater equality will require some form of direct transfer payments, and as we have seen, there is a tremendous, persistent need to reform dramatically the current system of transfer payments called welfare. An approach with particular appeal, we believe, is the credit income tax, which offers the promise of reforming the present AFDC system (by virtually eliminating it), providing local tax relief through federalization of all transfer payments, achieving tax reform, and establishing a decent minimum income all at a single stroke, and which promises to do so while reducing the taxes of almost 60 percent of American families.[22]

The credit tax rests on the principle of assigning each individual a credit that may vary with age but that does not vary with family income. For example, every child under eighteen in the country might provide a tax credit of $1,400 for his or her family, and every adult might produce a credit of $2,800. All families would owe the same percentage of their earned income —say, 50 percent—in taxes. Families with lower incomes and thus less cash to pay in taxes would find the individual credits either partly or entirely balancing out their tax bill. Those on very low incomes would find their sum of individual credits outweighing their tax liability and would receive a net additional income from the government. Thus, the interaction of credits and taxes would create a truly progressive tax situation, with the wealthy paying a higher percentage of their income in taxes. Under this illustrative plan, a two-parent family of four with no earnings would have a minimum income of $8,400—the sum of its tax credits. A similar family with earnings of $10,000 would have an after-tax income of $13,400, consisting of $10,000 in earnings, plus $8,400 in tax credits, minus $5,000 in tax liabilities. A family with earnings of $16,800 would have an after-tax income of $16,800 because its tax credit would cancel its tax liability. A family with earnings of $50,000, despite a tax liability of $25,000, would have an after-tax income of $33,400 because it, too, would receive the $8,400 credit against its tax bill.

The virtues of a credit tax plan can be briefly summarized:

1. Tax and credit levels can be set so that families with incomes up to roughly $24,000 would pay *less* in taxes than they do at present, even though they, like others, would lose some deductions and exemptions, which are replaced by the credits.[23] It is possible to combine tax relief for the middle class, income supplements for the "working poor," and a guaranteed minimum income for all.

2. Tax reform and welfare reform would be achieved simultaneously. A credit tax would close regressive loopholes; the

entire tax structure would be progressive, and the patchwork of federal welfare programs could be eliminated, along with the administrative mess and bureaucratic costs of welfare. (Some existing programs, such as Social Security payments to senior citizens or food stamps, might be retained if their complete submersion in the credit tax would result in a loss for some families or individuals.) The marginal tax rate—50 percent—would be the same at every level of earnings, so neither high marginal taxes at the upper end of the income distribution nor those implicit marginal taxes of up to 67 percent that face welfare recipients *at the other end of the spectrum* would exist as disincentives to work.

3. Relative poverty would be eliminated; no family's income would fall below the "low-income line" of 50 percent of the median for families of an equivalent size, and the overall distribution of income would be far more even. (The size of the credit would be pegged to the median to ensure this effect.)

4. The universal nature of the tax credit would get government out of the messy game of determining eligibility for public assistance and other welfare benefits. At the same time it would remove incentives for family breakup that characterize some aspects of the present welfare system. Since all earnings would be based at the same rate, taxes would be the same no matter who was living with whom. At a time when the meaning of family and the configurations of families are in considerable flux, this neutrality of the tax system to a highly sensitive and properly private aspect of social life would be exemplary.

5. It would be possible to install an equitable "work test" to establish eligibility for a tax credit.* Work requirements are onerous under the current welfare system since they apply only to the poor and since the supply of jobs is inadequate. But this work test would be applied to all adults, rich and poor alike, and full employment, plus the government's guarantee of a job, would eliminate the possibilities for abuse of the work test. Such a test could be administered fairly easily in either of a couple of ways. Individuals would be required to state on their tax returns

* Children, parents of small children, the severely disabled, and senior citizens would be exempt from such a requirement.

whether they were full-time participants in the labor force. This information, like all exemptional deductions now, would be subject to audit. An individual not employed but seeking work would be required to register with an employment office for certification, as persons receiving unemployment benefits are now required to do.

With a generous credit *and the guarantee of a job* under full employment conditions, there are no good reasons, in our view, to object to a work test requirement.

Is the Price Tag Too High?

The adoption of a program for income redistribution of this magnitude—one that would reduce the ratio between the top and bottom fifth of earners from its current eight to one to something like four to one—may sound like pie in the sky. The most popular tax reforms today seem to be those that benefit the affluent more than the poor—reforms such as decreases in capital gains tax and increases in personal exemptions.* Tax reduction and reduction of the welfare rolls, not tax reform and reform of the welfare system, are the hot political issues. That is, it may be too expensive politically for elected officials to advocate the kind of dramatic redistribution we have described, and it may continue to be too risky until the norms of fairness, equity, and economic prerogatives change.

It is worth pointing out that the obstacles are *not* basically economic. There is sufficient money to fund government operations and install a redistributive tax scheme if tax loopholes are closed (by replacing most exemptions and deductions with credits or by imposing a fair tax on wealth, which is now theoretically taxed at high levels through inheritance taxes, but is in fact scarcely taxed at all because of another set of loopholes).

Almost 40 percent of adjusted gross income disappears from

---

* Note that all exemptions and deductions in our tax system are regressive in impact since those in the highest tax brackets receive the highest savings. With a deduction of $1,000 for a dependent child, someone whose marginal tax rate is 50 percent receives a tax break of $500, while someone whose marginal tax rate is 15 percent receives only $150.

the tax rolls every year through deductions and exemptions. Some of these benefit almost exclusively the rich (e.g., exempt income from municipal bonds and capital gains exemptions), and all yield greater tax savings to higher-income families than to lower-income families. As one study, summarizing the effects of deductions and exemptions, put it in 1974, "The 160,000 taxpayers with incomes of $100,000 received an average of $45,662 each in tax relief, while the 9.9 million taxpayers earning between $15,000 and $20,000 saved an average of only $901 apiece. Those with incomes from $10,000 to $15,000 saved only $556, and the working poor with income under $3,000 saved only $267."[24]

What these figures suggest is that to a considerable extent, redistribution of income is a matter of redistribution of tax breaks by substitution of a tax credit for the current structure of exemptions and deductions. Additionally, the costs of redistribution will be partially offset by the current welfare payments and expenditures such a system replaces.[25] Beyond these sources of funds, if IRS definitions of income are broadened, an additional sum of roughly $100 billion is added to gross personal income.[26] If this untaxed nest egg, owned primarily by the wealthy, were taxed at the modest rate of 20 percent, it would yield enough funds to raise all individuals above the current government poverty line (with $3.8 billion in change).[27] An additional possibility, advocated by Lester Thurow, is imposition of a net worth tax on wealth, which, if applied at a very modest level (say, 2 percent annually) to only the top 2.5 percent of families, would yield sufficient funds to raise all families above our low-income line of half the median.[28] Cost is not the real issue. Economic justice in a liberal society is.

The Role of Services in an Egalitarian Family Policy

Services, by themselves, are not sufficient to reduce significantly the inequalities of condition that characterize our society or to alter the class- and race-associated life chances that children face. When services are advanced as an egalitarian strategy *in lieu of* direct redistributive measures, the results can be perverse. But services are important: a sick child needs care; an abandoned child needs a home; an abused child needs immediate attention and that child's family needs continuing help and support; all children need an education that honors their integrity, intrinsic worth, and diverse learning styles, that transmits cultural heritages, and that helps open the power and pleasure of thought.

Clearly the importance of services in American family life has grown with time. One of the major changes in family configuration over the past two centuries has been the increased role of service providers as adjuncts to the home in rearing and nourishing children. For better and for worse, the parent is less and less the sole guardian of a child's upbringing, more and more the managing partner in consort with teachers, doctors, and others who provide family services.

Each of the systems providing these services presents a maze of important issues for governance, accountability, staffing, programming, funding, and coordination. This book will not enter these mazes since its prime focus has been on the social and economic structure of inequality, a structure that services alter marginally, if at all. But there are some junctures at which issues of service delivery and issues of inequality do intersect. These deserve special attention as supplements to an egalitarian family policy.

For one, the practices of some service-providing agencies, regardless of intent, have a discriminatory impact on children from low-income and nonwhite families and produce "help that hurts." Arbitrary suspension from school, misclassification of students as retarded, emotionally disturbed, sociopathic, or otherwise deficient, and differential treatment at the hands of the juvenile justice system all affect low-income and nonwhite children especially, shaping their map of the world, their self-concept, and their ambitions.

For another, poverty remains a barrier to access to some vital services that should be universally available and the lack of which, again, has the power to shape the present and future of the poor children of this country. This barrier may exist because of a variety of structural reasons; for instance, the nature of market incentives often means that service providers do not locate in areas where low-income families are concentrated. Despite Medicaid and other government programs, health care remains a service to which access is maldistributed. Similarly, when the funding of service relies heavily on local wealth, as is typically the case with schooling, such service as is available may be inferior or impoverished.

Third, some parents are less able than others to play the role of managing partner effectively, for reasons that have more to do with their social and economic position than with their concern or competence. Middle-class or professional parents, individually and collectively, have a much easier time dealing with teachers and school officials if their child is having difficulty in school, or if the school is maltreating the child. Second chances, special arrangements, even a change of teachers can be negotiated. The parents of low-income children often face a triple disadvantage in efforts to work with professional service providers; if both parents are working hard to pay the rent and feed the family, they may lack the time to meet with school officials (usually at the latter's convenience), especially when multiple sessions are required. When they do meet, their knowledge of the institutional practices and protocols may be limited by the confines of class-bound experience and may place them at a disadvantage in discussion, negotiation, and problem solving. And there are imbalances in power and status that may intimidate parents, making it difficult for them to penetrate the barriers of professional mystique and institutional obduracy that can turn meetings between professional service providers and poor clients into exercises in domination and frustration. Finally, as we have already argued, the asymmetry of power that skews these transactions between individual parents and service providers, when writ large, is magnified by class and race differentials to create a fertile ground for stigmatization.

These four issues—discrimination, inadequate access, lack of power, and stigma—mark the major intersections of an egalitarian family policy and social services. Full employment, fair employment, and income supports as described above are partial steps toward solving these problems. Families with the cash, the security, and the status that these provide will be less vulnerable to disparities in power and access in the services they require. In the meantime (and perhaps beyond), a child and family support policy should acknowledge that access to vital services is a universal need of contemporary families, one that should be served as a matter of universal entitlement. In addition, continued and intensified attention should be given to ensuring that service providers are accountable to clients.

Beyond Money

Beyond the steps this chapter has proposed, large and substantial as the changes they envision may be, are still larger questions. Lack of money or a job is not the sole measure of inequality, although it is its most obvious and perhaps most damaging mark. A "one-shot" alteration of income distribution, a full-employment economy, a revamped system of services with a redistribution of power in that system, would be a considerable step toward making families and individuals more equal as consumers. But except for those at the very bottom of the distribution, it would not necessarily make people any more equal as producers or as social and political actors. It is certain that such a move would not usher in a classless society. Substantial inequalities in power, control of resources, control of time, richness of human experience and, correlatively, in the array of human potentials each individual has a chance to exercise would remain.

Such inequalities, which are inequalities in the basic content of day-to-day experience and human relations, may in fact prove to be the most important issues for the development of children. For instance, a parent's experience on the job and in the society probably has more influence on development than a parent's income per se. Beyond the redistributive strategies we have discussed here lie major issues that might well constitute the future themes of egalitarian policy. Ultimately, for instance, the achievement of an egalitarian society may well entail reorganization of the control of production and the social relations of the workplace; it may entail coming to grips with the increasing need for planning in an increasingly complex international economy—a need that, some pessimists predict with chilling plausibility, is most likely to be met through totalitarian and centralized systems of political and economic governance unless our "social technology" undergoes rapid transformations to catch up with the complex global technostructure. Democratizing the control of technology itself—both "hard" physical technologies and the "softer" technologies of human behavior and biogenetic engineering—may represent yet another such issue, for clearly technology offers enormous possibilities for both individual empowerment and individual exploitation. In the process of tangling with these enormous, complex issues, a continual concern will have to be how we resolve, or rework, the tension between meritocratic standards of human worth and more pluralistic ideals implicit in the concept that every person has an intrinsic worth the cultivation of which is the highest form of collective good.

Beyond economic redistribution, in short, lies the ultimate goal of an egalitarian society: to create a world in which each child and parent have the opportunity not only to make decent lives but, in making their lives, to help make history. This would be a world in which the power to influence and shape the collective destiny, a power now concentrated in the hands of relatively few, was diffused among the many who currently have little more than the power to "muddle through."

In a sense, that long-range goal and the recommendations of this chapter return us to the liberal idea the dark underside of which this book has criticized at such length. It is out of concern for the individual, ultimately, that this book is written, and it is from that concern for individual children that the great ideals of liberalism—justice, freedom, *and* equality—flow. Our argument has been that these three ideals are interrelated; one cannot exist without the other, and when one is given short shrift, all suffer. These ideals are indivisible, not confined to either the economic or the political realm. They reach across generations, for the child's development is bound up with history. They are ideals that individuals strive for, but that they can seize only when the context of social forces and structures makes them attainable.

Members of the Carnegie
Council on Children

KENNETH KENISTON, chairman and director of the Council, has undertaken extensive studies of social change, social protest, and alienated youth: *The Uncommitted* (1965), *Young Radicals* (1968), and *Youth and Dissent* (1971). Formerly a professor of psychology in the department of psychiatry at the Yale Medical School, he is now Mellon professor of human development at the Massachusetts Institute of Technology, where he is exploring the impact of modern society on patterns of human development.

CATHERINE FOSTER ALTER, a social planner, is director of the Council on Children at Risk, an agency that does research, planning, and program development in the area of child abuse, neglect, and other populations of children at risk because of environmental factors and that serves Rock Island County, Illinois, and Scott County, Iowa. She has worked with community-based agencies and with state and county governments to assure the rights of students and to set up youth advocacy agencies and home-based day care arrangements.

NANCY BUCKLER was formerly a child care worker in a residential treatment center for disturbed children. She is now master teacher at the Loyola University Day School in Chicago, a center working with severely disturbed children and their families, and is an adjunct faculty member at the National College of Education.

JOHN PUTNAM DEMOS, a professor of history at Brandeis University, is the author of *A Little Commonwealth* (1970) and other studies of family life in the American past. Formerly acting director of the Center for Psychosocial Studies in Chicago, he is trained in psychology as well as in history. His current research interests include witchcraft in early America and the human life cycle in relation to historical change.

MARIAN WRIGHT EDELMAN practiced law in Jackson, Mississippi during the early 1960s, where she founded and directed the NAACP Legal Defense Fund. In addition to handling test cases involving children, she now directs the Children's Defense Fund, a group she founded to document and challenge unfair treatment of children in schools, courts, and the welfare system.

ROBERT J. HAGGERTY, a pediatrician, is professor of health services and pediatrics at the Harvard School of Public Health and Harvard Medical School. While at the University of Rochester, he pioneered a child health program involving many disciplines and community agencies. The senior author of *Child Health and the Community* (1975), he is now director of a Robert Wood Johnson Foundation program to develop the field of academic general pediatrics.

WILLIAM KESSEN, professor of psychology at Yale University, has conducted numerous studies of how young children develop the abilities to perceive and think and has written about the history and philosophy of how social science approaches children. He is the author of *The Child* (1965), editor of *Childhood in China* and, with Marc Bornstein, *Psychological Development from Infancy* (1978).

LAURA NADER, professor of anthropology at the University of California at Berkeley, has studied law among the Zapotec of Mexico and the Shias in Lebanon. She has investigated extrajudicial complaint handling in the United States and is the editor of a forthcoming book on the subject. The author of *Talea and Juquila: A Comparison of Zapotec Social Organization* (1964), she has produced a film on Zapotec court procedure (1966). With her collaborators she has written *The Disputing Process: Law in Ten Societies,* and she has edited several books on conflict, social control, and health. She is currently working on the human factors involved in energy planning.

FAUSTINA SOLIS, associate professor of community medicine at the medical school of the University of California at San Diego, is the former deputy director of the California health department's Public Health Division. A social worker, she directed from 1967 to 1971 the first major expansion of state health services for migrant workers in California.

PATRICIA MCGOWAN WALD* is an assistant attorney general in charge of legislative affairs for the Department of Justice. Previously, as a public interest lawyer, she was litigation director of the Mental Health Law Project in Washington, D.C. She served as a consultant to the National Commission on Civil Disorders and the National Commission on the Causes and Prevention of Violence, as co-director of the Ford Foundation Drug Abuse Research Project, and as a member of the American Bar Association's commission developing new guidelines for children's rights.

HAROLD W. WATTS, director of the Center for the Social Sciences and professor of economics at Columbia University, formerly headed the Institute for Research on Poverty at the University of Wisconsin. He supervised the evaluation of the federally sponsored test in New Jersey of a negative income tax as an alternative to the welfare system and is currently directing a Carnegie Corporation–sponsored study of the social and economic status of American families.

* PATRICIA WALD, who participated in the discussions that helped shape the ideas in this volume, resigned from the Council upon appointment to her post in the Justice Department in February 1977.

Council Staff

Executive Director: Kenneth Keniston

Associate Directors: Peter O. Almond, Joan Costello, Richard H. de Lone

Senior Editor: Jill Kneerim

Director of Public Affairs: Christopher T. Cory
  Deputy Director of Public Affairs: Kathryn K. Toll

Managing Director: Cheryl R. Towers

Director of Public Relations: Adelina Diamond

Washington Representative: Virginia Fleming

Research Associates: Peter O. Almond, Robin Boger, Susan Bucknell, Alison Clarke-Stewart, Joan Costello, Richard H. de Lone, Peter Garlock, Mark Gerzon, John Gliedman, Rochelle Kessler, Michael A. Lerner, Katherine P. Messenger, John U. Ogbu, Hillary Rodham, William Roth, Elga Wasserman

Research Assistants: Chris Buckley, Deborah R. Chernoff, Ellen Chirelstein, Laura Eby, Francesca Gobbo, Georgia Goeters, Susan Hunsinger, Vera Wells Jones, Nina Kraut, Felicity Skidmore, Phyllis Holman Weisbard

Statistical Analysis: Georgia Goeters

Administration: Darlene Copeland, Susan Ellison, Arlene Gurland, Missle Wodajo Hankerson, Ethel Himberg, Jane Hyand, Margaret Jackewicz, Karin Kaminker, Marion Lincoln, Michele McLean, Sheila Meyers, Susan Mulford, Donna Piazza, Sylvia Rifkin, Laurie Rosenbaum

Television Planning: Donald Dixon

Notes

Introduction:
American Inequality

1. These odds derive from a number of sources. William H. Sewell, "Inequality of Opportunity for Higher Education," *American Sociological Review* (October 1971), found, when controlling for academic ability, that children in the bottom quarter of socioeconomic status were only one-fourth as likely to go to college as those in the top quarter. (Hence the odds separating Jimmy and Bobby, who are from the top and bottom tenth, are understated.) Samuel Bowles and Herbert Gintis, *Schooling in Capitalist America: Educational Reform and the Contradictions of Economic Life* (New York, 1976), found when controlling for ability that children from the bottom tenth in socioeconomic status are only one-twelfth as likely to complete college as those from the top tenth. Robert M. Hauser and David L. Featherman, "Equality of Access to Schooling: Trends and Prospects" (Working Paper 75-17, Center for Demography and Ecology, University of Wisconsin–Madison), compare the contribution of father's education, father's occupation, race, family size, and family income to probable years of schooling (again with ability controlled) and the factors that differentiate Bobby and Jimmy add up to about four years of education. Bowles and Gintis, "I.Q. in the United States Class Structure," in Alan Gartner, Colin Greer, and Frank Riessman, eds., *The New Assault on Equality* (New York, 1974), compute that when the statistics are controlled for ability, children from the top tenth of the income distribution have twenty-seven times the chance of those from the bottom tenth to end up in the top tenth as adults. (Their data show that only 4 of 1,000 children born in the bottom tenth make the Horatio Alger leap to the top tenth.) Similarly, John A. Brittain, *The Inheritance of Economic Status* (The

Brookings Institution, Washington, D.C., 1977), found, in a longitudinal sample of brothers in the Cleveland area, that while children who were born in the top tenth had a fifty-fifty chance of earning an income of more than $25,000 a year (in 1976 dollars) as adults, those born in the bottom tenth had only one chance in fifty of earning the same income. (Brittain also found that children born in the top 5 percent were twenty times as likely as children born at the median income of earning $35,000 or more.)

2. This assumes that a low-income standard of minimum decency is defined as 50 percent of the median, as discussed later in the text.

3. This estimate, a conservative one, is based on the conviction that all families living on less than half the median income for a family their size are suffering deprivation that will affect their children in a number of ways. (See the discussion of a low-income line in *All Our Children: The American Family Under Pressure*, by Kenneth Keniston and the Carnegie Council on Children [New York, 1977], pp. 26–32: "How Poor Is Poor.") In 1975, 17,814,000 of the children under eighteen living with their families (or 27.6 percent of all such children in the country) lived in households with less than half the median income. This figure represents the number living below 150 percent of the official poverty line, which was roughly equivalent to half the median. Figures came from Department of Commerce, Bureau of the Census, *Current Population Reports: Consumer Income*, Series P-60, No. 111 (April 1978), p. 11.

4. For more on the concept of relative deprivation, see W. G. Runciman, *Relative Deprivation and Social Justice* (Berkeley, Calif., 1966). The concept is not novel, for its lineage runs back to the nineteenth century, but it has been more often than not ignored when social policy is being made.

5. For a discussion of the genesis of the poverty line, its rather arbitrary nature, and its subsequent canonization—over the protests of its author—see Robert A. Levine, *The Poor Ye Need Not Have with You: Lessons from the War on Poverty* (Cambridge, Mass., 1970).

6. For example, see Ben Wattenberg, *The Real America* (Garden City, N.Y., 1974).

7. The evidence, drawn from public opinion polls, is reviewed in Lee Rainwater, "Poverty, Living Standards and Family Well-

Being," in *Studies in Public Welfare*, No. 12, Part II, U.S. Congress Joint Economic Committee (Washington, D.C., 1973).

8. U.S. Department of Commerce, Bureau of the Census, *Current Population Reports: Consumer Income*, Series P-60, No. 115 (July 1978).

9. See note 3.

10. That is, income distribution as measured by the Bureau of the Census and recorded in its annual *Current Population Reports*. Since World War II the top 20 percent have had somewhat over 40 percent of the after-tax income, and the bottom 20 percent have had about 5 percent, with only slight fluctuations. The middle three-fifths have stayed approximately the same as well (see table, page 9). The distribution of earnings of individuals in this period has actually become somewhat less equal for all groups of wage earners (including white males), so that increases in two-or-more-earner families have been required to keep family income distribution unchanged. (On the increase of inequality among individual earners, see Peter Henle, "Exploring the Distribution of Earned Income," *Monthly Labor Review* [December 1972].)

11. Most economists agree that the Depression and World War II had an equalizing effect (see, for instance, Lester Thurow, *Generating Inequality: Mechanisms of Distribution in the U.S. Economy* [New York, 1975]), although some argue that when fringe benefits, tax-exempt income, and "perquisite" income, such as expense accounts, which are not considered a part of an individual's income by the Census Bureau, are thrown in, there has been no increase in equality of income distribution since the beginning of the century. (Cf. Gabriel Kolko, *Wealth and Power in America: An Analysis of Social Class and Income Distribution* [New York, 1962], and Howard Tuckman, *The Economics of the Rich* [New York, 1973].)

12. See, for instance, Edgar K. Browning, "How Much More Equality Can We Afford?" *The Public Interest* (Spring 1976), and Congressional Budget Office, "Poverty Status of Families under Alternative Definitions of Income" (Washington, D.C., January 13, 1977).

13. See David Lyon et al., *Multiple Welfare Benefits in New York City* (Santa Monica, Calif., 1976).

14. Ibid.

15. Joseph A. Pechman and Benjamin A. Okner, *Who Bears the*

Tax Burden? (The Brookings Institution, Washington, D.C., 1974).

16. Cf. Kolko, op. cit.

17. U.S. Department of Commerce, Bureau of the Census, *Current Population Reports: Consumer Income,* Series P-60, No. 114 (July 1978).

18. Estimated on the basis of *Current Population Reports,* op. cit.

19. James Smith, "The Concentration of Personal Wealth in America, 1969," *Studies in Income and Wealth* (New York, 1972).

20. Wealth data are rarely collected. The latest survey showing wealth shares for all families is Dorothy S. Projector and Gertrude S. Weiss, *Survey of Financial Characteristics of Consumers* (Federal Reserve Technical Papers, Washington, D.C., 1966).

21. U.S. Department of Commerce, Bureau of the Census, *Current Population Reports: Consumer Income,* Series P-60, No. 114 (July 1978).

22. While poverty is most concentrated in inner cities, it is by no means confined to them. Of families considered poor by the government in 1976, 54.9 percent lived in central cities, another 12.9 percent were scattered through the remainder of standard metropolitan statistical areas (cities plus suburbs), and the remaining 32.2 percent lived in rural areas. See U.S. Department of Commerce, Bureau of the Census, *Current Population Reports: Consumer Income,* Series P-60, No. 115 (July 1978).

23. On mortgage redlining and its contribution to neighborhood decay, see Arthur J. Naperstek and Gale Cincotta, "Urban Disinvestment: New Implications for Community Organization, Research and Public Policy" (joint publication of the National Center for Urban Ethnic Affairs and the National Training and Information Center, Washington, D.C., 1975). Although recent federal legislation, spurred on by grass-roots lobbying, has taken some steps to stop redlining, the effectiveness of the legislation remains to be seen.

24. On insurance redlining and the inadequacy of government attempts to compensate for it, see "Homeowner's Insurance in Detroit: A Study of Redlining Practices and Discriminatory Rates" (study prepared by the office of Detroit City Council President Carl Levin in 1976, mimeo, undated).

25. See David Caplovitz, *The Poor Pay More: Consumer Practices of Low-Income Families* (New York, 1967).

26. The relationship between such jobs and poor physical and mental health is reviewed and documented at length in *Work in America* (report of a Special Task Force to the Secretary of Health, Education and Welfare, Cambridge, Mass., 1973).

27. On the correlation of mental illness with unemployment, see Heather Ross and Isabel Sawhill, *Time of Transition: The Growth of Families Headed by Women* (The Urban Institute, Washington, D.C., 1975), a report on correlations between unemployment and family breakup, providing survey evidence that is consistent with the anthropological findings of Elliot Liebow, *Tally's Corner* (Boston, 1967). Richard J. Light, "Abused and Neglected Children in America: A Study of Alternative Policies," *Harvard Educational Review* (November 1973), found unemployment to be more highly correlated with child abuse than any other factor. Although correlations do not necessarily prove causality, and in some cases causality may run the other way (mental illness can cause unemployment), the findings of these studies, which are consistent with many other studies, lead one to suspect that unemployment is a major causal factor in all these forms of personal devastation, given the cultural importance our society attaches to work.

28. Current evidence on infant mortality is reviewed in Children's Defense Fund, *Doctors and Dollars Are Not Enough* (Washington, D.C., 1976). Nationally, the infant mortality rate among blacks remains about twice as high as that among whites. National figures on the association of income and infant mortality are not routinely available, but local studies typically show higher rates, as reviewed by Charles U. Lowe and D. F. Alexander, "Child Health and Federal Care Programs," in Nathan B. Talbot, ed., *Raising Children in Modern America: Problems and Perspective Solutions* (Boston, 1976).

29. See, for instance, H. G. Birch and J. D. Gussow, *Disadvantaged Children: Health, Nutrition and School Failure* (New York, 1970), and Bonnie Kaplan, "Malnutrition and Mental Deficiency," *Psychological Bulletin* (November 1972).

30. The President's Committee on Mental Retardation, *Mental Retardation: Century of Decision* (Washington, D.C., March 1976). Also see Rodger Hurley, *Poverty and Mental Retardation: A Causal Relationship* (New York, 1969).

31. Karen Davis, "A Decade of Policy Developments in Providing Health Care for Low Income Families," in Robert H. Haveman, ed., *A Decade of Federal Antipoverty Programs: Achievements, Failures and Lessons* (New York, 1977).

32. Lowe and Alexander, op. cit.

33. American Public Health Association, *Minority Health Chart Book* (Washington, D.C., 1974).

34. Meharry Medical College, "Study of Unmet Needs for Health and Welfare Services: Phase I, the 1972–3 Study" (presented at American Public Health Association, 102nd Annual Meeting, New Orleans, La., October 1974).

35. Klaus J. Roghmann, "Recent Changes in Child Health Services: The Impact of Medicaid," in Robert J. Haggerty, Klaus J. Roghmann, and I. B. Pless, eds., *Child Health and the Community* (New York, 1975).

36. According to the Children's Defense Fund, op. cit., p. 10, 300 to 400 children a year still die of lead-paint poisoning, and 6,000 more suffer irreversible brain damage.

37. Stephan Thernstrom, *The Other Bostonians: Poverty and Progress in the American Metropolis, 1880–1970* (Cambridge, Mass., 1973). See Chapters 5 and 9 especially.

38. Peter Blau and Otis Dudley Duncan, *The American Occupational Structure* (New York, 1967).

39. Joseph A. Kahl, *The American Class Structure* (New York, 1957).

40. See evidence reviewed in *Manpower Report of the President* (Washington, D.C., April 1974), pp. 122–23. The report indicates graphically the difference in mobility rates that characterize different races between the first job held and the job held in the prime working years of ages forty-five to fifty-nine, as summarized in the following table:

	Upwardly Mobile (%)	Downwardly Mobile (%)	Same (%)
All male	55	16	29
White male	57	15	28
Black male	41	22	37

James J. Byrne, "Occupational Mobility of Workers," *Monthly Labor Review* (February 1975), gives a picture of such movements on a year-to-year basis. The strongest evidence for substantial intragenerational mobility comes from Bradley R. Schiller, who studied a large sample of men in the same age cohort using Social Security data from 1957 and 1971, a system that is somewhat flawed since it shows only earned income from persons paying Social Security, yields no data on the earnings record of the bottom 10 percent, and omits from the later year individuals who had dropped out of the labor force, were not otherwise paying into Social Security, or had dropped into the bottom tenth. However, Schiller shows data suggesting that among the 65 percent of white males who were upwardly mobile, the average white male who, in 1957, was in the eighteenth ventile of the income distribution (between the tenth and fifteenth percentile) had moved up to the fifteenth ventile by 1971 (with others, of course, dropping down to take his place). In dollar terms, this meant an increase in income from roughly \$1,200 to \$6,200. One can argue, as Schiller does, that movement up three-plus ventiles is a "very large movement." But one can, alternatively, look at the actual dollars involved, and the limits to the data, and be unimpressed. For black males, he shows only half as much upward mobility and, for black males who were at the top of the income distribution in 1957, much more downward mobility than for whites. See Bradley R. Schiller, "Equality, Opportunity, and the Good Job," *The Public Interest* (Spring 1976).

41. See, for instance, the reviews of recent studies from several countries in Raymond Boudon, *Education, Opportunity and Social Inequality: Changing Prospects in Western Society* (New York, 1974), and the overview of studies over time in Seymour Martin Lipset, "Social Mobility and Equal Opportunity," *The Public Interest* (Fall 1972).

42. On the substantially lower rates of intergenerational mobility for blacks see, for instance, Blau and Duncan, op. cit., and for their persistence into the 1970s, see Robert M. Hauser and David L. Featherman, "White-Nonwhite Differentials in Occupational Mobility among Men in the United States, 1962–72," *Demography* (May 1974). On intragenerational mobility, see also Hauser and Featherman, op. cit., and the *Manpower Report of the President* cited in note 40. Measuring the intergenerational mobility of women is complicated and filled with uncertainties, given that either marriage or occupation or both

may affect measurements used in most studies (see Andrea Tyree and Judith Treas, "The Occupational and Marital Mobility of Women," *American Sociological Review* [June 1974]), although some studies conclude they are similar to those of men.

43. This is true when status is measured (as indicated by the table in note 40), and it is also true when income measures are viewed on a cross-sectional basis: black males in their twenties have roughly the same earnings as black males in the years thirty-five to fifty-four, which are, for whites, "peak" earning years. See *Manpower Report of the President,* op. cit., p. 118.

44. This does not necessarily mean that blacks and women working side by side with white males in the same organization are paid or promoted differentially, although that is not infrequently the case. But it generally does mean that they are employed in lower-paying industries or in lower-paying job classifications within firms and industries.

45. U.S. Department of Commerce, Bureau of the Census, *Current Population Reports: Consumer Income,* Series P-60, No. 114 (July 1978).

1976 Income Distribution

Households	Lowest Fifth	Top Fifth	Mean Income
All races	Up to $7,441	Above $23,923	$16,870
White	Up to $8,073	Above $24,500	$17,525
Black	Up to $4,320	Above $18,271	$11,922

46. Robert Coles, *Migrants, Sharecroppers, Mountaineers,* Vol. 2, *Children of Crisis* (Boston, 1972).

Chapter One
Egalitarian Policy: Children as Bearers of the Dream

1. Mann's view of schooling as the "great equalizer" that prevents poverty is discussed in Chapter 2.
2. See the discussion of these distributions in the Introduction.
3. Stanley M. Lebergott, *The American Economy: Income, Wealth and Want* (Princeton, N.J., 1976), concludes that the median income of black families has been between 52 and 64 percent

that of white families since 1900. Occasionally this ratio has dipped up or down a few points, and in recent years there has been a dip up from 56 percent in 1965 to 64 percent in 1970; but in the 1970s this trend toward racial equality of family income has mildly reversed itself. (See Bernard E. Anderson, James R. Dimpson, et al., *The State of Black America, 1978,* National Urban League, p. 6). Since World War II the unemployment rate for black males has averaged about twice that of white males, with only modest fluctuations from this ratio, as many reviews of Bureau of Labor Statistics figures show.

4. See *Manpower Report of the President* (Washington, D.C., April 1975) or other reviews of Bureau of Labor Statistics data discussed in the Introduction.

5. This well-known correlation characterizes dozens of studies, some of which are discussed in Chapter 3.

6. Discussions of liberalism in this chapter and throughout this book draw generally on a large body of political theorists, with a special debt to Louis Hartz, *The Liberal Tradition in America* (New York, 1955).

7. A contrasting view has been voiced by Garry Wills, *Inventing America* (New York, 1978).

8. While Locke rejects the Cartesian concept of innate ideas and is popularly remembered for portraying the human mind as a *tabula rasa,* or blank slate, on which experience leaves its imprint through the senses, there did remain in his thought an implicit dualism, a belief that certain faculties of reason and judgment which operate on experience are innate, a dualism that subsequent radical empiricists tried to eliminate (see Ernst Cassirer, *The Philosophy of the Enlightenment* [Princeton, N.J., 1951], especially Chapter 3, for a discussion of these issues). The basic elements of this tension of ideas still reverberate in psychological theory.

9. On the development of American pedagogic theory in the nineteenth century, see Lawrence A. Cremin, *The American Common School: An Historic Conception* (New York, 1951), or Merle Curti, *The Social Ideas of American Educators* (Paterson, N.J., 1959). In addition to the ideas of Locke, the educational ideas of Rousseau, who represents the more radical and egalitarian path of development from liberal theory (in politics and in education), played, of course, a significant role in shaping these concepts.

10. The phrase is Louis Hartz's.
11. William Ryan, *Blaming the Victim* (New York, 1976).

Chapter Two
Political and Social Reform
in Three Eras

1. Arthur M. Schlesinger, Jr., *The Age of Jackson* (Boston, 1945).
2. Richard Hofstadter, *The American Political Tradition* (New York, 1948), Chapter 3.
3. This development is elegantly analyzed by Louis Hartz, *The Liberal Tradition in America* (New York, 1955).
4. Quoted in Schlesinger, op. cit., p. 10.
5. Richard Hofstadter, ed., *Great Issues in American History: From the Revolution to the Civil War, 1765–1865* (New York, 1958).
6. On the limited egalitarianism of the revolutionary era, when equality before the law was the dominant form of that ideal, see Bernard Bailyn, *The Ideological Origins of the American Revolution* (Cambridge, Mass., 1967).
7. One of the leading polemicists to strike this theme was William Leggett, a newspaper editor and leader of the "Equal Rights" or "Locofoco" wing of the Democratic party. Leggett's rhetoric often sounds like that of class warfare as he defends the "poor and laboring classes" against the "would be lordlings of the paper dynasty" (see Robert V. Remini, ed., *The Age of Jackson* [New York, 1972], p. 95). But as Marvin Meyers, among others, has pointed out, the substance behind Leggett's rhetoric resembles what would, in contemporary terms, be considered a conservative call for an absolute free market (see Marvin Meyers, *The Jacksonian Persuasion: Politics and Belief* [Palo Alto, Calif., 1957]).
8. For instance, in 1848 Horace Mann, a Whig political leader in Massachusetts before he became the leader of the common school movement, attacked bitterly the "main idea set forth in the creeds of some political reformers, or revolutionizers . . . that some people are poor because others are rich," labeled political unrest "the revenge of poverty against wealth," and attacked socialism as a scheme to divide up the wealth and, after the profligate had exhausted their share, divide it again. See Horace Mann, *The Twelfth Annual Report of the Board of*

Education, in *Life and Works,* Vol. 4 (Boston, 1891). The point is that despite the view of contemporary historians that the Jacksonian Democrats ("political madmen" Mann called them in his journal) were not radical levelers or proponents of class warfare, some Whigs took the rhetoric of men like Leggett at face value and seem to have grouped the Jacksonians with Jacobins, socialists, and men like Thomas Skidmore.

9. Remini, op. cit., pp. 81–82. Jackson's views on the relationship between inequality and wealth sounded a theme that has reverberated throughout American history, from (ironically) Madison's comments in Federalist 10 to the present day.

10. *The American Political Tradition,* op. cit., Chapter 3.

11. Ibid.

12. Meyers, op. cit.

13. Remini, op. cit., p. xix.

14. Hartz, op. cit.

15. Quoted in Schlesinger, op. cit., p. 105.

16. Ibid., pp. 269–70.

17. Ibid., Chapter 22, pp. 268–82.

18. Ibid., p. 271.

19. Horace Mann, *Third Annual Report to the Board of Education* (1839), in *Life and Works.* Vol. 3 (Boston, 1868).

20. Ibid.

21. Mann, *Twelfth Annual Report,* op. cit.

22. Ibid.

23. Quoted in Merle Curti, *The Social Ideas of American Educators* (Paterson, N.J., 1959), p. 112.

24. Ibid.

25. This "conflict of interest," to use latter-day terminology, did not go unnoticed at the time. Critics to Mann's political left, such as Orestes Brownson, charged Mann and the normal school with serving the interests of the industrialist Whigs, and on the religious right, conservative Calvinists saw his efforts as an attempt to use the machinery of the state to spread the new liberal Protestantism which many of these same Whig industrialists—epitomized by the Unitarians—were spreading. On Brownson, see note 26. On religious opposition, see Raymond Culver, *Horace Mann and Religion in the Massachusetts Public Schools* (New Haven, Conn., 1929).

26. Orestes Brownson, "Education of the People," *Boston Quarterly Review* (October 1839). Brownson, a mercurial thinker, was

then editor of the review and a leading Democratic theorist whom Hofstadter credits with being one of the few men of his time to have a sharper sense of social class issues. This article was a review of Mann's *Second Annual Report to the Board of Education*. Brownson urged Governor Morton, a Democrat elected in 1840, to oust Mann as education secretary, but the attempt failed. In addition, Michael B. Katz, *The Irony of Early School Reform: Educational Innovation in Mid-Nineteenth Century Massachusetts* (Cambridge, Mass., 1968), has produced impressive evidence that the educational reforms of that era, portrayed by early historians as a "triumph of democracy," were generally opposed by working-class members and artisans. In the past ten years a flood of books, initiated by Katz's work, have argued this position in various ways, resulting in a substantially changed historiography of education.

27. Horace Mann, *Lectures on Education*, in *Life and Works*, Vol. 2 (Boston, 1868).

28. Mann, *Third Annual Report*, op. cit.

29. On the development of the school curriculum as an instrument of moral control, see Katz, op. cit., Part II, "The Uses of Pedagogy."

30. As late as 1890, for instance, only 78.1 percent of school-age children (five to seventeen) were enrolled in school; few passed the eighth grade, and the average pupil attended only eighty-six days of school a year (barely more than half the current rate). See U.S. Department of Commerce, Bureau of the Census, *Historical Statistics of the United States, Colonial Times to 1970* (Washington, D.C., 1970).

31. On Mann's tremendous influence see, for instance, Curti, op. cit., or Lawrence A. Cremin, *The American Common School: An Historic Conception* (New York, 1951).

32. Hartz, op. cit., p. 111.

33. For instance, on the distribution of wealth in the 1860s, see Lee Soltow, *Men and Wealth in the United States, 1850–1870* (New Haven, Conn., 1975).

34. Cited in Cremin, op. cit. As Cremin points out, moral development, economic individualism, and patriotism were inextricably intertwined in nineteenth-century pedagogy, almost to the point of being considered synonymous.

35. See Hofstadter's essay "Abraham Lincoln and the Self-Made Myth," in *The American Political Tradition*, op. cit.

36. David M. Potter, *People of Plenty: Economic Abundance and the American Character* (Chicago, 1955). Friedrich Engels argued a similar point of view in an 1892 letter explaining why America never developed a strong socialist tradition (see Lewis Feuer, ed., *Basic Writings on Politics and Philosophy: Karl Marx and Friedrich Engels* [Garden City, N.Y., 1959]).

37. For this and similar antischool positions see Robert H. Bremner et al., *Children and Youth in America: A Documentary History* (Cambridge, Mass., 1970), Vol. 1 (1600–1685).

38. This movement, the nativist movement, gave rise to the Know Nothing party, which actually gained control of the legislature in Massachusetts and several other states. See Richard Hofstadter, *The Paranoid Style in American Politics and Other Essays* (New York, 1965). Also see Sidney Ahlstrom, *A Religious History of the American People* (New York, 1975), for an account of the relationship of nativism to Protestant religious movements at the time, especially their anti-Catholicism.

39. Katz, op. cit.

40. On the tremendous economic and social instability of this period see Robert Wiebe, *The Search for Order, 1877–1920* (New York, 1968), who interprets many of the Progressive reforms of the era as a response to this turmoil in search of order and harmony.

41. On the rapid growth of the corporation in the last five years of the nineteenth century, see Gabriel Kolko, *The Triumph of Conservatism, A Reinterpretation of American History, 1900–1916* (New York, 1963).

42. Richard Hofstadter, *The Age of Reform: From Bryan to F.D.R.* (New York, 1955).

43. Bureau of the Census, *Historical Statistics*, op. cit.

44. This quote, and others from Roosevelt, are from Hoftstadter, *The American Political Tradition*, op. cit., Chapter 9, unless otherwise noted. The brief portrait of Roosevelt draws heavily on Hofstadter.

45. Ibid.

46. Ibid.

47. For an excellent analysis of the ways in which the ideologies of efficiency and both moral and economic uplift were fused in reform ideology, see Samuel Haber, *Efficiency and Uplift: Scientific Management in the Progressive Era, 1890–1920* (Chicago, 1964).

48. Woodrow Wilson, *The New Freedom* (New York, 1913), quoted in Hofstadter, *The Age of Reform,* op. cit.
49. Quoted in Hoftstadter, *The Age of Reform,* op. cit.
50. Quoted in Hofstadter, *The American Political Tradition,* op. cit.
51. Wilson, op. cit. For a discussion of Wilson's views, see Hofstadter's chapter "Woodrow Wilson, the Conservative as Liberal," in *The American Political Tradition,* op. cit.
52. John Dewey, *The School and Society* (Chicago, 1956—originally published in 1867), pp. 10–11.
53. As Hofstadter put it in *The Age of Reform,* op. cit., the Progressive mind "was eminently a Protestant mind; and even though much of its strength was in the cities, it inherited the moral traditions of rural evangelical Protestantism."
54. Peter D. Garlock, "The Child-Saving Movement, 1870–1900" (background paper for the Carnegie Council on Children, October 1974).
55. Ibid.
56. On the influence of this period on the subsequent development of social services in general (many of which were born during it) see Murray Levine and A. Levine, *A Social History of Helping Clinic, Court, School and Community* (New York, 1970). On the impact on schools, in particular, see Lawrence A. Cremin, *The Transformation of the School: Progressivism in American Education, 1876–1957* (New York, 1961), and, with special emphasis on its impact on the canons of school administration, see Raymond E. Callahan, *Education and the Cult of Efficiency: A Study of the Social Forces That Have Shaped the Administration of the Public Schools* (Chicago, 1962).
57. Croly was the influential founder of the *New Republic,* and his book *The Promise of American Life,* Arthur M. Schlesinger, Jr., ed. (Cambridge, Mass., 1965—originally published in 1909), exhibits—even codifies—many of the reform concepts discussed here. The disjunctions between politics and economics, between individual and society that we have argued characterize liberalism are patent in this book, along with an attitude toward equality that is almost Hamiltonian. For instance, "Society is organized politically for the benefit of all people. Such an organization may permit radical differences among individuals in the opportunities and possessions they actually enjoy; but no man would be able to impute his own success or failure to the legal framework of society" (p. 180), and "Ameri-

can political thinkers have always repudiated the idea that by equality of rights they meant anything like equality of performance or power" (p. 181). Indeed, Croly goes further and criticizes the belief in the principle of equal rights as one that "does not bind, heal and unify public opinion. Its effect rather is confusing, distracting, and at worst, disintegrating" (p. 185). What Croly—who sees himself as a reformer and was so seen, ends up advocating as a transcendent ideal (and here he departs from traditional liberalism) is the concept of the nation-state, organized both politically and economically along lines of corporate efficiency (for instance, he wanted to do away with direct primaries on grounds that the mass of men could not exercise proper political judgment), which in broad outlines resembles the basic principles of fascism more than any other system of government.

58. Joseph Mayer Rice, *The Public School System of the United States* (New York, 1893).

59. This description of progressive school reform and the subsequent analysis of its perversity can be found in the work of many writers in addition to Cremin, especially David Tyack, *The One Best System: A History of American Urban Education* (Cambridge, Mass., 1974); Joel H. Spring, *Education and the Rise of the Corporate State* (Boston, 1972); Sol Cohen, *Progressive and Urban School Reform: The Public Education Association of New York City, 1895–1954* (New York, 1964); Michael B. Katz, *Class, Bureaucracy and Schools: The Illusion of Educational Change in America* (New York, 1975); and Samuel Bowles and Herbert Gintis, *Schooling in Capitalist America: Educational Reform and the Contradictions of Economic Life* (New York, 1976). On the impact of scientific management on school administration see Callahan, op. cit.; on the effort to scientize (and psychologize) the curriculum see Cremin, *The Transformation of the School*, op. cit. On the development of vocational education as the preferred mode for lower-class and working-class children see Marvin Lazerson, *Origins of the Urban School: Public Education in Massachusetts, 1870–1915* (Cambridge, Mass., 1971); David K. Cohen and Marvin Lazerson, "Education and the Corporate Order," *Socialist Revolution* (March–April 1972); and Sol Cohen, "The Industrial Education Movement, 1906–1917," *American Quarterly* (Spring 1968).

60. Cremin, *The Transformation of the School,* op. cit.
61. Ibid., especially pp. 303–8.
62. See his 1888 speech, "Can School Programs Be Shortened and Enriched?" in Charles W. Eliot, *Educational Reform* (New York, 1898).
63. As Curti, op. cit., points out, this fact was not lost on some teachers of the day, including an early organizer of teachers, Margaret Haley. See also the resistance of New York City teachers to installation of the so-called Gary Plan, one Progressive scheme for more efficient, individualized instruction, described in Callahan, op. cit. The Gary Plan is, in fact, an excellent case in point. Praised by Dewey (see John and Evelyn Dewey, *Schools of Tomorrow* [New York, 1915]) and radicals such as Randolph Bourne for its presumed benefits to children, combining individualized instruction with a wide range of activities supposed to simulate the organic environment of the lost rural community learning environment, it ended undergoing strange transformations at the hands of reformers. For instance, in New York it was seized on primarily as a cheaper form of education which made more efficient use of expensive school buildings by "platooning" children. In short order, what was first touted as an organic communal setting for learning was marketed as a cost-cutting management strategy, with much of the original spirit of the plan lost.
64. See Cremin, *The Transformation of the School,* op. cit., and sharper, more critical and class-conscious variants of this argument in Bowles and Gintis, op. cit., and Clarence Karier, "Testing for Order and Control in the Corporate Liberal State," *Educational Theory* (Spring 1972).
65. Quoted in Bowles and Gintis, op. cit., p. 191.
66. Elwood P. Cubberley, *Changing Conceptions of Education* (Boston, 1909). Cubberley, dean of the School of Education at Stanford University, was a prolific writer whose textbook on school administration was long a standard, as was his history of public education. The latter work codified the view widely held today (and now being challenged by many educational historians) that the development of public education in this country was a series of victories for democracy, the struggle of the common people and their advocates against vested interests of privilege. On Cubberley's considerable historiographic im-

pact, see Lawrence A. Cremin, *The Wonderful World of El-wood Patterson Cubberley* (New York, 1965).

67. Cubberley, op. cit., p. 15.
68. On the influence of Social Darwinism in general, see Richard Hofstadter, *Social Darwinism in American Thought, 1860–1915* (Boston, 1944). For its particular influence on educational theory, see Cremin, *The Transformation of the School,* op. cit.
69. Quoted in Levine and Levine, op. cit.
70. "What Is a Lynching? A Study of Mob Justice, South and North," Ray Stannard Baker on the condition of the Negro, in Richard Hofstadter, ed., *The Progressive Movement, 1900–1915* (Englewood Cliffs, N.J., 1963). Reformers such as Baker and Croly (see *The Promise of American Life,* op. cit., p. 81) simply took black inferiority for granted.
71. See Sol Cohen, *Progressive and Urban School Reform,* op. cit.
72. Christopher Jencks et al., *Inequality: A Reassessment of the Effect of Family and Schooling in America* (New York, 1972), p 14.
73. For a discussion of the confusion of goals within the Office of Economic Opportunity, the agency created to lead the War on Poverty, where it was rarely clear whether the "enemy" was poverty, inequality, or racial injustice, see Robert Levine, *The Poor Ye Need Not Have with You: Lessons from the War on Poverty* (Cambridge, Mass., 1970).
74. See Martin Deutsch, "Early Social Environment: Its Influence on School Adaptation," in Fred Hechinger, ed., *Pre-School Education Today* (Garden City, N.Y., 1966). Hechinger labels early education a "passport to equality."
75. Betty Caldwell, "The Fourth Dimension in Early Childhood Education," in R. Hess and R. Bear, eds., *Early Education: Current Theory, Research and Action* (Chicago, 1968), quoted in Stephen S. Baratz and Joan C. Baratz, "Early Childhood Intervention. The Social Science Base of Institutional Racism," *Harvard Educational Review* (February 1970).
76. See Maya Pines, "Head Head Start," *New York Times Magazine* (October 26, 1975).
77. For evidence that casts doubt on the proposition that parent education will have significant developmental payoffs for children (whatever benefits it may have for parents in easing day-to-day problems) see Arlene Amidon and Orville G. Brim, Jr.,

"What Do Children Have to Gain from Parent Education?" (paper prepared for the Advisory Committee on Child Development, National Research Council, National Academy of Sciences, mimeo, undated). One simple problem is reaching and retaining the involvement of so-called high-risk parents—see David A. Goslin, *Children under Three and Their Families: Implications of the Parent and Child Centers and the Parent Child Development Centers for the Design of Future Programs* (report to the U.S. Office of Child Development, April 30, 1974).

78. For a brief review of evidence on misclassification of minority students, see John U. Ogbu, *Minority Education and Caste* (New York, 1978), pp. 136–37. Also see the evidence amassed by the Children's Defense Fund, *Children Out of School in America* (Washington, D.C., 1974).

79. For a serious journalistic account of this movement and its abuses, see Peter Schrag and Diane Divoky, *The Myth of the Hyperactive Child* (New York, 1975). A careful academic assessment of the flawed diagnostic procedures employed in detecting learning disabilities, a study that questions the effectiveness of prevalent treatment approaches even when diagnosis is correct, is Lester Grinspoon and S. B. Singer, "Amphetamines in the Treatment of Hyperkinetic Children," *Harvard Educational Review* (November 1973).

80. Hans R. Huessy and A. H. Cohen, "Hyperkinetic Behaviors and Learning Disabilities Followed over Seven Years" (University of Vermont College of Medicine, mimeo, undated). This study was completed in 1974. We would not suggest it is a particularly good study—just a typical one.

81. Ibid.

82. See Marian Wright Edelman, "Winson and Dovie Hudson's Dream," *Harvard Educational Review* (November 1975).

Chapter Three
Help That Can Hurt

1. On the state of the art, see Kenneth Boulding and M. Pfaff, eds. *Redistribution to the Rich and the Poor: The Grants Economics of Income Distribution* (Belmont, Calif., 1972).

2. See Richard A. Musgrave and Peggy B. Musgrave, *Public Finance in Theory and Practice* (New York, 1975).

3. Joseph A. Pechman and Ben Okner, *Who Bears the Tax Burden?* (The Brookings Institution, Washington, D.C., 1974), calculated that in 1967 some $55 billion was lost to the treasury through these deductions—which in that year was some fifteen times the total AFDC bill. Presumably the ratio is still roughly the same.

4. See Franna Diamond, *For the Welfare of Children: Welfare Reform* (Washington, D.C., 1978).

5. Ibid.

6. William J. Lawrence and Stephen Leeds, *An Inventory of Federal Income Transfer Programs, Fiscal Year 1977* (White Plains, N.Y., 1978).

7. Carol Stack and Herbert Semmel, "The Concept of Family in the Poor Black Community." "The Family, Poverty and Welfare Programs: Household Patterns and Government Policies," in *Studies in Public Welfare*, No. 12, Part II, U.S. Congress Joint Economic Committee (Washington, D.C., 1973).

8. Joel F. Handler and Ellen Jane Hollingsworth, *The Deserving Poor: A Study of Welfare Administration* (Chicago, 1971), p. 78.

9. For varying views of the evidence on this point, see papers by Marjorie Honig, Lee Rainwater, Phillip Cutright and John Scanzoni, and Robert I. Lerman in "The Family, Poverty and Welfare Programs: Factors Influencing Family Stability," in *Studies in Public Welfare*, No. 12, U.S. Congress Joint Economic Committee (Washington, D.C., 1973). A study that, in addition to finding evidence that families break up because of this fiscal incentive, documents the negative impact of welfare and unemployment on many aspects of family life is Blanche Bernstein and William Meezan, *The Impact of Welfare on Family Stability* (New York, June 1975).

10. In most states the effective rate is lower, by virtue of discretionary state regulations, ranging between 25 and 40 percent. However, even the 25 to 40 percent marginal tax rate implicit in the structure of welfare benefit reductions is a higher marginal tax rate on earnings than that paid by other families until their net taxable income (after deductions and exemptions) exceeds $20,000 a year. Although there is no clear evidence that this fact actually constitutes a widespread disincentive to work, it is certainly unfair. On the actual implicit tax rate on earnings of AFDC recipients see Irene Lurie, "Estimates of Tax Rates

in the AFDC Program," *National Tax Journal* (March 1974).

On benefit-loss rates in other transfer programs see "Public Welfare and Work Incentives: Theory and Practice," in *Studies in Public Welfare,* No. 14, U.S. Congress Joint Economic Committee (Washington, D.C., April 1974).

11. On the belief that the poor in general and AFDC recipients in specific do not wish to work, see Leonard Goodwin, *Do the Poor Want to Work?: A Social-Psychological Study of Work Orientations* (The Brookings Institution, Washington, D.C., 1972). Also see findings of the New Jersey Income Maintenance Experiment in Joseph A. Pechman and P. Michael Timpane, eds., *Work Incentives and Income Guarantees: The New Jersey Negative Income Tax Experiment* (The Brookings Institution, Washington, D.C., 1975), which found that primary earners continued to seek work even with a guaranteed minimum income. On the relatively high turnover of the welfare rolls see James N. Morgan et al., *Five Thousand American Families— Patterns of Economic Progress: An Analysis of the First Five Years of the Panel Study of Income Dynamics,* Vol. 1 (Institute for Social Research, Ann Arbor, Mich., 1974). The average family remains on the welfare roles less than two years (although some may return subsequently) according to George Hoshino, "AFDC as Child Welfare," in Alvin L. Schorr, ed., *Children and Decent People* (New York, 1974). Numerous studies dispute the view that high welfare payments create migration of the poor from state to state. The conclusion reached by John G. Grumm, on this point, also adds to the evidence that the poor want to work: ". . . these data suggest that migrants prefer a state with high per capita income and relatively low welfare payments to one with relatively high payments and low income." See John G. Grumm, "Population Change and State Government Policy," in *Governance and Population: The Governmental Implications of Population Change,* Vol. 4 (The Commission on Population Growth and the American Future, Washington, D.C., 1972).

12. A 1975 interview with TV producer Mort Silverstein.

13. See Introduction, p. 9.

14. It is interesting to note, in this respect, that the vast majority of improper welfare payments are *not* the result of client dishonesty or fraud. In dollar terms, according to Peter M. Wynn, deputy commissioner for administration, New York State De-

partment of Social Services, improper Medicaid billings by doctors are the largest source of outright fraud in that state. Administrative error is the next largest source of improper payments, followed by minor (and perhaps unintentional) misstatements by clients. Deliberate fraud (e.g., outright lies, applying for welfare at more than one office, etc.) accounts for no more than 5 percent of improper payments—less than one-half of 1 percent of all welfare billings in New York State. (Wynn was interviewed by the author on October 17, 1977.)

15. U.S. Department of Health, Education and Welfare, National Center for Social Statistics, *Children Served by Public Welfare Agencies and Voluntary Child Welfare Agencies and Institutions, March, 1972* (Washington, D.C., 1974).

16. Phyllis H. Weisbard, "The Placement of Children in the Child Welfare System" (background paper, Carnegie Council on Children, New Haven, Conn., 1975).

17. On the reasons for placement and their inherent vagueness, see Robert Mnookin, "Foster Care: In Whose Best Interest?" *Harvard Educational Review* (November 1973).

18. Michael H. Phillips et al., *Factors Associated with Placement Decisions in Child Welfare* (Child Welfare League of America, New York, 1971).

19. Weisbard, op. cit.

20. Ibid.

21. Reported by a Carnegie Council research assistant, Nina Kraut.

22. David L. Bazelon, "Racism, Classism and the Juvenile Process," *Judicature* 53 (1970), pp. 373–78.

23. Herbert J. Wahlberg, Elaine Gee Yeh, and Stephanie M. Paton, "Family Background, Ethnicity and Urban Delinquency," *Journal of Research in Crime and Delinquency* (June 1974).

24. William F. Hohenstein, "Factors Influencing the Police Disposition of Juvenile Offenders," in Thorsten Sellin and Marvin Wolfgang, eds., *Delinquency: Selected Studies* (New York, 1969).

25. Edward Eldefonso, *Youth Problems and Law Enforcement* (Englewood Cliffs, N.J., 1972), estimates that about 75 percent of cases are handled informally.

26. Lois Forer, *No One Will Lissen: How Our Legal System Brutalized the Youthful Poor* (New York, 1970), cites Philadelphia data. Similar findings emerge in other studies: see William R. Arnold, "Race and Ethnicity Relative to Other Factors in

Juvenile Court Dispositions," *American Journal of Sociology*, Vol. 77 (September 1971).

27. Richard G. Kiekbusch, *Juvenile Court Intake: Correlates of Dispositioning* (dissertation, University of Notre Dame, 1933, in *Dissertation Abstracts 33A*, No. 7, January 1973), found disposition to be most severe the more "the adult make-up of the offender's family deviated from the nuclear model." Terence P. Thornberry, "Race Socioeconomic Status and Sentencing in the Juvenile Justice System," *Journal of Criminal Law, Criminology and Police Science* (March 1973), found that in one jurisdiction (Philadelphia) whites were roughly 1.5 times as likely as blacks to receive probation (instead of incarceration), a fact partially explained by socioeconomic status. Also see Arnold, op. cit.

28. A number of studies show this pattern to pertain in widely different geographic locales. The evidence is reviewed by Phyllis H. Weisbard, "Treatment of Minority Children in the Juvenile Justice System" (background paper, Carnegie Council on Children, New Haven, Conn., January 1975).

29. Joseph B. Treaster, "State Delinquent Center: No Punishment or Reform," *New York Times* (March 2, 1976).

30. Forer, op. cit., points to the use of such a rating scale by police in handling juvenile offenders, a scale based on social science studies, as one reason for differential treatment of whites and blacks at the station house in Philadelphia.

31. Stigma is a widely acknowledged concept that has been the subject of a rather limited literature. A basic treatment is Erving Goffman, *Stigma: Notes on the Management of Spoiled Identity* (Englewood Cliffs, N.J., 1963). A graphic study of the effects of stigma is Robert B. Edgerton, *The Cloak of Competence: Stigma in the Lives of the Mentally Retarded* (Berkeley, Calif., 1967). Most discussions of the phenomenon of stigma focus on such issues as the effects of labeling, the internationalization of stigma, or the interaction between healthy and stigmatized individuals, tending to downplay or ignore the differentials in power and the social class origins of those differentials, which we stress here.

32. Joan McCord, "A Forty Year Study of Behavior and Some Effects of a Treatment Program" (paper presented at Oberlin College, April 13, 1978). Also, Joan McCord, "Thirty-Year Follow-up of Treatment Effects," *American Psychologist* (March 1978). Her

study is a follow-up of the well-known Cambridge-Somerville Youth Study.

33. Ivar E. Berg, *Education and Jobs: The Great Training Robbery* (New York, 1970).

34. Beatrice G. Reubens, "Vocational Education for All in High School?" in James O'Toole, ed., *Work and the Quality of Life* (Cambridge, Mass., 1974), provides a comprehensive review of such evidence. Analogies between the career education movement and earlier versions, the ineffectuality and class-biasd outcomes of which give pause for thought, are probed in W. Norton Grubb and Marvin Lazerson, "Rally 'Round the Workplace, Boys: Continuities and Fallacies in Career Education," *Harvard Educational Review* (November 1975).

35. Studies that find little or no correlation between educational performance and performance in practice include Osler L. Peterson et al., *Analytical Study of North Carolina General Practice, 1953–1954* (Association of American Medical Colleges, Evanston, Ill., 1956); Kenneth F. Clute, *The General Practitioner, a Study of Medical Education and Practice in Ontario and Nova Scotia* (Toronto, 1963); T. B. Price et al., *Performance Measures of Physicians* (Salt Lake City, Utah, 1963). Also, the law school aptitude tests, assigned to predict performance in law school, a task for which tests are best suited, correlate with first-year grades at the .43 level. A slightly higher correlation, .5, means that tests scores predict performance 13 percent better than chance. On this point, and on legal credentials generally, see David White, "The Definition of Legal Competence: Will the Circle Be Unbroken?" (Childhood and Government Project, University of California at Berkeley, June 15, 1976), who argues that the net effect of legal credentialing systems is to screen out the poor and the nonwhite.

36. Samuel Bowles and Herbert Gintis, "I.Q. in the United States Class Structure," in Alan Gartner, Colin Greer, and Frank Riessman, eds., *The New Assault on Equality: I.Q. and Social Stratification* (New York, 1974).

37. For example, see Michael A. Wallach, "Tests Tell Us Little about Talent," *American Scientist* (January–February 1976).

38. It is not that no studies ever find correlates of teacher effectiveness. Many do. But there is no consistency in their findings, suggesting either that the studies are flawed or that teacher effectiveness is highly situational.

39. See, for instance, George Weber, "Inner-City Children Can Be Taught to Read: Four Successful Schools" (Council for Basic Education, Occasional Papers, No. 18, October 1971), and David Klepak, "School Factors Influence Reading Achievement: A Case Study of Two Inner City Schools" (State of New York, Office of Education Performance Review, March 1974).

40. For a persuasive critique of the methodology of most educational productivity studies, see Daniel F. Luecke and Noel F. McGinn, "Regression Analyses and Education Production Functions: Can They Be Trusted?" *Harvard Educational Review* (August 1975). An example of a second-generation study—although not a study exempt from some of the same methodological problems of earlier studies—is Anita A. Summers and Barbara L. Wolfe, "Which School Resources Help Learning? Efficiency and Equity in the Philadelphia Public Schools," *Business Review* (Federal Reserve Bank of Philadelphia, February 1975). This study, which had more detailed information on the school experience of children than most earlier studies, and also had longitudinal data, found that some school factors were associated with better school performance for some children. For instance, children with low aptitude scores performed somewhat better when they had inexperienced teachers, while children with high aptitude scores performed somewhat better with experienced teachers. But these effects, compared to the effects of social class, remain small and nothing in the Summers-Wolfe study suggests that schools can provide the magic pull that produces equality.

41. See, for instance, Harvey Averch et al., *How Effective Is Schooling? A Critical Review and Synthesis of Research Findings* (Santa Monica, Calif., 1972); Christopher Jencks et al., *Inequality: A Reassessment of the Effect of Family and Schooling in America* (New York, 1972); and Christopher Jencks and Marsha D. Brown, "Effects of High Schools on Their Students," *Harvard Educational Review* (August 1975).

42. See discussion in the Introduction, p. 17, and note 42 of the Introduction.

43. For an analysis of 423 occupations ranked by average income and educational level, see Dixie Sommers, "Occupational Rankings for Men and Women by Earnings," *Monthly Labor Review* (August 1974). Most of the highest-paying occupations require professional educations—sixteen or more years of schooling.

44. Jencks et al., op. cit., pp. 179–80, conclude that between 40 and 60 percent of the variants in adult occupational status can be explained by differences in educational attainment unrelated to ability or test scores. Note that "status" is not the same as income since the prestige of the occupation is a component of status. (In turn, educational attainment helps determine prestige, producing a correlation between the two.) However, years of education, regardless of ability or family background, do result in somewhat higher earnings. According to Jencks et al., p. 223, whose estimates are lower than those in some studies, an extra year of elementary or high school, when ability and family background are controlled, yields a 4 percent increase in income on the average; an extra year of college yields 7 percent; and an extra year of graduate school yields another 4 percent. It is also worth noting that Jencks et al., p. 145, found IQ differences to explain no more than 2 to 9 percent of variants in educational attainment.

45. In recent years this gap has closed somewhat if median years of schooling are the measure used since black rates for high school completion have increased. Whether this measure actually reflects greater equality is a matter of debate, however, since it can be argued that there is now relatively little competitive advantage to be gained in the labor force from a high school education. The more salient indicator may be college education. Here measurement is also complex. Again, the black-white differentials have diminished somewhat in terms of post–high school education, but most nonwhites attend two-year colleges, technical schools, or traditionally black colleges which confer less competitive advantage than four-year colleges, research universities, or prestigious private colleges. The gap remains barely dented at the level of professional education (postgraduate school). For a current discussion of these issues see Bernard C. Watson, "Education, in a report of the National Urban League, *The State of Black America, 1978.*

46. Torsten Husen, "The Inequality-Meritocracy Dilemma in Education," in Nelson F. Ashline, T. R. Pezzullo, and C. I. Norris, eds., *Education, Inequality and National Policy* (Lexington, Mass., 1976). A pertinent case in point is a recent article touting the gains in achievement by low-income black students in Chicago that resulted, apparently, from adoption of a curriculum designed specifically for low achievers. The article men-

tions in passing that it had some beneficial effects for students in a high-income district, too. Indeed, while second graders in the former schools were reading at grade level, the affluent students were at the fourth-grade level! See J. S. Fuerst, "Report from Chicago: A Program That Works," *The Public Interest* (Spring 1976).

47. On the role of crime and politics as avenues for upward mobility for immigrant groups see Daniel Bell, *The End of Ideology* (New York, 1965). For evidence that school attainment of the children of immigrant groups followed (i.e., did not cause) attainment of "middle-class" economic status see Colin Greer, *The Great School Legend* (New York, 1976).

48. These data are drawn from a report of the College Entrance Examination Board, "College-Bound Census, 1973–4" (Princeton, N.J., 1974).

49. Jencks et al., op. cit.

50. Jerome Karabel, *Inequality: A Reassessment of the Effect of Family and Schooling in America* (New York, 1972).

51. Jencks et al., op. cit.

52. William H. Sewell, "Inequality of Opportunity for Higher Education," *American Sociological Review* (October 1971).

53. On the contribution of parents' education to the likely attainment of children see Robert M. Hauser and David L. Featherman, "Equality of Access to Schooling: Trends and Prospects" (Working Paper 75-17, Center for Demography and Ecology, University of Wisconsin–Madison).

54. Samuel Bowles and Herbert Gintis, *Schooling in Capitalist America* (New York, 1976).

55. Children's Defense Fund, *Children Out of School in America*, (Washington, D.C., October 1974).

56. Nicholas Hobbs, *The Futures of Children: Categories, Labels and Their Consequences* (San Francisco, 1974).

57. See Children's Defense Fund, op. cit.

58. President's Committee on Mental Retardation, *Mental Retardation: Century of Decision* (Washington, D.C., March 1976).

59. L. Alan Sroufe and M. A. Stewart, "Treating Problem Children with Stimulant Drugs," *New England Journal of Medicine* (August 1973), quoted in Peter Schrag and Diane Divoky, *The Myth of the Hyperactive Child* (New York, 1975).

60. President's Committee on Mental Retardation, op. cit. On such practices, also see Children's Defense Fund, op. cit.

61. Cited in Children's Defense Fund, op. cit.

62. This literature is immense, ranging from the journalistic accounts of writer-teachers such as Jonathan Kozol, John Holt, and Herbert Kohl, to scholarly studies, such as those by Rist and Leacock, which are cited later. The important point is not that class or race bias are rampant in schools, although it is not difficult to find examples of both, but rather that differential treatment is built into the warp and woof of schools as they perform their screening and credentialing function, and as the brief discussion of professional education in Chapter 2 indicated, it is broadly rationalized through the ideology of "individualizing instruction," leading to accelerated classes, remedial tracks, and all manner of ability grouping in between.

63. These findings emerge, in composite, from the close anthropological observational studies of Eleanor Leacock, *Teaching and Learning in City Schools* (New York, 1969), and Ray Rist, *The Urban School: A Factory for Failure* (Cambridge, Mass., 1973), as well as Ray Rist, "Student Social Class and Teacher Expectations: The Self-Fulfilling Prophecy in Ghetto Education," *Harvard Educational Review* (August 1970). On differential treatment of black children see also John U. Ogbu, *The Next Generation: An Ethnography of Education in un Urban Neighborhood* (New York, 1974). Differential treatment is not limited to teachers; class, race, and ethnic bias has also been demonstrated in the behavior of school counselors. See, for instance, Aaron V. Cicourel and John I. Kitsuse, *The Educational Decision-makers* (New York, 1963), and Frederick Erickson, "Gatekeeping and the Melting Pot: Interaction in Counseling Encounters," *Harvard Educational Review* (February 1975).

64. Rist, "Student Social Class and Teacher Expectations," op. cit.

65. Leacock, op. cit.

66. Rist, *The Urban School: A Factory for Failure*, op. cit.

67. Leacock, op. cit.

68. The system described is in Philadelphia, where the author worked as an assistant to the superintendent from 1969 to 1971 and where he learned of the "star" class system as a parent in 1977.

69. While ability grouping may be administratively convenient— and most teachers do prefer it—the evidence suggests that it does not produce benefits for students—"fast" or "slow"—and

may actually retard the latter (perhaps because they are deprived the peer influence of better students or perhaps because of teacher expectations). The most comprehensive study remains Miriam L. Goldberg et al., *The Effects of Ability Grouping* (New York, 1966).

70. See, for instance, Jencks et al., op. cit., p. 144; Ogbu, op. cit.; and Jerome Kagan, "The Baby's Elastic Mind," *Human Nature* (January 1978). Typically, studies show fairly wide fluctuations in performance between grades 1 and 3, and then a pattern is set. Year-to-year correlations (grade 3 to grade 4, etc.) are often in the magnitude of .8 to .9, with correlations over time—between third-grade scores and high school scores, in the range of .5 to .6.

71. See Jencks et al., op. cit. Also Jerald Backman et al., "Adolescence to Adulthood: Change and Stability in Lives of Young Men" (University of Michigan, Institute for Social Research, May 1978).

72. See James E. Rosenbaum, "Contest and Tournament Mobility: Norm, Policy and Practice in an American School" (paper presented at the Annual Meeting, American Sociological Association, San Francisco, August 1975). Rosenbaum suggests that the apparent stability in career aspirations which exist through high school may reflect institutional practice—specifically, placement in curriculum tracks—not any "intrinsic" individual characteristics.

73. A simulation of this effect is provided by Raymond Boudon, *Education, Opportunity and Social Inequality* (New York, 1974).

74. Jencks et al., op. cit.

75. This is the conclusion argued by Bowles and Gintis, op. cit., and it is also the position advanced by Pierre Bordieu and other European sociologists.

76. Boudon, op. cit.

Chapter Four

**Child Development: American Theories
on the Sources of Inequality**

1. William Kessen, "Questions for a Theory of Cognitive Development," in Harold W. Stevenson, ed., *Concept of Development:*

A Report, Monographs for Research and Child Development, Serial No. 107, Vol. 11, No. 5 (1966).

2. For a fuller discussion of this history, see Sheldon White et al., *Federal Program for Young Children: Review and Recommendations,* Vol. 1, *Goals and Standard of Public Programs for Children* (Washington, D.C., 1973).

3. Benjamin Bloom, *Stability and Change in Human Characteristics* (New York, 1964), p. 88.

4. Whether the architects of Head Start were fully cognizant of these studies or whether these studies were subsequently used to "legitimize" Head Start may be arguable. But whatever the sequence, early childhood education programs and cultural deprivation theory became closely linked in the mid-sixties.

5. Follow-up studies are being conducted by Dr. Irving Lazar and associates at Cornell University. While work is still in progress, early reports on comparisons between Head Start and non–Head Start children show that in some school systems, for instance, Head Start children have less often been placed in special education classes than non–Head Start children and have been less often held back a year. However, the results are not consistent across sites; it is not clear whether findings on such measures demonstrate that Head Start children have superior cognitive development or whether they have been more fully socialized to the behavioral expectations of the school system; and, finally, these marginal improvements, while certainly desirable, do not in any way appear to constitute evidence that Head Start attendance will equalize life chances for children. (For a brief report on the Cornell studies see Joseph Michalak, "Head Start-Type Programs Get Second Look," *New York Times* [April 30, 1978].)

6. Arthur R. Jensen, "How Much Can We Boost I.Q. and Scholastic Achievement?" *Harvard Educational Review* (Winter and Summer 1969).

7. Cf. James S. Coleman et al., *Equality of Educational Opportunity* (U.S. Department of Health, Education and Welfare, Washington, D.C., 1966), and Christopher Jencks et al., *Inequality: A Reassessment of the Effect of Family and Schooling in America* (New York, 1972).

8. For a balanced, brief account of fifty years of controversy, see Lee J. Cronbach, "Five Decades of Public Controversy over

Mental Testing," *American Psychologist* (January and September 1975).

9. The history of black oppression is not doubted; but a priori it is as plausible to believe the oppression may strengthen family, and there is a considerable school of historical, anthropological, and journalistic evidence that this has often been the case, including the historical work of Herbert Gutman, anthropological studies by Carol Stack, Charles Valentine, and others, and the journalistic/psychological writings of Robert Coles, among others.

10. For this reason some psychologists have advocated that norm-referenced tests should generally be abandoned in favor of criterion-referenced tests, which provide some information about what an individual actually knows or can do at the time the test is taken. For example, in one widely used test, males score better than females in verbal ability, but females far outstrip males in English ability. See Sheldon White et al., op. cit., p. 181.

11. Test constructers today try to avoid using items that are actually taught in school, in pursuit of what may be an ephemeral distinction between aptitude and acquired knowledge, and sometimes the validity of tests is now determined primarily by comparing results of new tests with those of older tests. But ultimately the test results have to be compared with some other results to be meaningful, and historically the something else has most frequently been school performance or, at minimum, problems that in their general nature test the same kinds of problem-solving abilities schools try to teach.

12. Michael Young, *The Rise of the Meritocracy, 1870–2033: An Essay on Education and Equality* (Harmondsworth, England, 1958).

13. To the extent that such claims ever derived from empirical evidence, as distinct from social mythology, the basis would appear to be in studies done by early figures in the testing movement, such as Terman, which found that high-IQ children ended up as high-status adults. But such studies were methodologically primitive and typically failed to take account of such factors as social-class standing or years of education.

14. "I.Q. in the United States Class Structure," in Alan Gartner, Colin Greer, and Frank Riessman, eds., *The New Assault on Equality: I.Q. and Social Stratification* (New York, 1974).

15. For reviews of the literature which assert the extremely limited

predictive power of aptitude tests and tests of academic ability in general, see Michael A. Wallach, "Tests Tell Us Little about Talent," *American Scientist* (January–February 1976), and David McClelland, "Testing for Competence Rather Than for Intelligence," in Gartner, Greer, and Riessman, eds., op. cit. A noted proponent of aptitude testing, Ghiselli, in reviewing the predictive power of aptitude tests, found modest correlations between test scores and performance in training settings (most correlations falling between .25 and .4) but much lower correlations between test scores and actual proficiency in a job or trade (typically, correlations between .15 and .2 on various measures), cf. E. Ghiselli, *The Validity of Occupational Aptitude Tests* (New York, 1966).

16. In most samples this difference is about 15 points, roughly equivalent to one standard deviation. (This means that the average black score will be exceeded by 84 percent of whites taking the test.)

17. John C. Loehlin, G. Lindzey, and J. N. Spuhler, *Race Differences in Intelligence* (San Francisco, 1975).

18. Ibid., p. 12. See also Richard C. Lewontin, "The Analysis of Variance and the Analysis of Causes," *American Journal of Human Genetics*, Vol. 26, No. 3 (1974).

19. Jensen, it should be noted, does not limit himself to twin studies in arguing the genetic hypothesis, although these constitute his major source of data. Jensen also states in various articles his awareness of this fact, yet his conclusions seem to dismiss it.

20. Loehlin, Lindzey, and Spuhler, op. cit., pp. 128–32.

21. Ibid., pp. 126–28.

22. Barbara Tizard, "I.Q. and Race," *Nature*, Vol. 247 (1974), p. 316.

23. Warren D. Ten Houten, "The Black Family: Myth and Reality," in Arlene S. Skolnick and Jerome H. Skolnick, eds., *Family in Transition: Rethinking Marriage, Sexuality, Child Rearing and Family Organization* (Boston, 1971). In his massive in-depth study of welfare recipients, Samuel Z. Klausner found, in fact, that black families are more patriarchal than whites: "Six Years in the Lives of the Impoverished: An Examination of the WIN Thesis" (report submitted to the U.S. Department of Labor, Center for Research on the Acts of Man, University of Pennsylvania, 1978).

24. For example, Stephen S. Baratz and Joan C. Baratz, "Early Childhood Intervention: The Social Science Base of Institutional Racism," *Harvard Educational Review* (February 1970).

25. John F. Kantner and Melvin Zelnik, "Contraception and Pregnancy: Experience of Young Unmarried Women in the United States," *Family Planning Perspectives* (Winter 1973).

26. Heather Ross and Isabel Sawhill, *Time of Transition: The Growth of Families Headed by Women* (The Urban Institute, Washington, D.C., 1975).

27. Herbert Gutman, *The Black Family in Slavery and Freedom* (New York, 1976).

28. For example, Baratz and Baratz, op. cit.

29. See Carles A. Valentine, "Deficit, Difference and Bicultural Models of Afro-American Behavior," *Harvard Educational Review* (May 1971).

30. John U. Ogbu, *Minority Education and Caste: The American System in Cross-Cultural Perspective* (New York, 1978), especially pp. 44–46.

31. Ibid., pp. 21–25, 27–28.

32. Andrew M. Greeley and Peter H. Rossi, *The Education of Catholic Americans* (Chicago, 1966), Chapter 6.

33. Howard S. Erlanger, "Social Class and Corporal Punishment in Childrearing: A Reassessment," *American Sociological Review* (February 1974), reviews and reanalyzes the data of eleven major studies of this subject.

34. Melvin Kohn, *Class and Conformity, a Study in Values* (Homewood, Ill., 1969).

35. For a substantial review of this literature, see Alison Clarke-Stewart, *Child Care in the Family: A Review of Research and Some Propositions for Policy* (New York, 1977).

36. Urie Bronfenbrenner, "The Experimental Ecology of Education," AERA Award Address (Annual Meeting of the American Educational Research Association, San Francisco, 1976).

37. See, for instance, William Labov, *Language in the Inner City: Studies in the Black English Vernacular* (Philadelphia, 1972), and William Labov, "The Logic of Nonstandard English," in F. Williams, ed., *Language and Poverty: Perspectives on a Theme* (Chicago, 1970).

38. While many psychologists have begun to back off from this contention recently and in some cases have "rediscovered"

contrary evidence that was available all along, the influence of these ideas remains strong, our experience suggests, among academics and practitioners alike, as the continuing stream of studies reviewed by Clarke-Stewart (op. cit.) and the citation of Bloom's 1964 work as the prime basis for California's statewide early education program, begun in 1973, illustrate. (Cf. "The Early Childhood Education Proposal: A Master Plan to Redesign Primary Education in California," California State Department of Instruction, Sacramento, 1973.)

39. See, for instance, reviews of contrary evidence by Jerome Kagan, "The Baby's Elastic Mind," *Human Nature* (January 1978); Arlene Skolnick, "The Myth of the Vulnerable Child," *Psychology Today* (February 1978); Ann M. Clarke and A. D. Clarke, eds., *Early Experience: Myth and Evidence* (New York, 1977); and White et al., op. cit.

40. White et al., op. cit., p. 99.

41. In addition to the correlations in studies reviewed by Bloom, Jencks et al., op. cit., found a correlation of about .6 between elementary school grades and eventual educational attainment (p. 144); John U. Ogbu, *The Next Generation: An Ethnography of Education in an Urban Neighborhood* (New York, 1974), found grades awarded to elementary children varied very little from year to year, and Kagan (op. cit.) states that from the third grade on, most studies find correlations of better than .5 between elementary and high school scores. As Jencks points out, the correlations between early grades and school attainment are of roughly the same magnitude as correlations between social class and attainment.

42. See, for instance, Jean Macfarlane, "Perspectives on Personality Consistency and Change from the Guidance Study," *Vita Humana,* Vol. 7, No. 2 (1964), and those cited above in note 39.

43. Skolnick, op. cit.

44. In Chapter 5 we will return to the potential significance of this point.

45. See the studies reviewed by Kagan, op. cit.

46. See H. M. Skeels and H. B. Dye, "A Study of the Effects of Differential Stimulation of Mentally Retarded Children," *Proceedings of the American Association of Mental Deficiency,* Vol. 44 (1939), and H. M. Skeels, "Adult Status of Children with Contrasting Early Life Experiences," *Monographs of the So-*

ciety for Research in Child Development, Vol. 31, No. 3 (1966); and studies revealed in White et al., op. cit., pp. 148–49.

47. Kagan, op. cit.

Chapter Five
**Toward a Situational Theory of
Child Development**

1. Claude Lévi-Strauss, *The Savage Mind* (Chicago, 1966).
2. Ibid., p. 19.
3. Michael Cole, John Gay, Joseph A. Glick, and Donald W. Sharp, *The Cultural Context of Learning and Thinking* (New York, 1971).
4. Ibid., p. 187.
5. Ibid., p. 233.
6. Erving Goffman, *Asylums: Essays on the Social Situation of Mental Patients and Other Inmates* (Chicago, 1961). Also pertinent is Erving Goffman, *Frame Analysis: An Essay on the Organization of Experience* (Cambridge, Mass., 1974).
7. D. H. Rosenhan, "On Being Sane in Insane Places," *Science* (January 19, 1973).
8. For example, Roger Barker, *Ecological Psychology: Concepts and Methods for Studying the Environment of Human Behavior* (Palo Alto, Calif., 1968).
9. Frederick Erickson, Susan Florio, and Donald Breme, "Children's Sociolinguistic Performance and Teachers' Judgements of Children's Competence" (paper delivered at the annual meeting of the American Educational Research Association, Washington, D.C., April 2, 1975). Erickson and associates kindly permitted the author to view these videotapes.
10. William Labov, *Language in the Inner City: Studies in the Black English Vernacular* (Philadelphia, 1972). Also pertinent are studies showing that people of a given social class exhibit different linguistic behavior depending on the situation they are in. For instance, William Labov, *The Social Stratification of English in New York City* (Washington, D.C., 1966), found speech patterns of sales clerks varied to match the social classes of the characteristic clients of different departments in stores. Also see Courtney Cazden, "The Situation: A Neglected Source of Social Class Differences in Language Use," *The Journal of Social Issues* (Spring 1970).

11. Basil Bernstein, *Class, Codes and Control,* Vol. 1 (London, 1971). The developmental theory sketched out in this chapter, it should be noted, departs from Bernstein in its deemphasis of the crucial nature of early childhood and family behavior, and Bernstein's "codes" are not the same as the concept of situational code derived here from Cole and associates. On similarities and departures between Bernstein's work and that of Cole, see Sylvia Scribner and Michael Cole, "Perspectives on Language and Social Class: On Bernstein's Class, Codes and Control," *Reviews in Anthropology* (August 1974).

12. Given the usual exceptions to all generalizations, it is fair to say that anthropologists generally view intelligence as an adaptation to specific cultural and environmental imperatives, while psychologists tend to view it as a universal faculty with biological roots.

13. To some extent this is so by definition. That is, if one measures social class by a series of continuous variables (income, years of schooling, occupational prestige rankings), the result is inevitably a continuum. If, on the other hand, one works from a Marxist perspective and defines social class in "objective" terms, according to one's relationship to the control of the means of production, the lines may appear sharper, but the effort to make them appear so leads often to rather extreme positions. For instance, one neo-Marxist position is that in a corporate economy with control of productive decision making in the hands of relatively few, the great majority of citizens, including persons we typically think of as "middle-class," become members of the proletariat. There seems little point to trying to draw sharp lines between classes, however; once the birth-ascribed status of feudal societies disappears and the possibility of social mobility exists, the lines blur, but it remains clear that the life chances and experiences of individuals at different points on the continuum are sharply different.

14. This discussion of caste draws on John U. Ogbu, *Minority Education and Caste: The American System in Cross-Cultural Perspective* (New York, 1978), a Carnegie Council on Children monograph. Caste societies are usually defined as those in which society is divided into hierarchic groups, arranged from superior to inferior, whose membership is determined at birth. By law or by custom, almost all marriage occurs between members of the same caste. In the few cases where marriage occurs

across caste lines, the children of the marriage are always defined as members of the lower caste. Centrally important, adult social and economic roles are more or less assigned by caste; this results in very different prospective futures for children and different cultural requirements for development. Members of the lowest echelon in a caste society, referred to in the anthropological literature as the "pariah caste," are sharply restricted from improving their condition through the methods open to other members of the society, especially those based on training and ability. Members of the society's dominant group often point to the roles pariah minorities have been forced to play and the styles of coping they have developed as evidence that the latter are naturally suited for such low positions and cannot perform the more skilled and rewarding roles the upper castes have come to dominate. So whites invented the stereotype of the simple, "childlike" Negro (i.e., one who does *not* develop), and some blacks, as adults, were forced to exhibit these characteristics to survive in a racist society.

15. The Jim Crow laws that sprang up in the South after Reconstruction are the best examples, although it is less widely realized that such southern laws had northern antecedents in many cases. (See C. Vann Woodward, *The Strange Career of Jim Crow* [Oxford, 1974].)

16. The fullest treatment of this topic remains Gunnar Myrdal, *An American Dilemma* (New York, 1944). On the continuance of the job ceiling and its influence on black patterns of development, see Ogbu, op. cit.

17. Stanley Lebergott, *The American Economy: Income, Wealth and Want* (Princeton, N.J., 1975), p. 301.

18. See evidence discussed in the Introduction.

19. For example, see Bennett Harrison, *Education, Training and the Urban Ghetto* (Baltimore, 1973).

20. "A Study of Black Male Professionals in Industry," U.S. Department of Labor Manpower Administration Research Monograph (Washington, D.C., 1973), p. 12.

21. This finding was reported in a *New York Times* survey. See "Many Blacks Are Living in Dual World of Conflict," *New York Times* (June 2, 1976).

22. Ogbu, op. cit., Part II.

23. Larry H. Long and Lynne Meltman, "Income Differences Between Blacks and Whites Controlling for Educational Differ-

ences and Region of Birth," U.S. Department of Commerce, Bureau of the Census (paper prepared for the Annual Meeting of the Population Association of America, April 18–20, 1974). Recent black migrants to northern cities, the authors find, had higher incomes on the average than native-born (to the North) blacks despite lower levels of educational attainment.

24. On this point, which seems also to hold true in comparisons of Puerto Rican immigrants in comparison to those born on the mainland, see Michael J. Piore, "The Role of Immigration in Industrial Growth: A Case Study of the Origins and Character of Puerto Rican Migration to Boston," Working Paper No. 112, May 1973, Department of Economics, Massachusetts Institute of Technology. Piore suggests that the confinement of most minority groups to the secondary labor force blunts the drive of the second generation of migrants, who lose the belief in opportunity that migrants have even while they acquire higher expectations for economic well-being as they absorb the norms of their new setting

25. Thomas J. Cottle, *Black Children, White Dreams* (New York, 1974).

26. Ibid., p. 85.

27. This last point is derived from economic theory: in theory, not only will a more skilled work force be a more productive one, but the means of production will be altered to adapt to the skills of the work force. Note that, in line with this logic, it seems theoretically possible that equalizing the skills of everyone through education will produce equality in the work force (with any difference reflecting individual difference), but the point we are arguing is that in an unequal social structure there are limits on the ability to equalize skills.

28. It is important to note that there is a long line of psychological theorists—Piaget being the most distinguished recent example —who stress the interaction between child and environment. But the child's side of the interaction has not always been properly represented in the dominant professional (and popular) psychologies of this country.

29. The analogy to Piaget breaks down at another point: we would not suggest that there are invariant universal stages of development of such a theory (a Piagetian claim about intellectual development which remains controversial), for to do so is again to lift the child out of time and space, which we speculate are

crucial. (On the uncertainty of the evidence for the hierarchy and invariant nature of Piagetian stages, see D. C. Phillips and Mavis E. Kelly, "Hierarchical Theories of Development in Education and Psychology," *Harvard Educational Review* [August 1975], and the ambiguous empirical evidence reviewed by Patricia Teague Ashton, "Cross-Cultural Piagetian Research: An Experimental Perspective," *Harvard Educational Review* [November 1975].)

30. Michael Polanyi, *The Tacit Dimension* (Garden City, N.Y., 1966).

31. A few studies dispute this, but the preponderance show that Head Start has not had enduring results for children. See Chapter 4, note 5.

32. For instance, the studies supporting the continued plasticity of the child cited at the close of Chapter 4 can easily be interpreted as rather dramatic changes in situation—from war orphan to adopted American child, from institutionalized infant to ward of an institutionalized woman, etc.

Chapter Six
Changing the Situation: Steps Toward an Egalitarian Family Policy

1. Arthur M. Okun, *Equality and Efficiency: The Big Tradeoff* (The Brookings Institution, Washington, D.C., 1975), p. 36.

2. Hayek tries to distinguish between the necessary amount of coercion vested in the state to "secure a certain minimum of uniformity of conduct that assists individual efforts more than it impedes them" and coercion (political or otherwise) which "prevents a person from using his mental powers to the full and consequently from making the greatest contribution that he is capable of to the community." But there is neither a clear-cut ethical case nor a logical case nor an empirical case intrinsic to such distinctions which tells us when to draw the line between John D. Rockefeller "using his mental powers to the full" and the Standard Oil Trust exerting economic coercion that interferes with others. Cf. F. A. Hayek, *The Constitution of Liberty* (Chicago, 1960).

3. Robert Heilbroner, *Business Civilization in Decline* (New York, 1976).

4. On the desire of the poor to work, see Leonard Goodwin, *Do the Poor Want to Work?: A Social-Psychological Study of Work* (The Brookings Institution, Washington, D.C., 1972), as well as the findings of the New Jersey income maintenance experiments that a guaranteed minimum income did not dilute the work behavior of primary wage earners—see Joseph A. Pechman and P. Michael Timpane, eds., *Work Incentives and Income Guarantees: The New Jersey Negative Income Tax Experiment* (The Brookings Institution, Washington, D.C., 1975).

5. See Lester Thurow and Robert Lucas, "The American Distribution of Income: A Structural Problem," U.S. Congress Joint Economic Committee (Washington, D.C., 1972), and Lester Thurow, *Generating Inequality: Mechanisms of Distribution in the U.S. Economy* (New York, 1975).

6. See, for instance, Frank Newman et al., *Report on Higher Education* (Washington, D.C., 1971). Also, reviewing the historical evidence in one profession, David White illustrates how educational requirements have been used to keep the supply of lawyers down (and prices up) over the last one hundred years ("The Definition of Legal Competence: Will the Circle Be Unbroken?" (draft article, Childhood and Government Project, Berkeley, California, June 15, 1976).

7. See John K. Galbraith, *The New Industrial State* (Boston, 1971), for discussion of the extent of oligopoly in the economy.

8. See John Rawls, *A Theory of Justice* (Cambridge, Mass., 1971). To oversimplify dramatically, Rawls draws on social contract theory to argue that an individual in the "original position"— i.e., outside the social contract—would become a signator to the contract only if it ensured a considerable degree of equality. Some sense of the hornet's nest he stirred up can be gleaned by reading the series of articles responding to Rawls in *The American Political Science Review* (June 1975) and one of the leading critics of Rawls, Robert Nozick, *Anarchy, State and Utopia* (New York, 1974).

9. See George F. Break, "Taxation and Economic Choice," in *The Economics of Public Finance* (The Brookings Institution, Washington, D.C., 1974).

10. On labor supply response of income maintenance recipients see U.S. Department of Health, Education and Welfare, "Summary Report: Seattle-Denver Income Maintenance Experiment, Mid-experimental Labor Supply Results and a Generalization to the

National Population" (Washington, D.C., February 1978). On marital effects see John Bishop, "Jobs, Cash Transfers, and Marital Instability: A Review of the Evidence" (Institute for Research on Poverty, Special Report Series SR-19, Madison, Wis., 1978).

11. Kenneth Keniston and the Carnegie Council on Children, *All Our Children: The American Family Under Pressure* (New York, 1977).

12. The Humphrey-Hawkins bill, in its legislative journey from 1974, when first introduced, to its passage in 1977, gradually lost all language guaranteeing a job and watered down both its definition of full employment and the extent to which policy was to aim at that goal, turning a firm objective into a conditional target as the prerequisite for support. For the extraordinary opposition generated by an earlier effort, immediately following World War II, to make full employment a national goal (including a U.S. threat to drop out of the United Nations if that body's charter included the right to employment as a basic universal right), see Russell A. Nixon, "The Historical Development of the Conception and Implementation of Full Employment as Economic Policy," in Alan Gartner, Russell A. Nixon, and Frank Riessman, eds., *Public Service Employment: An Analysis of Its History, Problems and Prospects* (New York, 1973).

13. For instance, as this is written, news accounts of CETA scandals in Hartford, Denver, Miami, and Washington, D.C., among others, form a backdrop to congressional delay in 1979 appropriations—a replay of the previous year's script—and there is talk of considerably reducing public service employment authorizations from 750,000 to 600,000 jobs. The constant turmoil surrounding the CETA system since its inception in 1973 has no doubt hampered its effective implementation, but there are features built into the law which also impede it. For instance, jobs are supposed to be "transitional" in nature, leading to unsubsidized employment after one year. This fact constitutes a disincentive for public agencies to focus much effort on the qualitative nature of CETA jobs, and it quite simply ignores the fact that with high unemployment rates (especially in urban areas) there is often no job opening to which to make a transition.

14. Broad stimulus policies will have least impact in these areas,

where the recovery from recession is slowest and the descent most rapid.

15. Cf. Bennett Harrison and Sandra Kantner, "The Great State Robbery" (working papers, spring 1976).

16. The tax credit for hiring former welfare recipients seems to have had almost no impact, and fragmentary data suggest that the New Jobs Tax Credit of 1977 has had limited impact, perhaps primarily because of the time lag required for firms to become aware of it. There is, however, every reason to believe that tax credits or other forms of subsidy can induce firms to alter their hiring practices, if the subsidy is large enough, lasts long enough, and involves minimal red tape and other "hassles" for firms. But subsidies always face rough political sledding because of organized labor's opposition (fear of undercutting labor's price), and in any event, the impact of tax credits or subsidies on the willingness of firms to hire a targeted group of workers (e.g., the disadvantaged) on overall demand remains obscure. Cf. Richard H. de Lone, "Youth Employment and the Private Sector" (paper prepared for the National Commission for Manpower Policy, Conference on the Private Sector and the Structurally Unemployed, October 19–20, 1978).

17. For a comprehensive review of evaluations and assessments of the federal manpower effort, see Charles R. Perry, Bernard E. Anderson, Richard L. Rowan, and Herbert R. Northrup, *The Impact of Government Manpower Programs, General and on Minorities and Women*, Manpower and Human Resources Studies, No. 4 (Industrial Research Unit, The Wharton School, University of Pennsylvania, Philadelphia, 1976).

18. On procedural obstacles to enforcement of affirmative action, see Keniston, op. cit.

19. Ibid.

20. For a good basic introductory discussion of various approaches to income redistribution through the tax system, including the negative income tax, children's allowances, and the credit income tax, see James Tobin, "Raising the Incomes of the Poor," in Kermit Gordon, ed., *Agenda for the Nation* (The Brookings Institution, Washington, D.C., 1968).

21. Thurow and Lucas, op. cit.

22. The elements and the benefits of the plan described here in skeletal form are discussed at greater length in Keniston, op. cit.

23. This conclusion is based on comparing the average federal tax

bill for families grossing $24,000 a year with the credit tax they would pay. Of course, some families at this level pay less than the average—their tax bill would go up and vice versa.

24. Testimony of Bert De Leeuw, coordinator, Movement for Economic Justice, in *Tax Reform* (*Administration and Public Witness*) (Public Hearing before the Committee for Ways & Means, 94th Congress, Washington, D.C., 1975).

25. The extent of this offset depends on several factors; for instance, whether cash payments replace the cost of administering food stamps and the value of the stamps themselves, whether Social Security payments are subsumed under such a scheme or retained, etc. Some studies suggest that cashing out the costs of all such programs and incorporating them in a redistributive tax system could themselves raise all families above the government's poverty line.

26. Based on calculations in Joseph A. Pechman and Benjamin Okner, *Who Bears the Tax Burden?* (The Brookings Institution, Washington, D.C., 1974), adjusted for inflation from the 1966 data they use in 1976 levels.

27. In 1976 the gross income deficit for all households required to raise them to the government's poverty line was approximately $16.7 billion, according to data provided in U.S. Department of Commerce, Bureau of the Census, *Current Population Reports: Money Income and Poverty Status of Families and Persons in the United States: 1976*, Series P-60, No. 115, Table E (Washington, D.C., 1977).

28. Based on calculations estimated from Bureau of the Census, ibid., of the gross income deficit for families below the "low-income" line of half the median, and assuming that the wealth of the top 2.5 percent of families has increased from approximately $1 trillion to $2 trillion since 1969 (which underestimates what one would expect from the combined effects of inflation and economic growth). James D. Smith (study cited in the Introduction) calculated the wealth of the top 2.5 percent of families for 1969. A 2 percent net worth tax would yield $40 billion a year, which would raise all families above the median (at 1976 levels) with change.

Index

private labor market, 191–92
Progressive era, 21, 31, 32, 33, 49–65, 115, 116
Progressive party, 51
propertied class, 37, 38, 178
psychology, American, 29–31, 57–58
  child development theories of, 70, 113–40, 174–75
Public Education Association in New York, 65n.
public service employment, 189–90
Puerto Ricans, 67, 153

racial inequality, xiii, 4, 33, 34, 66–67, 76, 177
  in career advancement, 15–16, 66
  child welfare system and, 85–88, 94
  discrimination by expectation and, 107–10
  Great Society to present and, 65–73
  IQ tests and, 120–26 *passim*
  in juvenile justice system, 89–93, 94
  results of discrimination and, 16–19
  See also minorities; *names of minority groups*
racism, 64, 65, 76
Rawls, John, 182
recidivism, 97
redistribution of income, 9, 32, 66, 80, 183, 186, 188, 193–98
  credit income tax, 194–97
  transfer payments, 183, 193, 194
  wage policy, 193–94
  See also welfare
redistribution of power, 186–87, 201
redlining, 11
reform movements, American, 21, 31–34, 35–77, 115, 173
  bureaucracies as implementors of, 60–61, 74, 76, 81–82
  common qualities of, 73–74
  to "cool out" protest, 76
  Great Society to present and, 31, 32, 33, 65–73, 115, 136
  Jacksonian period, 31, 32, 33, 36–48
  limits of social programs, 93–97
  moralism of, 45, 51, 53–54, 56, 61, 65, 69, 70, 74, 84
  patrician quality of, 36, 40, 48, 51, 64, 73–74, 76–77
  Progressive era and, 21, 31, 32, 33, 49–65, 115, 116
  reasons given for failure of, 36, 64, 74
  "success" of, 74–77

regulated economy, 53, 54, 179, 191–92
Rice, Joseph Mayer, 58
Rockefeller, John D., 49, 51
role models, 162
Roosevelt, Theodore, 50, 51–52, 53, 58, 61, 179
Rosenhan, David H., 145
Ross, Heather, 129
Roth, William, 145–46

SAT (Standard Aptitude Test) scores and socioeconomic status, 102
Sawhill, Isabel, 129
Scarr, Sandra, 125
Schlesinger, Arthur, Jr., 36, 41
School and Society, The (Dewey), 116
schools. *See* education
scientific reform, 56–59, 74
  applied to schools, 60–61, 115
sexual discrimination, 16–18, 103
situational theory of child development, 141–70, 175–76
  caste as master setting, 153–60
  child's theory of social reality, 160–66, 169
  defining "situation," 145–46
  history, time and development, 167
  predictability and variability, 168–70
  situational code, 144–45, 161, 165
  situations within situations, 149–60
  social class as master setting, 151–53
Skeels, H. M., 138
Skinnerian behaviorism, 116
Smith, Adam, 28, 114
Social Darwinism, 64
Socialist party, 50
social mobility, 14–19, 48, 63
  discrimination and, 16–18
  intergenerational, 14–15, 16, 154
  intragenerational, 15–16, 154
  in U.S. versus Europe, 16
social programs
  Aid to Families with Dependent Children, 67, 79–84, 95, 193, 194
  child development theory and. *See* child development theory
  child welfare system, 85–88, 94, 188
  juvenile justice system, 55–56, 86, 88–93, 97, 107, 127, 199
  limits of, 93–97, 176–77
  misconceptions shaping, 21–24, 33, 73, 74–75, 77, 113, 118–19, 172, 173, 174
  premises of an egalitarian policy, 185–98
  reform movements and. *See* reform movements, American

welfare (*cont'd*)
  mythology of, 82–83, 84
  reform of, 75, 79, 185
Whig party, 36–37, 38, 39, 40–41, 46
White, Burton, 70
White, Sheldon, 136
White House Conference on Children,
  21
Wilson, Woodrow, 50, 52–53, 57, 179
Wisconsin, 103
Wiseman, Fred, 81*n.*, 145

women
  discrimination against, results of,
    16–18
  in Jacksonian period, rights of, 40
  salaries of, 16–18, 22
Work Incentives Program (WIN), 82

Youth Employment and Demonstration Projects Act of 1977, 65*n.*

Zelnik, Melvin, 128–29

DATE DUE

	1985		